# CENTRALIZATION AND SCHOOL EMPOWERMENT FROM RHETORIC TO PRACTICE

# CENTRALIZATION AND SCHOOL EMPOWERMENT FROM RHETORIC TO PRACTICE

**ADAM NIR**
**EDITOR**

**Nova Biomedical Books**
*New York*

**NOTICE TO THE READER**

LIBRARY OF CONGRESS CATALOGING-IN-PUBLICATION DATA
Centralization and school empowerment from rhetoric to practice / editor, Adam Nir.
p. cm.
Includes index.
ISBN 978-1-60692-730-4 (hardcover)
1. School autonomy--Cross-cultural studies. 2. Schools--Centralization--Cross-cultural studies. I. Nir, Adam.
LB2822.9.C43                                                                                                  2009
379.1'535--dc22                                                                                        2008050317

*Published by Nova Science Publishers, Inc.* ✤ *New York*

# CONTENTS

# FOREWORD

## *Brian J. Caldwell*

Educational Transformations
University of Melbourne, Australia

This book is published at an ideal time as far as developments in policy, professional and personal domains are concerned. In respect to policy, there is now ample evidence, as reported by the Organisation for Economic Cooperation and Development (OECD), that decentralisation in the form of school empowerment is a significant international trend. The same source also reports significant trends in centralisation. This is not a paradox – both can occur simultaneously but for different functions -- the policy issue is how to get the balance right in different contexts, acknowledging that the balance will differ from setting to setting and at different points in time. Given these trends, there are important implications for action in the professional domain. If authority and responsibility for important decisions are decentralised to the school level, what new knowledge and skills are required at that level and how should capacity be built to ensure that expectations are realised? The same question may be asked of those who work at the centre. In a personal sense the publication of this book coincides with the 30th anniversary of the start of my work in the field of decentralisation following doctoral research on school empowerment at the University of Alberta. Reading this book was important as I took stock of what has been accomplished.

Our own work on school empowerment is guided by a definition that reflects a balance of centralisation and decentralisation. It may serve as a framework for any of the developments described in this book. We adopted the concept of 'the self-managing school' for what is often described as school-based management or local management or site-based management. A self-managing school is a school to which there has been decentralised a significant amount of authority and responsibility to make decisions within a centrally-determined framework of policies, goals, standards and accountabilities. The domains of decision-making may include curriculum, personnel, finance, facilities or technology.

I have read much of the research and other scholarly work on decentralisation in recent times and I believe this book to be the most rigorous I have encountered. Some books deal with developments in a single country with authors seemingly unaware of what has occurred elsewhere. Some are only concerned with the most recent changes, which often result from initiatives of governments of a particular persuasion, and the authors either praise or criticise what has occurred on ideological grounds depending on their sympathy with proponents at the time. Some make little or no effort to report research on impact, especially the most recent, relying instead on early findings that were generally inconclusive. This book contains chapters from scholars who are at the top of their field and who provide perspectives from past and present in reporting on decentralisation. There is an evidence base to the extent that an effort has been made to draw on research. It is a special strength of the book that developments over time in nine countries in a particular region are addressed, with top-class framing and analysis by Adam Nir.

My review of developments about three decades ago identified four factors explaining early interest in decentralisation, working singly or in combination, representing demands for increased sensitivity to local needs, reversal of the effects of size and centralisation, heightened concern for accountability, and a desire for participative management. A decade later I added four more: interest in choice among schools in the public sector, emerging organisational theory that suggested decentralisation is an appropriate strategy in the face of diversity, in this case, recognition of the complex array of student learning needs at the local level; findings from early studies of school effectiveness; and interest in enhancing the professionalism of teachers and their leaders.

While there were many reasons for interest in self-management, much of the heat from often contentious debates about its efficacy has dissipated in the early years of the 21$^{st}$ century as most governments and system authorities settled on the enhancement of learning as its primary purpose. The logic of the argument is relatively straightforward: each school contains a unique mix of student needs, interests, aptitudes and aspirations, and those at the school level are best placed to determine the particular mix of all of the resources available to the school to achieve optimal outcomes.

A review of research suggests that there have been three generations of studies and it is only in the third that evidence of the impact of self-management on outcomes has emerged, and then only when certain conditions are fulfilled. The first generation was in times when impact on learning was not a primary or even secondary purpose. The second generation was when such purposes may have been to the fore but the database was weak. The third, emerging in the late 1990s and gathering momentum in the early 2000s, coincides with a pre-eminent concern for learning outcomes and the development of a strong database.

The most striking findings have come from recent analyses of school and school system characteristics in the Programme for International Student Assessment (PISA) conducted by the OECD. More than 400,000 students from 57 countries participated in 2006. School principals reported on the extent of autonomy on a range of matters. A model was constructed to explain the joint impact of school and system resources, practices, and policies on student performance. Of the 15 factors in the model, the system average on the school autonomy index in budgeting is by far the most powerful (OECD, 2007).

Even more striking are two studies on PISA 2003 conducted for OECD by staff in the Ifo Institute for Economic Research at the University of Munich, Department of Human Capital and Innovation. These were concerned with accountability, autonomy and choice, with one focusing on level of student achievement and the other on equity of student achievement. It was found 'that students perform better if schools have autonomy to decide on staffing and to hire their own teachers, while student achievement is lower when schools have autonomy in areas with large scope for opportunistic behaviour, such as formulating their own budget. But school autonomy in formulating the budget, in establishing teacher salaries, and in determining course content are all significantly more beneficial in systems where external exit exams introduce accountability'. As far as choice is concerned it was found that 'students perform substantially better in systems where private school operation creates choice and competition. At the same time, student achievement increases along with government funding of schools. A level playing field in terms of government funding for public and private schools proves significantly performance enhancing' (Wößmann, Lüdemann, Schütz and West, 2007).

The conclusions on equity of student achievement were equally noteworthy: 'Rather than harming disadvantaged students, accountability, autonomy, and choice are tides that lift all the boats … there is not a single case where a policy designed to introduce accountability, autonomy, or choice into schooling benefits high-SES students to the detriment of low-SES students' (Schütz, Wößmann and West, 2007).

Debates about school empowerment as described in this book are often conducted by participants who see power as a zero-sum game, that is, shifting power to schools means a loss of power at the centre. Experience is proving that this is a misleading game. Schools are acquiring more power to respond to the unique mix of student needs that exists in each setting but the centre has a more powerful but more sharply focused role in establishing a framework of goals, policies, curriculum, standards, accountabilities, funding and support.

We have recently completed a five-year project that commenced in early 2004 with a study of what had occurred in nations where self-management had been irreversibly institutionalised. We found that the new balance of centralisation and decentralisation had resulted in a new conceptualisation to the point that we needed to 're-imagine the self-managing school'. More than 70 workshops with about 4 000 school and system leaders were then conducted, laying the groundwork for the International Project to Frame the Transformation of Schools that was completed in 2008. We worked with teams of researchers in Australia, China, England, Finland, United States and Wales to study how secondary schools with a relatively high degree of autonomy were able to achieve transformation, defined as significant, systematic and sustained change that secured success for all students in all settings.

We found (Caldwell and Harris, 2008) that successful self-managing schools were adept at building four forms of capital (intellectual, social, spiritual and financial) and aligning them through good governance to achieve the goals of the school. Intellectual capital refers to the level of knowledge and skill of those who work in or for the school. Social capital refers to the strength of formal and informal partnerships and networks involving the school and all individuals, agencies, organisations and institutions that have the potential to support and be supported by the school. Spiritual capital refers to the strength of moral purpose and the degree of coherence among values, beliefs and attitudes about life and learning (for some schools, spiritual capital has a foundation in religion; in other schools, spiritual capital may refer to ethics and values shared by members of the school and its community). Financial capital refers to the money available to support the school. Governance is the process through which the school builds its intellectual, social, financial and spiritual capital and aligns them to achieve its goals.

The key to understanding how school empowerment should work in the 21st century lies in the new view of governance. The traditional view is characterised by a preoccupation with structures, roles, responsibilities and accountabilities. These are critically important considerations but the new view focusing on capital suggests a partnership of centre and school. In similar fashion the empowerment of schools has been marked by the same preoccupation and shifting the focus to how all of the resources at all levels of governance can be deployed to ensure success for all students in all settings. There is no one best way to do this; there will be a constantly shifting pattern of partnership with the student at the centre.

I think the book is quite outstanding and I wish this kind of book had been written for other regions around the world. The superb accounts of developments around the Mediterranean Basin in this book make clear that a $21^{st}$ century view of centralisation and school empowerment is emerging but the panorama is different in each country as is the process of creating it. For my part I am left with a sense of optimism that students will be the beneficiaries as the journey continues.

## REFERENCES

OECD (2007). PISA 2006 Science Competencies for Tomorrow's World. Paris: OECD. Pages 252-3.

Wößmann, L., Lüdemann, E., Schütz, G. and West, M.R. (2007). 'School Accountability, Autonomy, Choice, and the Equity of Student Achievement: International Evidence from PISA 2003'. Education Working Paper No. 13, *Directorate of Education*, OECD, September. Pages 59-60.

Schütz, G., Wößmann, L. and West, M.R. (2007) 'School Accountability, Autonomy, Choice, and Level of Student Achievement: International Evidence from PISA 2003'. Education Working Paper No. 14, *Directorate of Education*, OECD, December. Pages 34-5.

Caldwell, B.J. and Harris, J. (2008). Why not the Best schools? What we have Learned from Outstanding Schools around the World. Camberwell, Victoria: ACER Press.

In: Centralization and School Empowerment...
Editor: Adam Nir

ISBN 978-1-60692-730-4
© 2009 Nova Science Publishers, Inc.

*Chapter 1*

# SCHOOL EMPOWERMENT: MOVING FROM RHETORIC TO PRACTICE

## *Adam E. Nir*

The Hebrew University of Jerusalem, Israel

Public schooling. The ultimate institution established by developed societies for the purpose of educating the younger generation and preparing children for life as adults. Public education is expected to equip individuals with the knowledge, proficiencies and values likely to enable them to effectively cope with the main features and characteristics of their present and future daily lives. Promoting children's knowledge and skills in a vast number of areas, increasing their social involvement and awareness and, at the same time, developing their moral judgement and conduct are among the most popular expectations associated with public schooling.

However, since education presents a vague task in many ways, it is hardly surprising that public schooling is faced with various and at times contradictory expectations regarding its conduct and desired outcomes. Moreover, in line with the rising number of expectations associated with public schooling, schools also encounter criticism on account of the growing disappointment from their professional conduct and outcomes. Disappointment is not restricted only to children's achievements in national and international tests in various disciplines and subject matters such as reading and mathematics which are directly linked to schools' daily processes. Schools are also often accused of various anomalies that take place in the social context which are caused by many factors that have relatively little bearing on internal school processes. As a result, claims stating that the national investment in public schooling is not equal to the rate of return evident in school outcomes are often heard.

Not surprisingly, the growing disappointment and criticism directed at public schooling encourages educational policy-makers to seek remedies that will improve school outcomes and enable schools to better meet social expectations directly linked to public education.

In the academic sphere, this notion has led to the development of new disciplines – school effectiveness and school improvement, which became well established in the United States from the mid-1970s onwards and, later on, in various European countries. A significant increase in empirical knowledge in the field that followed established the belief that schools' performance can be modified and improved and, at the same time, it enhanced the public and political debate about the need to redesign educational policies and processes in ways assumed to improve schools' effectiveness and efficiency.

As the number of findings connecting various variables with school effectiveness began to accumulate, the articulation of various change strategies was boosted and educational reforms and restructuring initiatives gradually became the name of the game. Every once in a while, a new reform initiative or intervention program is born along with new hopes and expectations that it will bring about change which will finally improve public education and school outcomes.

Consequently, the restructuring of schools has nowadays become a major concern and schools are expected to constantly change, to enable their adaptation in an ever-changing and turbulent environment and improve the quality and relevance of the services they provide. This is followed by a continuous effort on the part of national level policy-makers to plan and implement new policy plans, although, so far, these restructuring initiatives have not led to a revolution in schooling.

# CONTROLLING PUBLIC EDUCATION

Control, one of the most prominent factors associated with reform initiatives and change strategies, is assumed to be a significant factor in altering public education and promoting school effectiveness. This line of reform initiatives evolves from a theoretical perspective that focused attention on the role of the state in controlling public schooling, which has long been at the heart of the debate in modern states. In particular, it centers on the conflict between centralized versus local control, attempting to reconcile these two clashing perspectives and determine what should be the right balance between them.

Although the power relations between central and local control have constantly been challenged, it is only in the last couple of decades that the tendency of centralized Western democracies to decrease central control over educational systems and to increase local-level autonomy has gradually evolved.

Centralized states are encouraged to follow this trend and to favor decentralization and the increase of school empowerment for several main reasons. It has long been realized that the tendency to maintain national central control over schools is ineffective and that school superintendents are unable to closely monitor the large number of processes that take place on a daily basis in every single school. Secondly, as we gradually move into the 21st century, more liberal voices are heard arguing against the uniformity of public education services and the need to promote pluralism in light of the variance existing among local communities and individual needs of children. Thirdly, increasing school flexibility and local level autonomy is assumed to promote school-level educators' sensitivity and attentiveness to local needs and to elevate their accountability and responsibility (Caldwell, 2003). Moreover, freedom of choice allows for authentic desires and views to dominate and shape individual performance and, therefore, is highly commended by individuals and organizations as a means for enhancing effectiveness. Fourthly, increased flexibility is also likely to allow schools to operate more efficiently and rapidly in comparison with the commonly described slow and cumbersome centralized structures, as flexibility allows a close and direct connection between needs and the means employed for the purpose of satisfying those needs. Finally, it is believed that decentralization will promote the participation and involvement of school-level educators in the various school processes and will increase the chances of plans to be implemented. Hence, decentralization is assumed to promote school productivity and effectiveness and to boost schools' relevancy and reputation, both vital assets for maintaining public schools' hegemony in the educational realm.

Although these arguments establish a strong case in favor of decentralization and school empowerment, this tendency towards increased local control is not free from criticism. Views opposing decentralization argue that the promotion of school empowerment may maintain and even increase existing social gaps and negatively affect the socialization power of the state if local needs overcome state-level considerations. Cynics argue, in addition, that the tendency toward decentralization and school empowerment mainly reflects governments' attempt to downsize potential criticism often pointed at them, by passing the ball to school-level educators and putting them on the hot spot regarding the educational services being provided and school outcomes. Nevertheless, it should be noted that although a school empowerment policy is likely to increase the degrees of freedom granted to schools at the local level, it eventually maintains steering from a distance by central authority. Moreover, delegated authority can be taken back by senior officials since powers still rest with that central authority (Bray, 1985).

And, in fact, even in most centralized governments and societies, there is a clear trend towards decentralization at all levels of education (Mazuerk and Winzer, 2006, p.16) with particular emphasis placed on school empowerment. These initiatives may appear in different shapes or under different names (for example – *school autonomy; site-based management; school-based management; self-managing schools*), although they all share a similar principle: the importance of local control and flexibility as a means of enabling schools to better and more quickly meet local needs and to increase the correspondence between aims and means by tailoring educational decisions to the needs of the local community. Hence, it is flexibility and extended degrees of freedom that are assumed to promote school relevancy and effectiveness.

In considering the advantages associated with decentralization and school empowerment, it is hardly surprising that many educational systems around the globe are tempted to follow decentralized countries and initiate policies of that nature. Yet, paradoxically, such reforms that imply major changes when implemented in centralized educational systems often spread, as fashion typically does, moving from one educational context to another in some mysterious way without being critically examined for their adequacy to a given educational context. As a result, they are adopted and implemented based on partial information or at times rumors, before their correspondence or potential contribution for a particular educational context is fully examined and appraised. This mode of operation fosters the use of trial and error strategies in which the relevance and value of a particular policy plan are assessed during or at times after implementation. No doubt such conduct enables many considerations other than educational ones to dictate which policy plan will be adopted and what will be the depth of implementation processes.

While this conduct hardly corresponds to the basic assumptions embedded in the rational model for planning and decision making and may be considered improper, it seems to rest on the belief that educational policies that are successful in promoting school effectiveness and efficiency in one particular social, economical, political and cultural context are most likely to work for schools operating in a different national context as well. Such a belief seems to lend itself to one major undermining assumption: successful policy plans may be viewed as *context-free*, therefore enabling them to migrate from one educational context to another regardless of the unique features existing in a specific educational system. According to this view, if school empowerment policies have qualities that benefit schools and educational processes, they are most likely to have a similar impact on all public educational systems and schools regardless of the unique features characterizing a particular national context in which schools operate.

## REFORM IN CONTEXT

Although unique contextual features are often ignored when educational reforms are considered, the significance of cultural, social and political context for organizational behavior is constantly gaining recognition. Through establishing a frame of reference for individuals who share a given culture (Wentworth, 1980, p. 84), the context creates what may be termed as the "relevancy zone," articulating an arena for human interpretation and behavior. The context presents an agreed-upon version of reality created through individuals' interactions in their social environment and, therefore, serves as a facilitator for human interaction. Hence, the context may be viewed as a membrane that absorbs changes and maintains meaning. Its significance is high not only in determining the appropriate qualities for a particular culture and social setting, but also in influencing and adjusting everything that goes through it (Goffman, 1961, p. 33). What follows is that citizens of the same nationality and social context are more likely to share comparable values (Gerstner and Day, 1994). Although all communities confront similar problems, various societies develop and expose their members during cultural socialization processes to different types of solutions for comparable problems (Hofstede, 1997).

Hofstede (1997) has identified four dimensions that may be used to differentiate among cultures: *power distance*, referring to an unequal distribution of power within a given society; *collectivism versus individualism*, referring to the degree of connectedness among members in a given society; *femininity versus masculinity,* referring to the extent to which social gender roles are distinct; and *uncertainty avoidance,* referring to the degree to which individuals feel threatened by uncertain circumstances. These dimensions enable a broad characterization of the properties of various social contexts and determine, for example, the way groups and individuals conceive and react in power-relation interactions. In considering that cultural socialization is the basic determinant of all values, it also affects individuals' values and attitudes that shape professional perceptions in work organizations. This may be best explained by considering cultural socialization as the "software of the mind" and as a "collective programming of the mind which distinguishes the members of one group or category of people from another" (Hofstede, 1997, p. 5).

Returning to the ongoing debate around school empowerment, it may be argued that the potential embedded in a decentralization reform to significantly alter a particular educational system is tightly associated with the unique social, political, cultural and economic features characterizing a particular society.

This book attempts to challenge the context-free notion following the variance existing in research findings regarding the implications of decentralization initiatives for public schools.

While this inconsistency in research findings may be caused by a large number of factors, one main factor that inevitably determines potential effects may be the magnitude and scope of implementation of school empowerment initiatives characterizing different national contexts. Logically, when a particular policy plan encourages only limited actions towards school empowerment in a given context, it is highly unlikely that significant effects will be created.

It is, therefore, suggested that contextual features have a crucial importance in determining the potential influence of policy plans and restructuring initiatives attempting to promote school empowerment. It may be concluded that "decentralization cannot be understood unless considering the context of the society's educational standards" (Hannaway and Carnoy, 1993).

## SCHOOL EMPOWERMENT IN CONTEXT

A main premise for this book is that the patterns of governance and control that have traditionally dominated a specific national context are one major contextual feature that must be taken into account both theoretically and practically, prior to the initiation of a school empowerment policy and when attempting to estimate its potential consequences for public education. Specifically, it is argued that decentralization and centralization create two very distinct starting points for school empowerment restructuring initiatives in terms of the structural features and belief system characterizing each national context. It is, thus, most likely that the number of obstacles that this restructuring initiative is likely to encounter will be much greater when implemented in a national context that has traditionally featured a highly centralized structure.

This last statement may be made clearer in light of the observation articulated by Watzlawick, Weakland and Fisch (1974), who differentiate between two types of changes which differ mainly in essence and scope: first-order and second-order changes. A first-order change is the permissible moving about within an unchanging system. A second-order change, in contrast, reflects a shift affecting the system itself, changing its goals, basic assumptions and values. In considering that school empowerment argues for the need to increase schools' autonomy and the degrees of freedom granted to teachers and school principals, it suggests a second-order type of change when implemented in centralized systems. Therefore, it may be understood why this restructuring initiative is most likely to encounter major constraints when implemented in centralized contexts.

Moving one step further, it is argued that the theoretical assumptions embedded in school empowerment reform initiatives may require some purification and adjustment when centralized structures are concerned. A new theoretical conceptualization may prove to be beneficial for three main reasons: Initially, adjusting the general assumptions for school empowerment according to the unique characteristics of centralized contexts may encourage policy-makers to better prepare the ground and to create more adequate conditions prior to planning and implementing school empowerment initiatives. This could be done through legislation and the establishment of new or different structural arrangements that may promote the chance of these initiatives to mature to a degree that will significantly alter school autonomy.

Secondly, recognition in the different challenges that centralized structures present for school empowerment initiatives may serve the development of corresponding strategies that are more likely to lead to a significant change in the dynamics within and between hierarchical echelons and, therefore, in the school conduct. Putting more emphasis on school-based evaluation processes as opposed to initiating a central testing system may serve as one example in this direction.

And finally and most importantly, adjusting the assumptions embedded in school empowerment in accordance with the unique characteristics of centralized contexts will better enable the establishment of realistic expectations regarding the process of policy implementation and its assumed consequences. Using the time frame as an example for one main feature of policy plans, it may be argued that the time perspective defined for the implementation of a school empowerment policy in a decentralized context may be shorter than the one defined in centralized contexts, assuming that planning takes into account the unique features and obstacles that this initiative is likely to encounter in various contexts.

While there is much logic in this line of thought which argues for the need to adjust the theoretical assumptions embedded in school empowerment in accordance with the contextual features characterizing particular educational systems, this logic still needs to be empirically supported. Such support may be gained if testimonies coming from different centralized national contexts will reflect similar patterns of action and similar consequences for school empowerment initiatives. Through employing a comparative strategy, the common denominators among different centralized states may be detected, therefore shedding light on the potentials and obstacles facing school empowerment initiatives in similar contexts. And, assuming that such common denominators actually exist, moving in this direction will provide the grounds for a more purified theory regarding school empowerment in centralized systems of education.

## MOVING ONE STEP FORWARD

This book is the result of an international project exploring the capacity of centralized structures to absorb change initiatives oriented towards school empowerment. It brings the stories of nine centralized national educational systems located around the Mediterranean Basin, systems that have attempted over the years to introduce various policies oriented towards increasing school empowerment.

Each of the chapters focuses on a single state, briefly describing its social, political and economical circumstances, the main features of the educational system, the main school empowerment initiatives taken in the last decades, the lasting effect of these initiatives in various areas and, finally, the potentials and constraints that these restructuring initiatives faced in the past and are likely to face in the future. Specifically, the book presents the cases of Malta, Cyprus, Greece, France, Turkey, Israel, Spain, Portugal and Italy.

Two common denominators may be initially identified among these countries: The first one is that they all traditionally featured a rigid centralized structure which characterized not only the educational system, but also and, not surprisingly, the government of the state as a whole. The second mutual characteristic is that, in recent years, in line with the worldwide tendency towards school empowerment, these countries initiated various policies, programs and actions, all attempting to alter the educational system and promote school empowerment and the degrees of freedom delegated to local-level educators.

Although these nine countries have different histories and are distinct in many ways, the fact that they were all centrally structured seems to have created similar influences on the way their educational systems were structured. Therefore, in spite of the uniqueness of each country, when reading the descriptions coming from these different countries, one cannot ignore one amazing feature that these educational systems all share: There exists a major gap between the rhetoric that supports school empowerment and what actually takes place in the educational system and schools. In short, it appears that much has been said, but little has actually been accomplished.

In addition to the rich descriptions presented in each chapter, the communalities among the various descriptions may be viewed and adopted as road signs for researchers, policy-makers and practitioners who wish to further explore school empowerment in centralized contexts. They point at the need to reexamine and refine the basic assumptions guiding policy plans and restructuring efforts oriented towards school empowerment in light of the uniqueness of centralized structures. Moreover, they imply the need to adopt a different scope when assessing the potential of school empowerment initiatives to significantly alter school conduct. This last statement may be better explained in considering that centralized socialization reinforces the reluctance of high-ranking officials to give up centralized patterns of operation and exchange them with ones that foster local level control while diminishing their own power and influence. At the same time, centralized socialization emphasizes the importance of obedience of individuals in subordinate echelons who are hardly encouraged to initiate or become involved in genuine endeavors that are locally based.

In line with previous observations stating that there typically exists a gap between rhetoric and conduct as far as school empowerment policies are concerned (Glickman, 1990), and based on the description of potentials and obstacles that school empowerment initiatives face in the nine centralized countries described, the concluding chapter of this book sets a theoretical framework likely to create a better correspondence between rhetoric and action when school empowerment initiatives are introduced in centralized systems of education.

## REFERENCES

Bray, M. (1985). Education and decentralization in less developed countries: A comment on general trends, issues and problems, with particular reference to Papua New Guinea. *Comparative Education*, 21 (2): 183-195.

Caldwell, B. J. (2003) A theory of learning in self managing school. In: A. Volansky and I. Friedman (eds.), *School-based management: An international perspective* (Jerusalem: State of Israel, Ministry of Education), pp. 93-116.

Gerstner, C. R., and Day, D. V. (1994). Cross-cultural comparison of leadership prototypes. *Leadership Quarterly*, 5 (2): 121-134.

Glickman, C. D. (1990). Pushing school reform to a new edge: The seven ironies of school empowerment. *Phi, Delta Kappan*, 63 (3): 9-28.

Goffman, E. (1961). *Encounters*. Indianapolis: Bobbs-Merrill.

Hannaway, J., and Carnoy, M. (eds.) (1993). *Decentralization and school improvement: Can we fulfill the promise?* New Brunswick, N.J.: Consortium for Policy Research in Education.

Hofstede, G. (1997). *Cultures and organizations. The software of the mind.* New York: McGraw-Hill.

Mazuerk, K., and Winzer, M. A. (2006). An introduction: Major themes. In: K. Mazuerk and M. A. Winzer (Eds.), *Schooling around the world: Debates, challenges and practices.* New York: Allyn and Bacon, pp. 3-28.

Watzlawick, P., Weakland, J. H., and Fisch, R. (1974). *Change: Principles of problem formation and problem resolution.* New York: Norton.

Wentworth, W. M. (1980). *Context and understanding: An inquiry into socialization theory.* New York: Elsevier.

In: Centralization and School Empowerment...
Editor: Adam Nir

ISBN 978-1-60692-730-4
© 2009 Nova Science Publishers, Inc.

*Chapter 2*

# EMPOWERING SCHOOLS IN CENTRALIZED STATES: EXPERIENCES FROM CYPRUS

*Petros Pashiardis*[1]
Open University of Cyprus, Cyprus

## INTRODUCTION

In an era of complexity and instability, education needs to adapt to contemporary trends and demands so as to secure its quality and sustainability. Undoubtedly, decentralization is a major trend nowadays and a promising initiative for empowering the self-managing school. This chapter seeks to provide an overview of the current, centralized educational system of Cyprus (a small island in the eastern Mediterranean), describe the efforts and changes observed towards decentralization as well as trace the catalysts and constraints favoring or inhibiting restructuring. On the whole, authority within the educational system of Cyprus emanates mainly from the Ministry of Education (through the Inspectorate) and schools and principals are obliged to obey without really questioning the system. Personnel and administrative management, curriculum issues and money allocation are mostly exercised by the Ministry without any significant deviation. Despite this situation, no major efforts have been noticed towards the empowerment of individual school units in Cyprus. Moreover, although principals are considered major catalysts in restructuring, their empowerment, mostly through training and budget allocations, seems to be insufficient and insignificant. The only initiative which promises a certain degree of devolution lies in the recently announced strategic plan of the Ministry of Education. Given the current situation of the educational system in Cyprus, decentralization and site-based management seem to be radical practices.

---

[1] I wish to acknowledge with thanks the assistance offered by my research assistant, Mr. Vassos Savvides, during the preparation of this chapter.

# THE CONTEXT: A BRIEF DESCRIPTION OF THE STATE AND THE EDUCATIONAL SYSTEM

We live in an era characterized by complexity and instability. Continuous change is the only factor that remains stable in our days. During the last few decades, we have witnessed numerous developments in every area of the human enterprise as well as demographic changes, state interdependence and globalization (Pashiardis, 1997a).

Educational organizations, when they operate as open, social systems interacting with and dependent on their environment, are the direct recipients of any innovations. Changes in the social environment inevitably have a tremendous impact on education, such as increased demands for effectiveness and quality in education which are the result of three main social trends: (a) recent developments in the educational and psychological sciences; (b) an increase in monetary expenses and bigger investments in education; and (c) increased accountability demands by parents and society at large for the provision of quality education (Pashiardis, 1996). As a result, educational organizations need to adapt to contemporary trends and demands.

## A Brief Description of the Social, Political and Economic Circumstances of Cyprus

Cyprus is an island in the north-eastern part of the Mediterranean with a total area of 9,251 km$^2$ (see Table 1). Cyprus is the third largest island in the Mediterranean: 226 km by 98 km. It is situated 380 km north of Egypt, 105 km west of Syria, 75 km south of Turkey, and 380 km east of the nearest Greek island, Rhodes. At the end of 2006, the estimated population was 867,600, with an ethnic composition of 76.1% Greek Cypriots (including a few Maronites, Armenians and Latins), 10.2% Turkish Cypriots and 13.7% foreign residents (Statistical Service of the Republic of Cyprus, 2007). These figures do not include Turkish settlers and military personnel, estimated at 150,000 and 40,000 respectively, who have moved into the Turkish-occupied areas since the Turkish invasion of Cyprus in 1974. At that time, one-third of the Greek population (about 200,000 persons) was expelled from their homes in the northern part of the island and was forced to resettle in the southern areas which are controlled by the government of the Republic of Cyprus. This *de facto* division of the island continues with little hope that there will be a reunification of the island. In any case, as of May 2004, Cyprus has become a full member of the European Union together with 10 other candidate countries.

The constitution of Cyprus recognizes Greek and Turkish as the official languages of the Republic. Under the constitution, the president, elected for a five-year term, exercises executive power together with his Council of Ministers. Cyprus is classified as a middle-income country, with a per capita income of 18,000 Euros. Total expenditure on public education in 2005 was about 937 million Euros, accounting for about 7% of GDP and representing 16% of the Government Budget (Statistical Service of the Republic of Cyprus, 2007).

**Table 1. Basic Information about Cyprus**

| Area of interest | Information |
|---|---|
| Location | North-eastern Mediterranean |
| Total area | 9,251 km2 |
| Estimated Population at the end of 2006 | 867,600 |
| Composition of the Population | Greek Cypriots (76.1%)<br>Turkish Cypriots (10.2%)<br>Foreign Residents (13.7%) |
| Per Capita Income | 18,000 Euros |
| Expenditure on Public Education in 2005 | 16% of Government Budget (about 937 million Euros) |
| Major economic factor | Tourism and services sector (77.6% of the economic activity) |

The economy of the island depends mainly on its tourism, which may be regarded as the major economic activity of Cyprus. Indeed tourism (and in general the service sector) account for about 77.6% of the island's economic activity (Statistical Service of the Republic of Cyprus, 2007). The quality and standard of life are high and the standards of health provision, the functioning of other social institutions and the provision of public education can be favorably compared to those of the rest of the European Union.

In 1959, after the London and Zurich Agreements, Cyprus became an independent state (in 1960), and subsequently a member of the British Commonwealth and of the United Nations. The provisions of the Agreements placed education under two parallel Communal Chambers, one for the Greek community and one for the Turkish Community. The system of local school committees continued to function under the same rules and regulations as those during the British era (Anastassiades, 1979).

In any case, the Greek Community aimed at strengthening the cultural and emotional links with Greece. A new curriculum for the public schools was developed similar to the Greek schools' curriculum and, also, the Teachers' Training College was modelled after the Pedagogical Academies of Greece and was renamed as the Pedagogical Academy of Cyprus (Persianis, 1981). This was the main college for the training of elementary school teachers in Cyprus until 1992 when the Department of Education at the University of Cyprus took over the preparation of elementary school teachers as well as part of the pedagogical training of secondary school teachers. However, the majority of secondary school teachers continue to be educated in Greece.

## A Description of the Educational System

In 1963, violent actions broke out between the two communities (Greek and Turkish). As a result of those disturbances, the parallel system of the two Communal Chambers was abolished and, furthermore, the two communities took steps towards separation. Following the de facto separation in 1965, all the administrative functions of the Greek Communal Chamber were transferred by law to a new ministry, the Ministry of Education. The Ministry of Education was (and still is) responsible for all Greek schools, and for the schools of all the other ethnic groups, which aligned themselves with the Greek community. Our discussion throughout this paper pertains only to the schools supervised by the Ministry of Education of the Republic of Cyprus. The Ministry of Education, which was renamed as Ministry of Education and Culture in 1994, is the policy making and administrative body of the government for education. It is responsible for the enforcement of educational laws and the preparation of educational bills to be voted by the House of Representatives. It prescribes syllabi, curricula and textbooks. It regulates and supervises all the institutions under its jurisdiction. The education budget became part of the national budget, and public education came under the control of the central government. Private schools are owned, administered and financed by individuals or bodies but are liable to supervision by the Ministry of Education and Culture. They also receive some money and free textbooks from the government.

Appointments, transfers, promotions and discipline of all teaching personnel and the Inspectorate of the Public Education System are the responsibility of the Educational Service Commission, a five-member independent body, appointed by the President of the Republic for a period of six years. The public educational system in Cyprus is highly centralized, with the Ministry of Education and Culture (MOEC) being responsible for the implementation of educational laws and the preparation of new legislation, as mentioned above. Public schools are financed from government funds, while private schools raise their funds primarily from tuition and fees along with some government assistance. Private schools are administered by voluntary bodies or private individuals but supervised by the Ministry, as mentioned above. Education is provided in pre-primary, primary,[2] general secondary, technical and vocational secondary schools and in special schools.

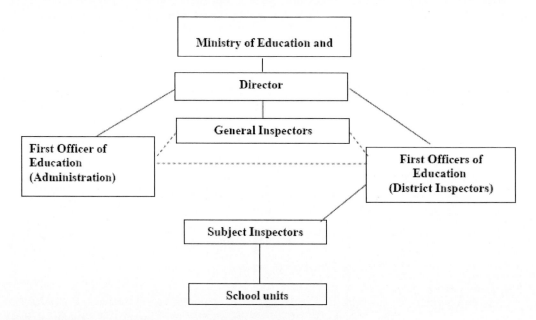

Figure 1. Organizational Structure of the Educational System in Cyprus.

---

[2] In this context the terms "primary" and "elementary" are used interchangeably. They refer to the schooling of pupils from age 6 to 12. Pupils in secondary and technical schools are approximately from age 12 to 18.

**Table 2. Basic Figures of the Educational System of Cyprus in 2005-2006**

| Level of Education | No. of schools | No. of pupils | No. of teachers |
|---|---|---|---|
| Pre primary | 443 | 19, 485 | 1, 302 |
| Public | 242 | 9, 849 | 621 |
| Community | 65 | 1, 833 | 96 |
| Private | 136 | 7, 803 | 585 |
| Primary | 365 | 59, 401 | 4,348 |
| Public | 338 | 55,879 | 4,054 |
| Private | 27 | 3,522 | 294 |
| Secondary | 158 | 65, 660 | 6, 942 |
| Public | 122 | 56, 573 | 6, 084 |
| Private | 36 | 9, 087 | 858 |

Figure 1 depicts a simplified version of the structure of the educational system of Cyprus. At the top of the chart is the Ministry of Education and Culture which constitutes the main decision-maker in important educational matters. The Director of each level of education (elementary, secondary, and technical/vocational) organizes and supervises the school units at the macro level while the General Inspectors have the responsibility of the general inspection of school units and the coordination of all the inspectors. The first officers of education are in charge of the school units within their district while one of them has administrative duties at the Director's Office. Lower in the hierarchy are the subject inspectors who are in charge of evaluating specific school units assigned to them. Finally, it must be pointed out that the structure described pertains to each separate level of education.

Pre-primary education is offered in kindergartens for children up to the age of five years and eight months, and is under the jurisdiction of the Ministry of Education and Culture. There are public, community and private kindergartens. Approximately 88% of children aged three to five are enrolled in some form of pre-primary education (Statistical Service of the Republic of Cyprus, 2007). As of the 2005-2006 school year (see Table 2), there were 242 public kindergartens, 65 community kindergartens and 136 private ones registered with the Ministry of Education (the number for private kindergartens is much greater, although not all are registered with the Ministry of Education and, thus, are not counted). The number of pupils for the year 2005-2006 reached 19,485 (9,849 in the public kindergartens, 1,833 in the community and 7,803 in the private ones) while the number of the teachers is 1,302 (621 in the public kindergartens, 96 in the community and 585 in the private ones). Children begin free, compulsory, primary education from the age of five years and eight months. As of the 2005-2006 school year (see Table 2), there were 365 primary schools (338 public and 27 private) with 59,401 pupils (55,879 in the public schools and 3,522 in the private schools) and 4,348 teachers (4,054 in the public schools and 294 in the private schools). About 94% of elementary school children attend public schools and about 6% attend private ones, with 69% of the students enrolled in urban schools and 31% in rural schools. Public Primary education has been free and compulsory since 1962.

Secondary education is pursued in public and private schools. Public Secondary education extends over six years and is divided into two cycles: the lower, which is called the *Gymnasium*, with pupils between 12 to 15 years old, and the upper, *Eniaio Lykeio*, with pupils between 15 to 18 years old. The lower cycle is free and compulsory, while the upper one is free but not compulsory. Secondary Technical and Vocational schools accept pupils who graduated from the Gymnasium at the age of 15. Each school has two departments, technical and vocational. They provide local industry with technicians and craftsmen. The lyceum comprises grades 10 to 12. As of the 2005-2006 school year (see Table 2), there were 158 secondary schools (122 public and 36 private) with 65,660 pupils (56,573 in the public schools and 9,087 in the private schools) and 6,942 teachers, 6,084 in the public schools and 858 in the private ones (Statistical Service of the Republic of Cyprus, 2007). Enrollments in public schools accounted for about 86.2 % and private schools for about 13.8%. Some 81% of secondary school leavers attend tertiary institutions either in Cyprus or abroad, mainly Greece, the UK and the USA.

The structure of the public educational system, suffers from (1) discontinuity at Primary – Secondary transition, (2) lack of communication and coordination because of the artificial splitting of a number of primary schools into two cycles, a junior and a senior primary school, each with a different principal, albeit operating in the same buildings, and (3) from the total control that is exerted to all schools from the Ministry of Education. Private Secondary education is focused on general, commercial and vocational education and the preparation for examinations such as the GCE, etc. There are also a very limited number of religious schools on the island. Mainly, these are private schools not necessarily affiliated with any particular religion.

The teaching of religion is compulsory and there is public prayer in all public schools in Cyprus. Where there are students of other faiths, they do not need to pray as the requirement is for the Greek Orthodox students; however, they need to stand in observance and maybe pray silently or just stand still. Further, students of other faiths can be excluded from religious teaching and they will be involved in other activities during such teachings and observances at their particular school. Every now and then, during major church celebrations, the students may all go to church en mass with their teachers and even receive Holy Communion.

# Major Restructuring Initiatives Towards School Empowerment

Undoubtedly, current trends in the field of educational leadership and accountability favor the empowered school unit and the need for skillful educational leaders who can cope with the multifaceted character of schooling. Decentralization and site-based management constitute major trends nowadays regardless of the fact that they have not yet been proven more successful with regards to student achievement (Bimber, 1994). According to the OECD (2004), devolving responsibility to the front line constitutes an important policy lever for empowering school units. Decentralization entails that the authorities entrust the school site with a number of responsibilities favoring the creation of the self-managing school. Therefore, educational leaders should be prepared to cope with multifaceted responsibilities that include financial, instructional, planning and evaluating functions (Massialas, 2000). In sum,

Decentralisation is driven by the idea that removing constraints on schools and enabling staffs to make decisions about instructional matters will produce more school charters, and other variations on the decentralisation theme; all share the assumption that reducing controls exercised by state authorities will prompt school staffs to exert greater initiative and to better tailor instruction to the needs of students (Bimber, 1994, p. 1).

Willingness of authorities to share power is a necessary prerequisite for successful decentralization. As Reynolds (1997) argues, "site-based management is perceived as a 'bottom-up' strategy for change, but its success requires leadership and supportive change from the top" (Reynolds, 1997, p. 23). The management team of the school including the principal, teachers, parents and sometimes students and other community members should be afforded release time to improve the quality of educational programs of their school unit.

Currently, the main philosophies that underpin the educational system in Cyprus are that of (a) centralization of powers and of (b) seniority within the system. Power emanates mainly from the Ministry of Education through the Inspectorate, and the schools and their principals are obliged to obey without really questioning the system and its authority. The second main philosophy is the one that tells everybody that they need to be patient and eventually (usually a few years before retirement which is age 60) they will reach higher administrative positions within the educational bureaucracy.

## Centralization-Decentralization under the British Rule

The educational system in Cyprus, however, was not always so centralized. Indeed, under the British rule of the island (1878-1959) it went through various eras of centralization and decentralization. Initially, the system was very decentralized and the local communities had almost total control as to whom they employed as teachers, how much they paid them and for how long they employed them. There were School Councils, Community Councils and District Councils as well as the Education Council for the whole island. In any case, the educational system of the island was separate for the two communities (Greek and Turkish) and quite autonomous until October 1931 (Spyridakis, 1952).

In October 1931, when the Greek-Cypriots rebelled against the British rule and burned down the British Governor's house in Nicosia, the British Administration imposed a new law in 1933 (Education Law No. 18 of May 27, 1933) taking complete control of the island's educational system. That law reiterated that the British Governor of Cyprus had total command and authority for the provision of elementary education in Cyprus. He had every right to change the books used, he changed the curriculum (which until then was aligned with the curriculum of elementary schools in Greece) and imposed the English language as the main teaching tool for the Greek population of the island. Further, through this law, the Archbishop and the Greek Orthodox Bishops were stripped of their right to chair the Education Council (which had been their prerogative until 1933). Further, through another law in 1935, the teaching of Greek history was prohibited and the British National Anthem was substituted for the Greek. In order to exercise more control over the educational system, the British administration abolished the two Teacher Training Schools that trained Greek teachers and created a new Teachers' College with English as the medium of instruction. Both Greek and Turkish Cypriot teachers were trained there (Myrianthopoulos, 1946;

Spyridakis, 1974). In essence, the educational system of Cyprus remained very centralized during the rest of the period until independence, in 1960. However, even after independence was granted, under the new constitution, which created the Republic of Cyprus, education was considered to be a separate affair for the two main communities of the island (Greek and Turkish). As mentioned before, the Ministry of Education was created in 1965 and all the centralized structures that were created by the British Administration were kept in place.

## Movements towards more Devolution of Powers

Recently, in December 2007, the Ministry of Education publicized a policy document promulgating its intentions for strategic planning in education (Ministry of Education and Culture, 2007). The implementation of this plan includes "the granting of administrative and educational autonomy to the school units in such a way so as to promote the improved use of human resources in education." According to the Ministry of Education (2007), centralization hinders the introduction of innovations while granting more power to the school units will provide them with the flexibility to handle and satisfy their local needs and particularities.

The implementation of the Ministry's strategic objective concerning decentralization involves a focus on specific action fields. In particular, the Educational District Offices are to be given authority to handle issues relating to the daily function of the school units. This devolution of powers will serve the immediate and better response to the everyday problems faced by schools. Moreover, it is proposed that the District Offices are given the responsibility for teachers' transfer and placement within the urban areas while the recruitment for the schools in rural areas will remain under the jurisdiction of the Educational Service Commission. Further suggestions for decentralizing educational authority include the establishment of procedures for the self-evaluation of school units, the introduction of in-service development programs for teachers at school level and the redistribution of the teachers' working and instructional time so that they respond to the new multifaceted role required by an autonomous school unit, such as conducting action research projects and designing self improvement action plans. In such a context, school organizations will have the opportunity to undertake activities which will respond to their own particularities and priorities.

The strategic plan for creating autonomous school units seems to be a promising initiative in laying the foundations for school empowerment. A considerable number of bureaucratic procedures will be cleared away and (as a result) principals will be able to concentrate more on their pedagogical and instructional mission instead of having to manage routine tasks. Moreover, the more active involvement of all stakeholders will create conditions for fostering organizational learning and building capacity within the individual organizations. Such an evolution in the Cyprus educational system would also bring parents and society closer to the real school life. The accountability movement demands the provision of quality education and thus, makes collaboration among all stakeholders necessary. Parents and other stakeholders should be an integral part of the school management team and (in general) become more actively involved in the educational processes taking place in the school unit (Ministry of Education and Culture, 2007). However, it has to be pointed out that while this is a positive step towards decentralization, still more has to be done in order to promote further devolution of educational structures. For example, the current plan does not provide for each school unit selecting its own personnel or making decisions about curriculum issues. Moreover, any initiatives may only be undertaken in coordination with the District's Senior Officers. As a result, it may be concluded that power will be partly devolved to the district level and to a lesser extent to the school level.

Further developments in the direction of school empowerment have also been observed recently. These include the training of administrative staff, the introduction of postgraduate degrees in Educational Administration and the provision of a small budget to principals to deal with routine, everyday tasks. Although important, these initiatives are not considered as major restructuring plans but rather more of a piecemeal kind of reform scheme.

It cannot be argued that site-based management or other decentralization practices are a panacea. However, given the highly centralized character of the educational system, small steps towards decentralization might be the starting point for the creation of a healthier educational system. Indeed, given the current situation of the educational system in Cyprus, the aforementioned decentralization and site-based management initiatives seem to be radical practices.

In closing this section, it must be emphasized that even though the Ministry of Education is now taking steps towards decentralization and more devolution of powers to the individual school units, it is doing so with great reluctance. The reasons for the Ministry of Education's reluctance to increase school principals' authority and school-level autonomy are not quite evident. It appears that everyone in Cyprus agrees that increasing school autonomy will benefit schools, yet initiatives in this direction fail to materialize. In my view, the main reasons for this reluctance and delay are: (a) the school leaders are not prepared at all through any kind of training to assume more responsibilities and, therefore, they keep their distance from increased powers, as more powers mean greater responsibility, with which they are afraid they will not be able to cope, (b) the center (i.e., the Ministry of Education) does not really wish to relinquish its own powers or authority, as schools have always been used as policy instruments by every government in Cyprus, and the thought is that with greater autonomy, the government will lose some of its controlling mechanisms, thus making it more difficult to implement educational policy, and (c) the unions do not want more autonomy at the school level, because they also feel that if school leaders acquire more powers, they (the school leaders) will be able to exercise more control over the teachers, as opposed to the unions exercising more control over them, as is the current situation.

## THE LASTING EFFECT: IN WHAT AREAS WERE CHANGES NOTICED AND IN WHICH OTHER AREAS SHOULD CHANGES BE INITIATED?

Unfortunately, there are numerous examples of policy changes and policy implementation at the national level, where those who need to implement them do not know or have not been informed about the content of the changes. The usual approach in Cyprus is for all educational innovations to be introduced in the top-down approach without the involvement of those who will need to implement them. For example, when the whole effort of introducing national standards began, not even the Ministry inspectors knew about this development. Only a handful of people who had developed the ideas and the then Minister of

Education himself were cognizant of this new development. In short, the policy-making role of school administrators in Cyprus is non-existent, as they do not help formulate policy, but are merely called upon to implement it once it has been decided.

As indicated through research worldwide, one of the most important catalysts for the introduction of innovations and empowerment at the school level is the school unit's leadership, i.e., the principal, assistant principals, etc. Unfortunately, even at this level, the Cyprus educational system has not done much in order to empower principals and provide them with the tools necessary to lead and introduce change at the school level. On the contrary, based on how school leaders are selected in Cyprus, maybe it is not possible for them to play the role of catalyst. Therefore, it is important to examine the status of the principalship in Cyprus and try to relate it to changes aimed at their empowerment.

## Selection and Appointment to the Principalship: Waiting in Line

Researchers in the field of educational leadership have found very interesting notions among the Cypriot principals about how they are promoted to the post as well as the extent to which they feel empowered to do their job and introduce change in their schools (Pashiardis, 1993; 1997b; Pashiardis and Orphanou, 1999; Pashiardis and Ribbins, 2000; 2003). What is evident is that the main criterion for promotion to the principalship is the age of the candidate; limitations of space here preclude a full treatment of the "long climb." In any case, none of principals participating in the research regards himself as working to a career plan designed to lead to a principalship at the earliest opportunity. In part, no doubt, this can be explained as a sensible response to the perceived existence of powerful systemic forces designed to inhibit early promotion to principal. In such a situation, there may be little point in striving for a goal, which is hard to hasten, and which will, in time, be "achieved" anyway. This is a view that the UNESCO auditors evidently share:

> Personnel management is a major weakness ... perhaps the greatest weakness [of the educational system in Cyprus]. Neither the method of appointing teachers for the secondary sector nor the promotion system ... focused on the needs of the education system... (Drake, Pair, Ross, Postlethwaite and Ziogas, 1997, p. 58).

Indeed, selection methods for educational leaders in Cyprus are either obsolete or non-existent. What is essential is the introduction of improved selection methods and the readjustment of job description qualifications in order to comply with the current needs of our educational system. Basically, we need radical reforms. The selection of potential educational leaders could be implemented through assessment centers, which, according to Hoy and Miskel (2008), enable the identification of individuals displaying the personality traits and the motivation to lead. It cannot be argued that assessment centers are a panacea. However, *"they do promise to create personnel selection practices that are based on more sound scientific evidence"* (Pashiardis, 1993, p. 34).

The utilization of assessment centers has also been proposed by a consortium appointed to design a new teacher appraisal system (called "Athena") for the educational system of Cyprus. According to this scheme, the Educational Service Commission will take up the responsibility to organize appraisal events in the form of an Assessment Center. The evaluators at the Assessment Center will have as a primary goal the observation and appraisal of the candidates while they go through various exercises and simulations that relate to school management and leadership. The proposal concerning the introduction of assessment centers seems to have been seriously taken into account by the Ministry of Education since it is treated as one of the main objectives in its strategic plan (Ministry of Education and Culture, 2007).

## Preparing for the Principalship in Cyprus

A practically non-existent system of school leaders' preparation can be seen as the black hole of the Cyprus educational system. Even though research findings emphasize the advantages of pre-appointment training (McHugh and McMullan, 1995), at present, few, if any, potential leaders receive training which adequately prepares them for leadership responsibilities. The majority of school principals are prepared to assume their position through an *apprenticeship model*. Interestingly, according to research (Pashiardis, 1998; Pashiardis and Orphanou, 1999) conducted among primary school principals in Cyprus, most of them believe in the trait theory of leadership, and that, at the same time, there is a felt need to improve in areas such as professional growth and development and personnel management. These findings reflect the inadequacy in the preparation (or lack thereof) procedures of educational leaders in Cyprus. The Ministry of Education offers a few induction seminars through the Pedagogical Institute, but even those short courses and seminars that are available are not found to be helpful, based on the Institute's own internal evaluations.

Taking into account the existing status of the preparation of principals, some changes were introduced with regard to university degree preparation programs. More specifically, the Departments of Education both at the University of Cyprus and at the Open University of Cyprus have initiated graduate programs in the area of Educational Administration, apart from the aforementioned post hoc training programs and short courses for principals. Such efforts are highly promising; however, they must be intensified, expanded and enriched. Simultaneously, research programs investigating the influence of the local culture in educational leadership must be designed. Those involved, such as the State Universities and the Pedagogical Institute, could do it through close collaboration. Research among these institutions can contribute to the successful resolution of challenges for the educational system of Cyprus (Pashiardis, 1996). Research concerning educational leadership within a specific cultural context is definitely necessary in order to prepare our leaders in the best possible way. This kind of research should be intensive, diagnostic, and developmental, in order to predict needs and to develop new approaches to educational leadership. It should also be critical and evaluative in order to place existing theories under scrutiny and absorb functional ideas and practices.

In the context of the strategic plan of the Ministry of Education a "School for Principals" will also be created in order to train the selected principals for their new position (Ministry of Education and Culture, 2007). Their training will last for one year during which the principals will be released from their duties. The "School for Principals" will also be in charge of the systematic in-service of the principals throughout their career. Through the empowerment of these school officials, it is possible that the educational system will move towards more decentralization and autonomy at the school level once the school leaders are equipped with the necessary knowledge and skills to be able to lead their schools towards new directions.

## Financial Autonomy

In addition to personnel selection and preparation, some changes were noticed in the area of financial autonomy. Although budget allocation is a task exercised by the center, there has been a move towards granting principals a small budget to distribute in accordance to the school unit's needs (Ministry of Education and Culture, 2005; 2006). This effort, although it encountered resistance in the beginning, was finally successfully introduced. It cannot be claimed that schools are financially autonomous, but it is a first move towards the financial empowerment of the school unit. Further devolution in financial issues is expected to occur with the future implementation of the strategic plan of the Ministry.

## Managing the Curriculum

It is also important to note that principals and the school unit in general have no authority over curriculum issues. No significant developments were noticed in regard to this domain of school autonomy. The content of the curriculum and to a great extent the instructional methodologies are prescribed by the Ministry of Education. The principal and teachers may only choose to give emphasis to selected goals and instructional methods or engage in European projects. Nevertheless, these adjustments are not sufficient to account for the school's unique characteristics.

## National Educational Standards

It is widely accepted among all stakeholders in education that, especially in our educational system, there is no explicit articulation of what a student should know and be capable of at each grade level. This acknowledgement is also mentioned in the UNESCO report on the evaluation of the educational system of Cyprus (Drake et al., 1997). The absence of clear performance indicators leads to a subjective treatment of the educational product offered to our students.

As a response to this deficiency of the educational system, the Ministry of Education decided, as of 2001, to proceed with the determination of National Educational Standards in the subject areas of Mathematics, Greek Language and Science, both in the primary and secondary levels of education. This change was introduced partly in an attempt to empower principals and school units to improve their individual performance. If principals had in their hands scientific tools of the actual standards of their students then they could establish mechanisms and procedures for the self-evaluation and improvement of their school unit. This initiative, although essential, was resisted by the teachers' unions which indefensibly asserted that this innovation would only lead to the intensifying of inequalities in education. This strong resistance of the teachers' unions was the main cause for the freezing of the procedures for establishing national educational standards back in 2004, after the committees had produced a large amount of work.

It is interesting to note that the teachers' unions resisted this effort when they realized that the Standards Committee was ready to begin testing students at any level of the educational system that the Ministry wished to do so. Their rationale for this resistance was that they did not want teachers to take all the culpability and discussion that would follow in case the results of the students' testing would be low. They felt that teachers would get more pressure and that they would become the "victims" for the educational system's perceived inadequacies and deficiencies. It must be stressed that the majority of parents in Cyprus have the perception that the public educational system does not really serve their children well and there is a shift towards private schools. When the Committee insisted that its goal was not to "name and shame" but only to establish the current level of students' achievement in Cyprus in order to suggest solutions and remedies, teachers were not convinced and they threatened the (then) Minister of Education with a strike if the Committee proceeded with testing; therefore, the whole effort was halted. What is now happening is that there was a change of government in Cyprus after the February (2008) presidential elections and the current Minister of Education was a member of this Standards Committee, as well as the author of this chapter. It will be interesting to wait for future developments on this issue.

## "Athena" - the Proposed Appraisal System

The high degree of centralization as well as the limited powers of principals, especially with regard to personnel management, creates a disproportionate practice of internal and external evaluation with the latter being significantly preferred at the expense of the former. For example, although the principals complete an annual report for each teacher in their school, this ultimately ends up in the hands of the school inspectors who are in charge of the external, summative evaluation. Moreover, the principals do not have the time to be the kind of instructional leaders they would like to be due to the many routine tasks they have to perform on a daily basis (Pashiardis, 1998). Nevertheless, as is indicated through findings from the effective schools research, leadership has an essential role in the life of a school. Educational leaders are considered to be the heart and soul of their schools (Pashiardis, 1993) and, thus, their role in teacher evaluation must be analogous.

Based on the aforementioned, a reform scheme called "Athena" has been devised so as to rectify the current state of teacher evaluation in the educational system of Cyprus. The Proposed System of Evaluation aims at empowering schools by transforming them into learning organizations. More specifically, the Instructional Leader (Assistant School Head) will be responsible for supporting teachers in the instructional domain and providing them with appropriate professional development opportunities. Great emphasis will be placed on in-service training within the school, and a connection to the self-appraisal of the teacher with the system for professional development will be established. Moreover, the principal's role itself will be greatly enhanced.

Within the framework of the Proposed Appraisal System, it is anticipated that internal evaluation processes such as self assessment and mentoring will form the basis on which improvement and self development will be enhanced. External evaluation will no longer drive out internal processes which will now be at the core of the evaluation system. As a result, teaching as well as management personnel will have the opportunity to reflect on their practices, learn from their mistakes and achievements and plan their future actions for improvement.

From what has been described so far, it is apparent that changes are neither vast nor substantial, thus leading to trivial effects on the educational system of Cyprus. For example, we have witnessed partial progress in the areas of the preparation of principals and their financial autonomy, while no advancement has been observed with regard to the management of the curriculum at the school itself. Additionally, the introduction of national standards has been blocked in the course of the implementation of the reform while the end products in the domains of the appointment of principals and the Proposed Appraisal System remain to be ascertained with the implementation of the strategic plan of the Ministry and the "Athena" scheme in particular.

This situation illuminates the disadvantaged position in which the Cyprus educational system is at the beginning of the new century. The system lacks the means and the vision for keeping pace with emerging needs and increased societal pressures for quality provision of education. *"It appears that there are some gaps that need to be closed in anticipation of changes in the 21$^{st}$ century"* (Massialas, 2000, p. 9). There is a pressing need for courageous political decisions and reforms to confront the challenges of our times. Thus, the new millennium signals the necessity for new leadership and more autonomy in our schools, as evidence of the past 50 years is consistent in pointing out the importance of quality leadership and local control in order to attain successful schools (Creissen and Ellison, 1998).

## RESTRUCTURING CONSTRAINTS AND CATALYSTS

In this section, a description of the main constraints and catalysts related to school empowerment will be attempted. Initially, as the UNESCO auditors (Drake et al., 1997) argued in their report on the Cyprus educational system, the following themes can be underlined that probably formulate the philosophy and values of this system:

### Money

The system is very centralized and everything is required to go through the Director of Primary or Secondary Education respectively within the Ministry of Education. Written authorization is needed for everything. School principals (generally) are not allowed to handle money. As principals often mention, the country trusts them with the education of its children but it does not trust them with handling of even small sums of money. Yet, recently the Ministry of Education has made an effort for partial devolution in the case of financial issues (Ministry of Education and Culture, 2005; 2006). Specifically, principals are to be trusted with a small budget for the smooth functioning of their school units. Although principals in Cyprus initially were against this initiative (perceiving it only as an extra burden on their already tight schedules), after advice from their unions they finally seemed to understand the importance of this measure. Therefore, the principals themselves constitute a major catalyst in enhancing decentralization efforts, whereas their unions may sometimes present themselves as obstacles to the introduction of new ideas.

## Personnel Management

One of the biggest obstacles to being an effective school and creating a distinct school culture and ethos is that the principals have no say in the appointment of personnel to their schools. Whatever the specialization of a specific teacher and whoever is sent to them by the Education Service Commission and the Ministry of Education, principals must accomodate. Therefore, the centralized nature of transfers of teachers in the various schools as well as the (almost) yearly redistribution of personnel constitutes a major obstacle in achieving any meaningful feeling of group cohesion at the school level.

## The Power of the Center

The third theme, running strongly through the others, is the power of the Ministry of Education and the lack of empowerment of the principal at the school level. Many principals nowadays argue both that the principal should have greater authority and that the school should be more autonomous. Moreover, as is indicated through findings from effective schools research, leadership has an essential role in the life of a school. *"A school's leadership is its heart and soul"* (Pashiardis, 1993, p. 27). However, teachers in public schools continue to be appointed, transferred and promoted by the Educational Service Commission. School inspectors from the Ministry of Education visit schools at all levels and offer consultations, advice and supervision. School evaluation is also their responsibility. Moreover, in-service education for primary school teachers is not mandatory after their university years. For secondary school teachers the only mandatory training is a one-year program (prepared and delivered by the University of Cyprus as of September 2007) prior to appointment to their first teaching post. The Pedagogical Institute and the Ministry of Education offer a variety of professional development programs for teachers. These usually consist of ongoing guidance from inspectors and principals and are taken on a voluntary basis during afternoons and after school. No organized, compulsory and systematic in-service training takes place after appointment to the education service. At this point, it is important to discuss in more detail the notion of centralization in relation to four critical elements: principalship, curriculum, examinations and inspection.

## Centralization and Principalship

As mentioned previously, school principals have no authority with regard to the appointment of their staff, the selection of textbooks, the setting of examinations and the development of their own curricula because of the centralized system of education in Cyprus. In fact, Cypriot principals' main functions revolve around routine administrative matters (OELMEK, 1999). They direct and supervise deputy principals and coordinators and delegate roles and responsibilities to them. Written authorization must be obtained by the director of

Primary or Secondary Education within the Ministry for most of the functions and activities organized at school level. The principals work in continuous cooperation with the Ministry, the Church, the school committees, the parents' association, the pupils' union, the counselling and careers guidance service and other welfare agencies both within and outside the Ministry of Education. They are responsible for developing a collaborative climate in the school. They supervise teaching staff, technicians and ancillary staff. They also encourage staff to initiate staff development activities. They attend and observe teachers' lessons and try to evaluate them, albeit not in any organized fashion or with any particular instrument.

Deputy principals are "middle managers" in the administrative structure of the school organization. They play supporting roles for the principals by handling school discipline matters and routine administrative tasks such as timetable changes, pupils' standards of work, attendance record keeping, implementation of school examinations and arrangement of educational visits and overseas journeys (OELMEK, 1999). Coordinators are responsible for implementing and delivering the curriculum and for developing departmental policy on issues such as the direction of homework and the assessment of pupils. They communicate frequently with the principal and the inspectors and coordinate the staff-team towards implementing the targets set by the inspectors for each school year.

Based on the above description of government policies and the duties of principals and deputy principals, it is evident that the notions of self-management at the school level or decentralization are non-existent in Cyprus. The system is highly centralized and schools have to operate within the close control of the Ministry of Education and the District Education Offices that are staffed by School Inspectors. However, the principals' willingness to embrace the new strategic objectives already mentioned will certainly be a catalyst to their successful implementation.

## Centralization and the Curriculum

Each department at the Ministry of Education (i.e., Primary, Secondary and Technical) had its own curriculum development unit even though recently there was an effort to create only one unit which would be responsible for all levels of public education. In fact, this unit became a single operating entity as of 2002. The same curriculum, a national curriculum, is applied to all schools, both primary and secondary, in Cyprus. At school level, there is no flexibility for curriculum changes except when teachers take their own initiative to create papers and handouts for the enrichment of the education process. All modifications to the curriculum, if necessary, come as a direct result of policy decisions emanating from the Ministry of Education and Culture.

The curriculum is exactly the same for all students up to the last grade of the Gymnasium (up to 15 years of age). After that students are offered the opportunity to choose some of their subjects according to their interests. This is a new development as of 2000, when the concept of the Comprehensive Lyceum (*Eniaion Lykeion*) was developed. In any case, even the teaching and curriculum delivery methodologies used by teachers are often prescribed either by the Ministry or by the inspectors, and there is not much room for deviation or experimentation, thus rendering the curriculum completely centralized. It must be noted that the curriculum is mainly directed towards preparing the students for Greek-speaking higher education institutions (either in Cyprus or in Greece). In contrast, the curriculum does not account for students wishing to pursue further studies in a foreign institution (other than Greece). Textbooks are produced locally by the departmental (i.e., primary or secondary) curriculum development units, or are donated by the Greek government.

## Centralization and Examinations

There are no state examinations for elementary education except for some diagnostic and formative examinations performed by the teachers themselves. Every student gets a school-leaving certificate at the completion of 6th grade. There is also an exam for university entrance during the last year of secondary education. At grade level there are also examinations which count for a percentage towards the student's total performance which determines whether the student is to proceed to the next grade or not. These final exams are prepared at school level. The only difference occurs at the end of the last grade of the upper secondary education where the exams are prepared by the Ministry of Education and Culture and are exactly the same for all students. Throughout all grades the norm is that only under extraordinary circumstances will a student fail to be promoted to the next grade.

At the end of the last grade of the upper secondary education (12th year of schooling), students had the option until 2005-2006 to take university entrance exams for the University of Cyprus and Greek universities. As of 2006-2007 the university entrance and school leaving exams became unified so as to simplify the process and release students from extra and, to a great extent, unnecessary stress. These exams are prepared and administered by the Ministry of Education and Culture and the subjects differ based on the university department or discipline for which the students are applying. Therefore, the subjects examined are different for students applying to the Department of Education than those students applying to medical schools, for instance.

Examination results are kept by each school for their own year-to-year performance assessment practices. No official mechanism for interschool comparison exists and, actually, any such comparison is avoided by Ministry of Education officials (at least formally). A factor that could make a difference in the interpretation of the results is the students who choose to attend a university outside Cyprus or Greece. The requirements for entering such institutions are not covered by the curriculum. Nevertheless, a considerable number of students choose to enter a British (about 23% of students studying abroad) or an American university (about 12% of students studying abroad) and usually these students do not appear on any report.

Thus, there are no examinations as a means whereby the educational system or the school demonstrates accountability. As long as there are no national standards, schools do not feel compelled to indicate any form of accountability towards society at large. The effort to introduce National Standards for the Cyprus Education System began in 2002, yet the process failed to be completed due to opposition of the educational unions. The unions were concerned with the negative implications such a process might hold in fostering inequalities in education, as they perceived them.

## Centralization and Inspection

Each education department in the Ministry has its own team of inspectors (some 40 inspectors in primary and some 45 inspectors in secondary), which inspects teachers, deputy principals and principals during a wider inspection for the whole school, the so-called *General Inspection*. General Inspections are undertaken by a team of inspectors (usually three inspectors per team), who carry out a "whole-school" inspection, which in reality is an inspection of the work done by the principal. In essence, these whole school inspections will give the principal a grade based on which the principal may be promoted to inspector.

Inspections for newly-appointed teachers are supposed to be done twice a year until they become permanent civil servants. Then, inspection becomes erratic, and not so important until the twelfth year of service for a particular teacher when (by law) the teacher must be inspected in order to earn a grade for promotion that usually happens around the 18th-20th year of service in the educational system. Recently, teachers at the elementary level have been promoted even as early as during their 15th year of service, but this is due to periodic cycles because of retirements and not to any structural changes in the system.

Furthermore, inspectors take part in curriculum development activities, the production of textbooks, the identification of other curricular resources, and the setting up of the joint examinations for the school-leaving certificate and the university entrance. In a sense, inspectors act as a link between the Ministry and the individual school units. They are in essence the policy implementation unit for the Ministry of Education. Although their role is all-encompassing and very important for the functioning of the educational system, they generally lack the necessary training and other qualifications to successfully exercise their duties.

It is also important to mention that School Inspection is mainly summative in nature, i.e., exercised for control and promotion purposes of the principalship. This should be done as well, but in the case of Cyprus, where schools lack any mechanisms for self-evaluation, this is at the expense of the school's empowerment and improvement. Therefore, it is imperative to include procedures for the self-evaluation of the school unit.

# A LOOK TOWARDS THE FUTURE

Now that education has entered the new millennium, today's educational needs necessitate that the structures at school level be redesigned and modified in a way that will reflect these new needs and guarantee further improvement in the years to come. Obviously, the bureaucratic and highly centralized structure of the Cyprus educational system is ineffective and must be redesigned. Principals must be motivated towards self-improvement and school improvement. It would seem logical for such motivation to be offered to teachers also in order to create an attitude fostering self-improvement among all teachers.

Principals are very important to the education enterprise and their preparation, evaluation and overall treatment must be offered the place they deserve. Change in educational matters becomes manageable if there are principals who can manage change. No change in the educational scene can be successful unless, at the same time, some areas of principals' work and their preparation are modified as well.

I believe that we are already past the computer and information era and are well into the biogenetics era. Based on the above and on the complexity of the environment around us, we should try to see the present as a function of the past and of the future. In essence, we in education need to be able to envision the future and use that vision to transform present teaching. We need to be able to see society at least 30, 40 or 50 years ahead, when our present students will be adults, in order to make the necessary changes in our school leadership, curricula and methods which will assist these children of today to live in the global and multicultural world of tomorrow.

It is imperative, though, that selection methods, evaluation, preparation and professional development of educational leaders engage substantial attention of those concerned with the improvement of educational provision in every country and that educational leaders become central figures to any efforts towards empowerment. It seems that in Cyprus we urgently need to take gigantic steps forward in structural and organizational reforms so that existing drawbacks do not constrain the educational system from successfully encountering current changes. Principals should be flexible enough to allow teachers to take part in rational problem solving and be responsible for widely shared decision making. Teachers should not have to become principals in order to influence policy; they should be provided with the opportunity to work with administrators as partners and to share power. Principals' authority derives from their staff. Therefore, their competence in delegating responsibilities would reinforce their position within the organization they lead. Furthermore, principals should always remember that only those who are qualified for the post they possess would be accepted and respected by their staff.

In lieu of a conclusion, given the accession of Cyprus to the European Union, the current educational system should be harmonized with European and global educational practices, albeit paying close attention to the local culture and character of education in Cyprus. In view of this development, tensions between local and European elements and other forces are expected to emerge. However, Cyprus, as a member of the multicultural European Union, should have the necessary readiness to respond to the challenge of multicultural education and this can mainly be accomplished through decentralized structures. During the twenty-first century, educational institutions will have to become multicultural in their perspectives given that Cypriot society has been confronted with unprecedented diversity in its population over the last decade. Many groups have either emigrated or come to Cyprus for short periods to work. Consequently, students with diverse cultural profiles, color, religion and language needs are already enrolled in our schools. It is the school's duty to provide an educational environment that will be effective for all students, regardless of their background. However, in order for schools to be able to do that, they need to be empowered and become autonomous to the greatest extent possible within the bounds of a national educational system. Looking at the issue from another perspective, we can easily foresee that, with the abolishment of protective labor regulations, Cypriot teachers will be in direct competition with foreign teachers, mainly Greeks from Greece because of proximity, language and familiarity. It is not unlikely for a graduating Greek teacher to have Cyprus as an option of appointment. When taking all of the above into consideration, it is easy to see that centralization will not take the educational system far. In essence, we will be forced to move towards more decentralization and empowerment at the school level and, therefore, the sooner we move towards that direction, the better off the education system will be.

# REFERENCES

Anastassiades, A. (1979). *The development of the administration of elementary education in Cyprus*. Nicosia: Theopress.

Bimber, B. A. (1994). *The decentralisation age. Comparing decision making arrangements in four high schools*. Santa Monica: Rand.

Creissen, T., and Ellison, L. (1998). Reinventing school leadership - back to the future in the UK? *International Journal of Educational Management, 12* (1), 28-38.

Drake, P., Pair, C., Ross, K., Postlethwaite, T., and Ziogas, G. (1997). *Appraisal study on the Cyprus educational system*. Paris: International Institute for Educational Planning.

Hoy, W.K., and Miskel, C.G. (2008). *Educational administration. Theory, research and practice* (Eighth Edition). New York: McGraw-Hill.

Massialas, B. (2000). *Educational reform in the Balkans and Eastern Mediterranean: School leadership in the 21ˢᵗ century. Advancing curriculum, instruction and assessment*. Paper presented at the Pedagogical Institute, Nicosia, Cyprus.

McHugh, M., and McMullan, L. (1995). Principal or manager? Implications for training and development. *School Organisation, 15* (1), 23-34.

Ministry of Education and Culture (2005). *The new law for the school councils* – 27/09/2005 (in Greek).

Ministry of Education and Culture (2006). *The modal law for the school councils of 2005. Administration of the New Institution "The Principal's Cash-In-Hand."* - 17/02/2006 (in Greek).

Ministry of Education and Culture (2007). *Strategic planning for schooling*. Retrieved on December 21, 2007 from http:// www.moec.gov.cy (in Greek).

Myrianthopoulos, C. (1946). *Education in Cyprus during the British rule (1878-1946)*. Limassol (in Greek).

OECD (2004). *Raising the quality of educational performance at school*. Policy Brief. OECD Observer.

OELMEK. (1999). *Educational laws*. Nicosia: OELMEK.

Pashiardis, P. (1993). Selection methods for educational administrators in the U.S.A. *International Journal of Educational Management, 7* (1), 27-35.

Pashiardis, P. (1996). *The Cyprus educational system and contemporary trends*. Speech presented at Skali, Aglantzia, Nicosia, Cyprus.

Pashiardis, P. (1997a). Higher education in Cyprus: Facts, issues, dilemmas and solutions. *Higher Education in Europe, 22* (2), 183-192.

Pashiardis P. (1997b). Towards effectiveness: What do secondary school leaders in Cyprus need? *Journal of In-service Education, 23* (2), 267-282.

Pashiardis, P. (1998). Researching the characteristics of effective primary school principals in Cyprus. *Educational Management and Administration, 26* (2), 117-130.

Pashiardis, P., and Orphanou, S. (1999). An insight into elementary principalship in Cyprus. *The International Journal of Educational Management, 13* (5), 241-251.

Pashiardis, P., and Ribbins, P. (2000). *On Cyprus: The making of secondary school principals*. Paper presented at the ACEA, CCEAM, NZEAS, PNGEA, TSPA, Hobart, Tasmania. September 9-13.

Pashiardis, P., and Ribbins, P. (2003). On Cyprus: The making of secondary school principals. *International Studies in Educational Administration, 31* (2), 13-34.

Persianis, P. (1981). *The political and economic factors as the determinants of educational policy in independent Cyprus (1960-1970).* Nicosia: Pedagogical Institute (in Greek).

Reynolds, L.J. (1997). *Successful site-based management. Practical guide* (Revised Edition). Thousand Oaks, California: Corwin Press, Inc.

Spyridakis, C. (1974). *Studies, lectures, papers. Second volume.* Nicosia (in Greek).

Spyridakis, C. (1952). *Educational policy by the Cyprus English administration (1878-1952).* Nicosia (in Greek).

Statistical Service of the Republic of Cyprus (2007). *Statistics of Education 2005/2006.* Retrieved October 10, 2007, from http://www.mof.gov.cy/mof/cystat/statistics.nsf index_gr/index_gr? OpenDocument.

In: Centralization and School Empowerment...
Editor: Adam Nir

ISBN 978-1-60692-730-4
© 2009 Nova Science Publishers, Inc.

*Chapter 3*

# DEVOLUTION, PARTIAL DECENTRALIZATION OF EDUCATION IN FRANCE AND IMPROVEMENT IN THE RUNNING OF SCHOOLS

## *Jean-Louis Derouet and Romuald Normand*

National Institute for Pedagogical Research University of Lyon 2, france

## INTRODUCTION

To understand the place of schools in the French educational system, it is necessary to put this question into perspective. The situation in the late 1960s and early 1970s conveys an image of over-centralization when schools were solely implementing the national policy of catchment areas – families had to enroll their children in the school nearest their home. This systematization reflected a new construct as the instruction of the French population had long been guaranteed by schools where each had a particular status, curriculum and, above all, clientele. Systematization was initiated in the 1960s and was questioned in the late 1970s because over-centralization had made the system unmanageable. Devolution and partial decentralization started in the 1980s to meet the demand for diversification. It is in this framework that the recommendations of international organizations concerning school improvement have been imported into France. This trend has only just begun. What role can it play in the diversification process and in the transformation of the complex relationships of competition and cooperation between schools?

## THE FRENCH EDUCATIONAL SYSTEM

The French educational system is under the authority of two ministries – the Ministry of Education and the Ministry of Higher Education and Research. Schooling is compulsory from 6 to 16.

There are four types of schools:

- Children as young as 2 can go to the *maternelle* (kindergarten).
- Pupils from 6 to 10 are taught in primary schools. Education for pupils with specific needs (school inclusion) is partly under the supervision of the Health ministry.
- Pupils from 11 to 15 attend junior high schools (*collège*). They have been placed in the same classes regardless of their respective level (*college unique*) since the Haby Act was passed in 1975. At the end of 9th form ($3^{ème}$), pupils sit the *brevet des colleges* (O level). Handicapped pupils are taught in *SEGPA* (vocational and general education adapted to handicapped pupils).
- Pupils from 16 to 18 go to *lycée (high school)*. General, technological, and vocational education is provided respectively in *lycées d'enseignement général, lycées technologiques* and *lycées professionnels*. All pupils in *lycées* sit the *baccalauréat* at 18. The 1989 Education Act holds that all pupils living in France should leave the educational system with a qualification and that 80% of a generation should reach baccalaureate level.

**Table 1. Number of school in the French public educational system**

| Number of primary, lower and upper secondary schools | 67,581 |
|---|---|
| Number of primary schools | 56,158 |
| Number of lower secondary schools | 56,158 |
| Number of upper secondary schools | 2,625 |
| Number of vocational schools | 1,708 |
| Number of local schools with specific education | 80 |

**Table 2. Evolution of the number of pupils**

| | School years | | | | School year 2006/2007 | | |
|---|---|---|---|---|---|---|---|
| | 2002/2003 | 2003/2004 | 2004/2005 | 2005/2006 | Public | Private | total |
| Primary education | | | | | | | |
| Kindergarten | 18,445 | 18,151 | 17,885 | 17,618 | 17,217 | 121 | 17,378 |
| Primary schools | 39,365 | 39,069 | 38,770 | 38,529 | 33,108 | 5,042 | 38,355 |
| | | | | | | | |
| Secondary education | | | | | | | |
| Lower secondary education | 6,988 | 7,003 | 7,005 | 7,021 | 5,239 | 1,706 | 7,031 |
| (*Collèges*) | 1,486 | 1,491 | 1,501 | 1,506 | 1,444 | 66 | 1,510 |
| Among which (number) have a class for students with specific needs (*SEGPA*) | | | | | | | |
| Upper secondary education | | | | | | | |
| (*lycées*) | 2,883 | 2,895 | 2,900 | 2,900 | 1,711 | 898 | 2,906 |
| Among which (number) have vocational classes | 616 | 655 | 667 | 684 | 525 | 164 | 689 |
| Vocational *lycées* (*Lycées professionnels*) | 2,070 | 2,056 | 2,040 | 2,033 | 1,153 | 418 | 2,034 |

# Table 3. Main streams in the French educational system

| General baccalaureate | Technological Baccalaureate | | Vocational Baccalaureate | | Vocational certificate (CAP) |
|---|---|---|---|---|---|
| Upper sixth (*Terminale générale*) | Technological upper sixth (*Terminale technologique*) | | Vocational upper sixth (*Terminale professionnelle*) | | CAP |
| Lower sixth (*Première générale*) | Technological lower sixth (*Première technologique*) | Première d'adaptation | Vocational lower sixth (*Première professionnelle*) | | CAP 2 ans |
| 5th form (*seconde générale et technologique*) | | (*BEP*) | | | |
| | | (*Terminale BEP*) → | Vocational 5th form (*Seconde Professionnelle*) | | |
| **Ordinary level (*Brevet*)** | | | | General and vocational education for children with specific needs (**SEGPA**) | |
| 4th form (*Troisième générale*) | | | | | |
| 3rd form (*Quatrième générale*) | | | | | |
| 2nd form (*Cinquième*) | | | | | |
| 1st form (*Sixième*) | | | | | |
| 5th year in primary school (*CM2*) | | | | | |
| 4th year in primary school (*CM1*) | | | | | |
| 3rd year in primary school (*CE2*) | | | | | |
| 2nd year in primary school (*CE1*) | | | | | |
| 1st year in primary school (*CP*) | | | | | |
| 3rd year in kindergarten | | | | | |
| 2nd year in kindergarten | | | | | |
| 1st year in kindergarten | | | | | |

**6 ans**

Educational spending represents 6.8% of GDP. This investment has long been considered an imperative. The economics of education was little developed and the question of educational return was not raised. It is the *DEP* (the department of assessment and forecast) within the Ministry of Education which launched the first tenders on this question in the early 1990s. In turn the *INSEE* (French institute of statistics) conducted a survey on the educational investment of families. These works suggested several evolutions. First, France is faced with the same contradictory problem as other developed nations. Labor training is a major asset in international competition but if it represents a financial burden on the State budget, tax pressure may result in the relocation of jobs. Consequently the challenge is to maintain, even raise spending while distributing it differently – cutting the share of the State and raising that of *régions* (local authorities) and families. Since the early 1980s, State spending has remained high (63%, including teacher pay) but the share of local authorities has increased dramatically from 7 to 20%. In addition this minority share can play a decisive role as the schools which want to develop innovative contributions are funded by local authority subsidies; so for a relatively modest allocation, local authorities can help make the difference.

There has also been a considerable evolution on the side of families. Although education is theoretically free, families have long been asked to contribute to outings, trips, even to the purchase of material, and solutions are found to help families in financial difficulty. The situation is much different for private lessons. Well-off families offer tutorials to their children. It was often public education teachers who provided this service. Now private providers offer families a complete package from homework aid to the younger to additional lessons (foreign languages, computing, etc.) to the older. Measuring this spending accurately is not easy but it has definitely become considerable. Overall, a new distribution of educational spending is looming. The State tends to focus on basic learning – literacy and mathematics – and leave arts to local authorities or families for funding.

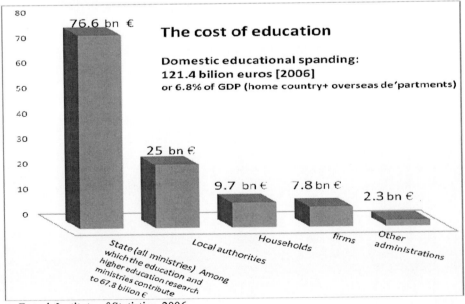

Source: French Institute of Statistics, 2006.

Diagram 1. The cost of education.

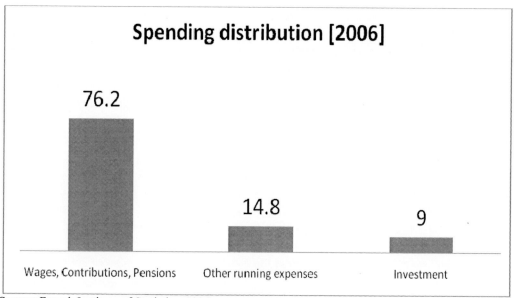

Source: French Institute of Statistics, 2006.

Diagram 2. Spending distribution on education [2006].

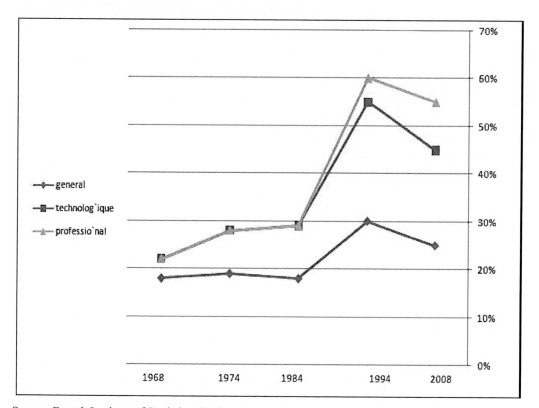

Source: French Institute of Statistics, 2008.

Diagram 3. Evolution of the annual rates of access to baccalaureate level.

France has a dual higher education system: students are mainly taught in universities but some apply to be admitted to a *classe préparatoire* which prepares students in two years for a very competitive admission test to a prestigious *grande école*.

Since the academic year 2006-2007, universities have offered a new course scheme. It is called *LMD*, L standing for license (BA), M for master (MA) and D for doctorate (PhD). It takes three years to complete a *license*, two additional years for a *master*. The *master* can be either labor market-oriented (*master professionnel)* or research-oriented (*master recherche)*. Finally, a student is awarded a doctorate degree (three years after the *master*) after writing a dissertation.

The *baccalauréat* holds a place of tremendous importance in the French educational system. It is both the top secondary education degree and the lowest higher education degree. Any baccalaureate holder has a right of access to university. In 1984, the ministry of Education made clear it wanted to bring 80% of an age-group to baccalaureate level. In addition to the general and technological baccalaureates, the vocational baccalaureate was created in 1985. A massive intake of pupils in *lycées*, and therefore of baccalaureate holders, took place in the years 1985-1995. After a sharp increase during this period, the baccalaureate pass rate first leveled off, and then decreased. Now around 63% of an age-group passes this diploma. There is no clear explanation for this stagnation. It probably reflects a crisis of the democratization model. This model was originally designed for bourgeois children and middle-class children adhered to it from the 1950S to the 1970s. Yet this model does not make sense for working-class children.

## From Networks of Diversified Schools to Systematization: Planning in the 1960s

The first schools were set up by the Church and supported by local communities during the Ancien Régime. The French Revolution and the Empire put schools under the control of the State but it did not result in centralization. One particular anecdote has to be taken cautiously: A minister of Public Instruction under the Third Republic –his name remains unsure – took out his pocket watch and asserted: "It's 8 o' clock on Monday and all French pupils start their moral lesson." This assertion may not have been made and, if it was, it has never been more than a project. Indeed, diversity was still the hallmark until the 1960s. A project of standardization linked to the ideal of equal opportunities emerged in the early 20th century. Following the First World War, the (*Compagnons de l'Université Nouvelle*) denounced the existence of two parallel instruction orders: one educated working-class pupils until they sat for the (*brevet)* at 16. The other welcomed middle-class children from the earliest age in the primary classes of (*lycées)* and brought them to matriculation (*baccalauréat)* in most cases (Garnier, 2007). Initially, there was no connection between the two networks: Latin, the major discipline in *lycées*, was not taught in the primary network. The *Compagnons* suggested that this organization into two parallel orders be replaced by a succession of levels: *école* (primary education) from 6 to 10, *collège* (lower secondary education) from 11 to 15, and *lycée* from 16 to 18. Entrance into a higher level was marked by the selection of the most talented. It is this very program which was gradually implemented until the Haby Act, the law modernizing the French educational system passed in 1975. In the eyes of its promoters, this long march (75 years) towards equality and rationality was aimed to guarantee the offer of equal educational and, in turn, equal opportunities. In addition, as 5th Republic governments were faced with a sharp rise in student intakes as a result of the baby boom, they opted for a rational, planned organization in the form of catchment areas: the area from which a school's pupils are drawn. Such a system implied that all schools had the same status, the same teaching body, the same curricula and provided the same services.

This ideal had already been given a blow when it was applied. In 1975 public opinion was familiar with the works of the sociology of reproduction and nobody believed that selection was possible irrespective of social background. Worse, historians even suggested that the former organization had a more positive impact on democratization than the ensuing standardization. The movement towards the extension of the schooling period for working-class students started in the late 19th century. The role of local communities and of guild chambers was essential to the creation of "people's colleges" (*collèges du peuple*) (Briand and Chapoulie, 2000). In the wake of the First World War, the early signs of democratization came in various forms in *lycées* (Prost, 2008). The creation in 1941 of modern classes in *lycées* was the opportunity for the best pupils in primary education to access matriculation classes. This measure initiated a rampant democratization process that was ended when the State introduced the first recommendations towards the (*collège unique*) (Prost, 1986).

The reform failed when it was systematized. French decisions followed OECD's recommendations towards the establishment of comprehensive schools. While France was one of the last countries to implement this reform, it was strictly applied and had side effects. British or Belgian governments also presented comprehensive schools as a system to modernize society but families still had some options left. In France the combined effects of the 1975 Haby Act and of catchment areas made the system binding at least in public education.

## From the Crisis of the Centralized System to the Pursuit of a New Order: The Ambiguous Interest in Local Policy-making

A report by the board of chief inspectors published in 1980 suggested that the 1975 Haby Act was not really applied. The *collège unique* implied heterogenous classes, but half of the principals made up their classes from pupils' record sent by primary schools principals. Consequently "strong" and "weak" 6th form classes coexisted. Middle-class parents, who were aware of this phenomenon, started developing alternative strategies. This misapplied law disorganized daily life. Teachers, parents, students argued that they had lost their bearings. The systematization had reached its limits and alternatives were under consideration. The first measures of devolution and school autonomy were taken when the Left came to power in 1981. School autonomy was part of the same philosophy as education priority areas. The purpose was to use local resources to attract working-class students to knowledge and to an academic organization from which they were distant. However, the measures implemented in 1981 and 1982 were prepared under the previous government. Christian Beullac succeeded René Haby in 1978. He was coming from the corporate world and applied to the French educational system (the *Éducation Nationale)* the principles of devolution and accountability of production units. Managerialism and the concern for the means to renew equality were going hand in hand. The transition between the Left and the

Right was made by the sociology of organizations. Michel Crozier's (1964; 1987) criticism of the "bureaucratic phenomenon" was very popular and inspired Alain Savary, the left-wing Education Minister. Dominique Paty (1996), one of Crozier's disciples, published *Twelve Junior High Schools in France* (*Douze collèges en France*). This book showed that schools were run in many different ways in a period of centralization. She was appointed adviser at the department for junior high schools within the French Ministry of National Education.

Another crisis revealed the emergence of school consumerism. Private – mostly Catholic – schools coexist with the State education system. They are largely subsidized by the State and accordingly the secular Left demanded their integration into the State sector. This demand was part of François Mitterrand's platform when he ran for President in 1981. It soon appeared that most French people remained attached to the autonomy of private education. Religious traditions still played a role but the rise in consumerism was gaining ground (Ballion, 1982). Private education provides an alternative for middle-class families when they disagree with the decisions made in the State sector (Langouët and Léger, 1994). The resistance to the bill on the unification of the public and private sectors of education was so fierce that François Mitterrand eventually abandoned the project he had initiated.

The years 1975-1984 marked the break of the pact concluded in the 1930s between the supporters of the *école unique* and the middle classes. The latter supported the project of lengthening the study period for all students because they expected access for their children to middle-class schools. Their demand was met in the 1960s and 1970s, but the 1975 Haby Act scared them because of the large-scale growth of the educational system. Their demands reversed accordingly. They sought selective procedures in a supposedly standardized system. Their first demand was school choice. This lobby was all the more active because the working classes were not in a position to suggest an alternative or a democratization project corresponding to their interests.

A new period of diversification opened with a local focus on schools, despite a few ambiguities. First these measures extended the 1982 Decentralization Act endorsed by Deferre but within the French educational system, power was devolved to *académies* and schools. Some capacities were transferred from the central administration to rectors; schools were granted more autonomy and were given the status of local State schools (*Établissement Public Local d'Enseignement*). This transfer of capacities was specific to the educational system and decentralization implied a transfer of capacities to local communities. Such a transfer concerned the building of schools and the management of real estate.

The focus on local interests is also politically ambiguous. Left-wing governments in the 1980s presented the territorialization of education as a means to give a fresh boost to the ideal of equality. The procedure was still in line with the tradition of the welfare state even if another objective was already present. Alain Savary was willing to reduce bureaucracy and undermine what he considered teacher corporatism. He thus gave new rights to other partners such as pupils' parents. This orientation was confirmed by Michel Rocard's decree specifying how the 1989 Modernization of Public Services Act should be enforced. Today families mainly demand the right to choose the school where their children will be taught. European recommendations endorse this orientation: the notion of governance legitimizes users' rights and the publication of league tables concerning the effectiveness of schools and teachers helps families make a choice. Other analyses highlight the break introduced by the report, *A Nation at Risk*, issued in 1983 in the USA. In the wake of its publication, educational and training policies underwent major changes. The main objective was no longer pursuing equality or maintaining social cohesion; rather it consisted of preserving the country's rank in international competition. The interest in the training of elites and performance obligations was renewed. These principles were adopted by the European Union during the Lisbon Conference in 2000 (Lawn and Nóvoa, 2005). Member states set themselves the target of becoming the most competitive and dynamic knowledge-based economy by 2010. They spurred competition through benchmarking criteria: The least competitive countries must adopt the "good practice" of those who are successful. In that light, the focus on local interests in France reflects the evolution of the notion of public service towards a quality-based regulation.

## Grandeur and Fall of the School Project (1981-1995)

The notion of school projects was introduced experimentally in 1982. It quickly gained ground and the 1989 Education Act made it central in the regulation of the educational system. It did not concern staff status, teaching hours, or curricula, as these points are included in laws or national regulations. The Education Act provided that each school had to find the best educational means to allow their students to reach targets set at national level. It was a challenging objective but it may have been doomed to failure in advance. Was it possible to work on means without first reconsidering the objectives set? School projects were undeniably successful in what is called scholastic life (*vie scolaire*) in France, that is, all that takes place in schools outside classrooms. They had a positive impact on the reorganization of canteens that have become real school restaurants, on the arrangement of the midday break, and on the organization of public transport, etc. They also focused on autonomous work in school libraries and the development of reading tutorials. In any case, they do not concern what happens in classrooms or curricular content.

The 1989 Education Act also strove to use school projects as a means to stem the rise in school consumerism. The balance of the system rests on a negotiation between the project of students or families and the school project. Rectors are in a position to make catchment areas more flexible.

The growing autonomy of schools goes hand in hand with the development of evaluation. The State exerts its control via ex-post assessment rather than through ex-ante regulations. The Ministry of Education had long established a statistics department designed as a planning and management tool. In the late 1970s this statistics department was gradually turned into an assessment instrument and the assessment and forecast department (*DEP*) was officially set up in 1986. In the 1989 Jospin Act (in the name of the then Education Minister), assessment served the purpose of "preventing possible abuses" and the IPES system (indicators measuring the performance of schools) was created accordingly. IPES shows that market regulation is more effective in France than in other countries, although inequalities among schools increase (Trancart, 1998). IPES may be considered an example of the ambiguities of the time: While they contribute to know more of how (in)equality in education develops and tends to orient state welfare policy towards a democratization process, they make enlightened consumers even more knowledgeable. In the late 1970s, the press started publishing league tables for schools. The publication of these gross figures reflects reality to some degree. The prestigious schools that recruit already selected students deserve little credit for obtaining good examination results. To know how good a school is, it is necessary to cross its results with the characteristics of its cohort of students, and maybe analyze how this school is run. Instead, *DEP* and several researchers made great efforts to determine the value that each school adds for its students. Although they tried to explain the difference between assessment and league table to public opinion (Thélot, 1994), social uses are hard to change.

## The Emergence of the Managerial State: International Benchmarking and local governance (1995-2007)

From 1995, the school project policy became a mere administrative obligation. Other changes occurred. Local communities, which were initially cautious in their approach to the "teaching fortress," started including education and training in their projects of local development. The State transferred a part of educational spending to local communities and families. It remains the principal financial contributor since it pays civil servants, but its share was cut from 69.5% in 1980 to 63.6% in 2005, while that of local communities increased from 14.2% in 1980 to 21.2% in 2005. The transfer of spending implied a transfer of competences. New forms of governance emerge and schools find themselves at the heart of a network with different interests and stakeholders – those of the educational system's civil servants (managers, teachers, administrative staff, etc.), but also those of parents, local communities, firms, etc. "Good governance" is the result of a circulation of knowledge between the different partners without any predominance of the public sector over the private sector (Koiman, 1993).

The Lisbon conference in 2000 marked France's entry into a new type of regulation based on performance obligation. This is not the retreat of the State in the face of the market but rather a compromise inspired by Britain's Third Way – what Anglo-Saxon researchers call the managerial State (Clarke, Gewirtz and McLaughin 2000; Gewirtz, 2002). It is no longer based on the welfare state model, but is the resulting combination of two rationales that each has their own legitimacy: The market rationale on one side combines individual choice and competition between schools when New Public Management seeks to promote new partnerships and a networked organization based on mechanisms to assess the quality and effectiveness of services. This evolution comes under two different forms in the French educational system: the Finance Act (*LOLF*) and the abandonment of catchment areas.

The Finance Act was passed in 2001 and is the direct consequence of the benchmarking strategy decided in Lisbon. Technical preparation was necessary before its implementation, which is why it has only been gradually applied in education since January 1st, 2006. The budget is no longer organized in sectors (health, education, transport, etc.), but rather in missions. Each department falls within one or several missions and has to set objectives and provide performance indicators. The *LOLF* is mainly implemented at *académie* level. The indicators concerning the effectiveness of schools remain basic but there is no doubt that they will become more sophisticated in the coming years.

The consumerism of middle-class families developed in the late 1970s. The governing Left in the 1980s prevented it from turning into a purely market form. The 1989 Modernization of Public Service Act introduced the notion of "rights of users." Users are both customers that defend particular interests and citizens who are concerned with the public good. This compromise, which reflects the French political socialization, paved the way for a smooth evolution. In the 1990s, the principle of catchment areas was not challenged but rectors could grant exemptions. This compromise was questioned during the 2007 presidential campaign. For the liberal Right, the constraints of catchment areas correspond to outdated planning. Some left-wingers point out that its strict application only makes urban segregation worse (van Zanten, 2004). The abandonment of catchment areas was part of Nicolas Sarkozy's presidential platform and is being gradually implemented despite administrative resistance. For the beginning of the school year 2008, the Minister of Education asked that the *rectorats* put online the main characteristics of each *collège* and *lycée* – school structure, exam pass rates over the last past years, the strong points of their school project, and the priorities of their educational policy. It is on this basis that each family can ask for an exemption in order to school their children in the school of their choice. The limit to school choice is of course the number of students a school can accomodate. Decisions are based on a number of priority criteria: handicapped children, grant holders, students in need of medical care, those who are close to the school of their choice but still outside the area.

## New Public Management at School Level: The School Improvement Movement

At international level, schools hold center stage in the implementation of the principle of performance obligation. In the United States, several studies published in the 1980s suggested that the improvement of educational systems implied the improvement of school performance. This conviction first took the form of "school effectiveness." Basically the spirit of initiative is promoted, bonuses to successful teachers are granted, and failing schools are punished. The limits of this approach soon showed. Pressure to boost performance leads to poorer teaching methods (teaching for testing) and to an exit of some teachers and students. International perspectives moved from the school effectiveness to the school improvement movement.

Finally, the transformations of the school market, the introduction of a performance obligation are meant to bring schools to think more about their offer and to the improvement of their practice towards innovation and performance. This evolution will probably be endorsed by the Ministry, as illustrated by the development of the plan, "On the Road to Success" (*Ambition Réussite*) for education priority areas or the recognition of a right to experimentation in Article 34 of the 2005 Education Act. It now stands for a fact that the model of democratization based on a "school form" does not include working-class students (Vincent, 1980). The middle-class school managed to include middle-class students in the years following the Second World War. Since the late 1990s, it is faced with the exit of working-class students, a factor of permanent disorder. The building of a new democratization project cannot overlook this fact.

The expression of differences and their recognition are also an important challenge. Religion, ethnicity, handicap and gender bring new rights (Caillé, 2007) that the educational system hardly recognizes, but they already affect the teacher-student relationship. However, the institutionalization of differences in an equality-based school regime specific to the Republican ideal is still a problem. Questions of discrimination and exclusion also arise and question the adjustment of the school system to a multiethnic and multicultural society. Accordingly, the diversification of teaching methods and the individualization of school paths have more and more shown tremendous success in the public space that increasingly takes minorities into account.

How can these new demands link up with the growing influence of an Anglo-Saxon model of educational quality? This approach, supported by the school improvement and school leadership movements, aims to break away from centralism and bureaucracy, create incentives and spur competition between schools. The judgement on the quality of their school becomes the main motivation of managers and their teams just as it strongly influences parental choice and the amount of funds furthering autonomy and the completion of educational projects. Are schools able to comply with the drive towards diversification and thus adapt to differences? Or will they favor a market-based approach that would result in a two-tier school system?

Schools apparently go in the second direction. It is easy to show the convergence between the new organization of schools and local communities on one side and the evolution of capitalism on the other: a project-based philosophy, performance-driven management, the requirements of flexibility and mobility, etc. (Boltanski and Chiapello, 1999). However, it is too early to draw conclusions. The works of historians have suggested that the former networked organization fared as well as the standardization that succeeded. The culture of teachers and education managers should also be taken into consideration.

The evolution that has been traced above is in keeping with the transformations of the role and missions of managers at local level. They not only have to implement procedures and directives defined at national level, but they must also include the variety of interests and preferences of other actors (Barrère, 2006). They are expected to put their greater autonomy into the service of the coordination of actions. They are thus led to assess the appropriateness of structures and resources for student success along preset objectives oriented on effectiveness.

Managers are therefore faced with a new culture of assessment (Thélot and Joutard, 1999) that range from the concerted inspection of teachers around the school project to the application of national assessments through audits conducted by boards of inspectors. Assessment will soon be extended to all the aspects of how a school is run (student pass rates, quality of teaching, discipline, use of material, management, etc.) and to the measurement of how effectively an *académie* is managed. In parallel, self-assessment procedures could soon develop.

These evolutions mark a shift in the school form and cause new hardships that New Public Management will have to take into consideration. One of them is about the pedagogical coordination within schools. Beyond the sharing of tasks between the principal and his deputy, the few responsibilities taken by teachers outside their classrooms are regarded as a opportunity for innovation, to the development of projects, and to the tutoring of students with learning difficulties. These secondary functions of volunteer teachers will become a major resource in the promotion of what each school offers educationally. This evolution will probably compel decision-makers to rethink the division of labor between school administration and teaching as well as the sharing of responsibilities.

# CONCLUSION

The emergence of New Public Management in education faces a complex reality (Walzer, 1997; Wuhl, 2002). The variety of educational goods to distribute, the diverse forms of initiatives and participation inside and outside school, the plurality of cultural influences call for an equitable system of justice and regulation by the State. The notion of "complex equality" refers to plural forms of equality and to fair compensation that may prevent social cohesion from breaking apart while not resting only on an indifference to differences. Governing this complex equality is not easy as New Public Management must do with the critical capabilities of actors who are familiar with the knowledge disseminated by social sciences (van Haecht, 2004). New Public Management also has to mobilize experts and scientists whose capacity to reduce the complex relationship between economic and social issues is increasingly challenged. Finally it must rest on a system of information stable and reliable enough to help policy-making in an increasingly heterogeneous and multilevel environment (Hutmacher, 2005).

# REFERENCES

Ballion, R. (1982). *Les consommateurs d'école. Stratégies éducatives des familles.* Paris: Stock.

Barrere, A. (2006). *Sociologie des chefs d'établissement. Les managers de la République.* Paris: PUF.

Boltanski, L., and Chiapello, Y. (1999). *Le nouvel esprit du capitalisme.* Paris: Gallimard.

Briand, J.-P., and Chapoulie, J.M. (2000). *Les collèges du peuple.* Paris: Eds du CNRS.

Caillé, A. (2007). *La quête de reconnaissance.* Paris: La découverte.

Clarke J., Gewirtz S. and McLaughlin, E. (Eds.). (2000). *New managerialism, new welfare?* London: Open University Press and Sage.

Crozier, M. (1964). *Le phénomène bureaucratique.* Paris: Le Seuil.

Crozier, M. (1987). *État moderne, État modeste.* Paris: Fayard.

Garnier, B. (2007). *Les fondateurs de l'école unique à la fin de la première guerre mondiale: l'Université nouvelle, par les Compagnons.* Revue Française de Pédagogie, n°159, INRP

Gewirtz, S. (2002). *The managerial school: Post-welfarism and social justice in education.* London: Routledge.

Hutmacher, W. (2005). Enjeux éducatifs de la mondialisation. In: Derouet, J-L., and Derouet-Besson, M.-C. (coordinator) *La sociologie de l'éducation à l'épreuve des changements sociaux, Éducation and Sociétés,* n° 16. Paris: De Boeck-INRP.

Koiman, J. (1993). *Modern governance, new government society interactions.* New York: Sage.

Langouët, G., and Léger, A. (1994). *École publique ou école privée?* Paris: Fabert.

Lawn, M., and Novoa, A. (Eds.) (2005). *Fabricating Europe. The formation of an education space.* Dordrecht/Boston/London. Paris: Harmattan.

Paty, D. (1996). *Douze collèges en France. Le fonctionnement réel des collèges publics.* Paris: La Documentation Française

Prost, A. (1986). *L'enseignement s'est-il démocratisé?* Paris: PUF.

Prost, A. (2008). A paraître, La diversité sociale de l'enseignement secondaire entre les deux guerres. Derouet, J.-L., and Derouet-Besson, M.-C., coordinator. *Repenser la justice dans le domaine de l'éducation et de la formation.* Berne: Peter Lang.

Thélot, C. (1994). *Évaluation du système éducatif.* Paris: Nathan.

Thélot, C., and Joutard, P. (1999). *Réussir l'école. Pour une politique éducative.* Paris: Seuil.

Trancart, D. (1998). L'évolution des disparités entre collèges publics. *Revue française de pédagogie, 124,* 43-53.

Van Haecht, A. (2004). (coordintor) *La posture critique en sociologie de l'éducation,* Éducation and Sociétés n 13, Paris: De Boeck-INRP.

Van Zanten, A. (2004). (coordinator). *Les classes moyennes, l'école et la ville: la reproduction renouvelée,* Éducation and Sociétés, n 14, Paris: De Boeck-INRP

Vincent, G. (1980). *L'école primaire française. Étude sociologique*: Presses universitaires de Lyon.

Walzer, M. (1997). *Sphères de justice.* Paris: Seuil.

Wuhl, S. (2002). *L'égalité; Nouveaux débats. Rawls, Walzer,* Paris: PUF.

In: Centralization and School Empowerment...          ISBN 978-1-60692-730-4
Editor: Adam Nir                                  © 2009 Nova Science Publishers, Inc.

*Chapter 4*

# CENTRALIZATION PARADIGM OF TRADITION VERSUS DECENTRALIZATION AS THE IMPOSITION OF MODERNITY IN TURKISH EDUCATIONAL SYSTEM

## *Selahattin Turan*

Eskisehir Osmangazi University, Turkey

## INTRODUCTION

Throughout the 2,000 years of Turkey's existence as a distinct cultural entity, its 113 states have had a tradition of centralized management structured within its societal and cultural roots. When the Turkish people first appeared on the pages of history, they were leading nomadic lives in which the use of power and the decision-making processes were under the strict control of the Khan, who could only be supervised by a council of mature and knowledgeable people. Upon accepting the Islamic faith and after their expeditions into Anatolia, Turks, with an admixture of Islamic and authentic Turkish culture, composed of a core of Seljuk and Ottoman traditions, produced a relatively decentralized administrative structure with a federative system comprising the central power domain of a state. The centralized features of administration which fused into a unique culture were also explicitly demonstrated in the administration of educational institutions. After the declaration of the Turkish Republic on October 29, 1923, the public administration system, including education, was restructured according to modern Western civilization and gradually adopted institutions and elements imported from the West. This was actually a transitional period starting from the late Ottoman era and it would lead to a drastic paradigm shift in which national and centralized State ideology were rebuilt. In the early years of the Republic, three significant reform laws were adopted and put into force, by which the government defined and legitimized the legal framework of central public administration. The laws, which include the Law on the Abolishment of the Ministry of Religious Affairs and Foundations, the Law on Unification of Education and the Law on the Abolishment of the Caliphate, formed the base of the secular and central educational administration.

In the early years of the new Turkish state, through the newly-adopted laws, the national sovereignty and secular characteristics of the Republic were formed. Within such a social, political and economical context, the foundations of an education system based on national culture, national solidarity and scientific principles were worked out (Akyuz, 2007; European Commission, 2006/07). Although after World War II, the second critical transition, in which the multiparty political system was introduced as a requirement for democracy underlined a more liberal and democratic atmosphere in the country, the centralized tradition in State and government bureaucracy was preserved. From the 1950s until the second half of the 1980s, following the military coups in the 1960s, 1970s and 1980s, Turkish society as a whole suffered from several crises, economic, social as well as educational. In order to overcome them and to maintain the State's economic development attempts towards industrialization and ideological inheritance, the State Planning Organization (SPO) was established as a macro-organizer of society to embrace the centralized structure and policies. In line with the establishment of the SPO, a new constitution was written based on the former one, which aimed to preserve and emphasize the secular structure of the State. In the second half of the 1980s, neo-liberal economic policies, efforts aimed at integration into Western markets, particularly into the European Union, and raising trends towards internationalization as a necessity of globalization resulted in decentralization attempts of the government via reforms.

## THE TURKISH EDUCATIONAL SYSTEM

Since the declaration of the Turkish Republic in 1923, the main goals of the Turkish National Educational System have been stated clearly in constitutions, laws, and other related legal and official documents. According to Basic Law on National Education No. 1739, adopted in June, 1973, the main goals of the Turkish National Educational System are to increase prosperity of Turkish citizens and society, to support and accelerate the economic, social and cultural development in accordance with national unity and integrity, and to produce constructive, creative and distinguished citizens, participants in a democratic society. In fact, during the early years of the Republic, the founders invited many leading scholars from around the world to restructure and determine the basic goals of education. One of them was a leading American philosopher, John Dewey, who was invited to Turkey in 1924. He prepared two reports about the Turkish educational system. In one of them, he stated that (Dewey, 1983a, p. 264):

> The first and most important point is to settle upon the aim and purpose of the schools of Turkey. Only when this is done is it possible to be clear upon the means to be used and to lay down a definite program of progressive and gradual development. A clear idea of the ends which the schools should attain will protect the schools from needless changes which are no sooner effected than they are undone by other so-called reforms, which lead nowhere. Positively, a clear idea of the end will reveal the steps which need to be taken, afford a check and test for measures proposed, and reveal the order in which the successive steps in education should be taken. Fortunately, there is no difficulty in stating the main end to be secured by the educational system of Turkey. It is the development of Turkey as a vital, free, independent, and lay republic in full membership in the circle of civilized states. To achieve this end the schools must (1) form proper political habits and ideas; (2) foster the various forms of economic and commercial skill and ability; and (3) develop the traits and dispositions of character, intellectual and moral, of men and women for self-government, economic self-support and industrial progress; namely, initiative and inventiveness,

independence of judgment, ability in think scientifically and to cooperate for common purposes socially. To realize these ends, the mass of citizens must be educated for intellectual participation in the political, economic, and cultural growth of the country, and not simply certain leaders.

Turkish education is regulated and governed by education and training laws, development plans, national education councils and government programs (Akbaba-Altun, 2007; MoNE, 2007a). The Ministry of National Education (MoNE) consists of central, provincial and overseas structures as well as other related establishments. It assumed its present structure under Law No. 3797 dated April 30, 1992. The central organization includes the board of education, basic service units, consultancy and inspection units, auxiliary units and permanent committees. The provincial organization includes provincial directorates and district directorates of national education. The overseas organization includes Education Counselors, Educational Attachés and Turkish Cultural Centers. In addition, in the capital city, affiliated with the Ministry of National Education, there are related establishments including the National Education Academy, the General Directorate of Higher Education Loans and Dormitories and the Directorate of Education Technologies. According to the Basic Law on National Education, the Turkish educational system consists of two main divisions, formal education and non-formal education. Categorized as formal education, the school system has four levels: pre-school education, primary education, secondary education, and higher education (MoNE, 2003, 2006b, 2007b). Graph 1 presents the general structure of Turkish education system.

*Pre-school Education:* Pre-school education in Turkey is not compulsory. Children who have not yet reached school age may attend pre-school. Pre-schooling was not attached much importance until recently, but with Turkey's admission into the European Union, there have been many more efforts to increase the attendance rates and school numbers.

*Primary Education*: Primary education is compulsory in the Turkish Constitution and includes 8 years of schooling. Children ranging in age from 6 to 14 are obliged to attend primary school, whose costs are provided completely by the State. Primary education anticipates a process which takes into consideration interests, maturation, talents and vocational values in accordance with the aims of contemporary educational principles. Until now, school attendance rates have not reached a hundred percent.

*Secondary Education*: The aim of secondary education, which includes general and vocational technical high schools, is to provide students with general culture through various programs and to prepare them for higher education, for life and for the business world in accordance with their interests and talents. Secondary education is divided into two: General High Schools and Vocational/Technical High Schools. General High Schools aim to prepare students to contribute to the country's economic, social and cultural development and to prepare them for higher education. Vocational/Technical High Schools are institutions which train young people in the commercial and vocational fields and prepare them for higher education. These schools, which function under the General Directorate of Vocational and Technical Education, train young people as semi-skilled labor for national industry. Though, in theory, students graduating from these schools have the chance to attend higher educational institutions, in practice they have great difficulty in doing so because of the Higher Education Council's recent decisions, which caused a reduction in demand for these schools. On the other hand, vocational and technical schools have been regaining what was previous popularity in the last five years with the financial support and educational policies of the European Union.

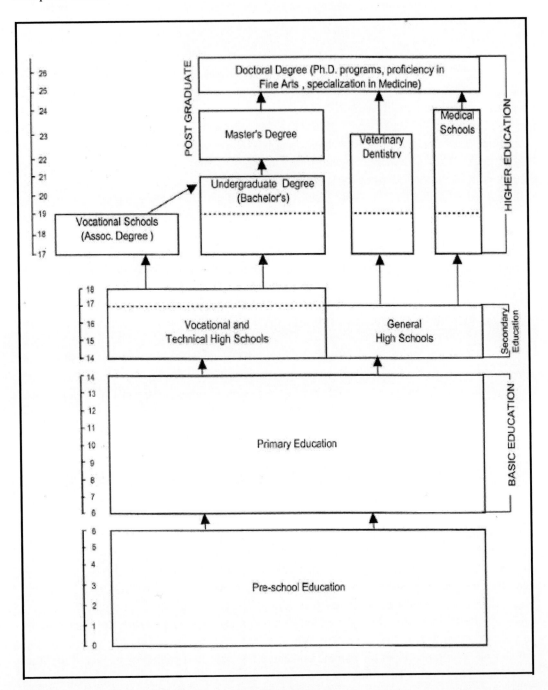

Graph 1. The Structure of the Turkish National Education System.

**Table 1. Number of Schools, Enrollment and
Teachers by Level of Education: 2006-2007**

| Education Level | # Of Schools | # Of Students | | | # Of Teachers |
|---|---|---|---|---|---|
| | | Total | Boys | Girls | |
| PRE-SCHOOL, EDUCATION | 3,222 | 640,849 | 334,252 | 306,597 | 10,016 |
| Public | 1,267 | 486,529 | 252,798 | 233,731 | 4,580 |
| Kindergarten | 786 | 80,767 | 42,572 | 38,195 | 3,217 |
| Nursery-Class | 792 | 482,212 | 250,696 | 231,516 | 13,018 |
| Other Institutions | 481 | 17,357 | 8,956 | 8,401 | 1,363 |
| Private | 1,955 | 60,513 | 32,028 | 28,485 | 5,436 |
| Kindergarten | 583 | 19,401 | 10,185 | 9,216 | 1,888 |
| Nursery-Class | 661 | 16,999 | 9,052 | 7,947 | 1,741 |
| Social Services and Child Protection Institution | 1,372 | 24,113 | 12,791 | 11,322 | 3,548 |
| PRIMARY EDUCATION | 34,656 | 10,846,930 | 5,684,609 | 5,162,321 | 402,829 |
| Public | 33,898 | 10,346,509 | 5,408,525 | 4,937,984 | 381,354 |
| Private | 757 | 213,071 | 116,099 | 96,972 | 21,475 |
| Open Primary | 1 | 287,350 | 159,985 | 127,365 | 0 |
| SECONDARY EDUCATION | 7,934 | 3,386,717 | 1,917,189 | 1,469,528 | 187,665 |
| Public | 7,216 | 2,946,363 | 1,663,955 | 1,282,408 | 174,748 |
| Private | 717 | 86,458 | 47,180 | 39,278 | 12,917 |
| Open Education High School | 1 | 353,896 | 206,054 | 147,842 | 0 |
| General Secondary Education | 3,690 | 2,142,218 | 1,156,418 | 985,800 | 103,389 |
| Public | 2,993 | 1,775,244 | 942,561 | 832,683 | 90,716 |
| Private | 696 | 85,547 | 46,509 | 39,038 | 12,673 |
| Open Education High School | 1 | 281,427 | 167,348 | 114,079 | 0 |
| Vocational Technical Secondary Education | 4,244 | 1,244,499 | 760,771 | 483,728 | 84,276 |
| Public | 4,223 | 1,171,119 | 721,394 | 449,725 | 84,032 |
| Private | 21 | 911 | 671 | 240 | 244 |
| Open Education High School | | 72,469 | 37,706 | 33,763 | 0 |
| NON-FORMAL EDUCATION (3) | 10,576 | 4,508,564 | 2,545,004 | 1,963,560 | 79,370 |
| Public | 1,833 | 2,141,389 | 1,043,308 | 1,098,081 | 10,190 |
| Private | 8,743 | 2,367,175 | 1,501,696 | 865,479 | 69,180 |
| TOTAL | 56,388 | 19,383,060 | 10,481,054 | 8,902,006 | 679,880 |

Source: Turkish Ministry of National Education, 2007a.

*Higher Education*: The main goal of Turkish Higher Education, which aims to reach world standards of higher education both in quality and quantity, is to meet the requirements of an educated society for skilled persons at various levels. Although many important developments in higher education have occurred since the proclamation of the Republic, in the last ten years higher education in Turkey has been the focus of serious ongoing debates, and there has been a resistance to reforms and restructuring efforts of the government in the universities by some circles, especially university rectors and Higher

Education Council officials. Teacher training in Turkey is also the responsibility of universities, and universities offer programs to equip would-be teachers with subjects' knowledge, general culture, and pedagogical skills. Following graduation, they are appointed for various parts of the country in accordance with the needs determined by the Ministry of National Education.

*Non-Formal Education*: Non-formal education, one of the two basic divisions of the national education system, covers education, training, guidance and applied activities for those who have never had a formal education, or who are currently at a particular stage. The basic aim of non-formal education is to provide adults with literacy skills and basic knowledge, to further develop acquired knowledge and to create new opportunities for improving their standards of living. Table 1 indicates the current number of schools, enrollment and teachers by level of education (MoNE, 2006b, 2007a, and 2007b).

## REFORM AND DECENTRALIZATION EFFORTS IN TURKEY

The Turkish educational system has a centralized organizational and administrative structure. In the last two decades, there have been many efforts to decentralize the Turkish educational system and restructure it, but these efforts have not been put into practice. Studies in Turkey show that such a centralized administrative structure has many drawbacks (Cınkır, 2002; Coker, 1995; Eryılmaz, 1995; Kurt, 2006; MoNE, 2006b). A decrease in the feasibility of services, an unfair distribution of the resources among the provincial administrations because of political concerns, red tape, participation of the public and educational leadership have underlined fiscal, financial and administrative drawbacks.

One of the most critical concepts in discussions in Turkey as to decentralization, restructuring, reform and teacher empowerment is participation. Reports prepared by the Ministry of National Education have indicated that high participation leads to some changes in school administration. Family participation in educational policy-making, both financial and administrative, is at the forefront, and it is expected that the implementation of the policies will be more legitimated when families participate in the process. Moreover, influences of central authority on education will be reduced through decentralization, and more independent and autonomous educational provinces and schools will be possible. Besides, in any process of collective negotiations about education, civil society will be given the opportunity to participate. Finally, decentralization in education may help those who are currently excluded from society, like the poor and the disadvantaged, to participate in decision-making processes and benefit from equal opportunities (Kiran, 2001; MoNE, 2006b; Weiler, 1990; Wissler and Ortiz, 1986).

In Turkey, although concepts such as restructuring, reform and decentralization are used interchangeably, the efforts made by central government, up until now, have underlined the restructuring process aiming to increase organizational effectiveness and services for schools. Besides, especially with emergence of decentralization as a main tendency due to the political discourse of central governments and policy-makers, it has come on the scene as a hot topic for school organizations.

Within the last two decades, many projects aiming to restructure the school system have been constructed, discussed and implemented. School-based administration, for instance, is one such project in Turkey initiated a decade ago and several theoretical and then practical studies on this subject have appeared in Turkish education administrative literature (Aytac, 2000; Erdogan, 1996; Kurt, 2006). In general, school-based administration aims at authorizing and empowering the school principal and teachers to make decisions concerning the school and the education environment. These decisions essentially include budget, human resources and school curriculum.

## INCUBATION PERIOD OF EDUCATIONAL REFORMS THROUGH DECENTRALIZATION

Although since the second half of the 1980s, the party programs of almost all governments have given priority to decentralization of public administration, including governance of education; attempts have recently gained momentum with the integration process of Turkey into the European Union. Despite some proposals to rehabilitate centralized State structure through decentralization, the problem has emerged with the implementation of reforms. The 59th and 60th cabinets, the latter still in power, initiated a program and urgent plan of action for restructuring the public sector, which has not had any outcomes as yet. In this context, restructuring efforts in the Turkish education system are being discussed and many proposals have been made. The party currently in power since 2007 has a plan called the Urgent Action Plan, also a result of the EU integration process. Realization of comprehensive local administration reform including education, culture, social welfare, public works, communication and services has been expressed as the ultimate goal in the urgent action plan of government (Prime Ministry of Turkish Republic, 2007).

Within the last decade, the EU integration process has imposed structural educational reforms, financed by EU funds, as a requirement for EU candidate status. In fact, about ten years ago, the Urgent Action Plan introduced within the 57th Government Program emphasized the importance of restructuring the Ministry of National Education before any decentralization efforts in the system. Restructuring of central and provincial organizations of Ministry of National Education, of higher education and teacher training, reconstruction of secondary education and improvement of basic education for all, called "Support for Basic Education Program" (SBEP), have emerged as the joint restructuring projects of central governments and the EU to ameliorate the system (MoNE, 2007a).

Among those reforms, SBEP has been given critical importance because of its impact on following reform efforts, its being a prerequisite for the realization of European Union reforms and its requirement for comprehensive collaboration among national and international experts. Since it aims to create a reform capacity and implementation at all educational levels in the national context, SBEP is seen as a way to enhance quality of education to transform schools into learning centers. The SBEP was a five-year program with a grant of 100 million Euros that began on September 11, 2002, after the signing of an agreement between the Republic of Turkey and the European Commission dated February 8, 2000 and ended in August 2007. The total amount of the budget was a grant provided by the European Union Mediterranean Fund. SBEP was a program that aimed to ensure access to education to those who were affected by poverty, were living in underdeveloped areas of urban cities and who were not included in the education system, especially girls, adults and children at risk. It aimed to increase the quality of education and to sustainable increase the enrollment in formal and non-formal education. These aims were realized by enhancing the infrastructures of schools and increasing the quality of education (SBEP, 2007, pp. 1-4). The Objectives of SBEP were as follows:

a) To increase access to education and improve the quality of education as targeted by focusing on reforms and the enhancement of capacity at the central level.
b) To support the decentralized management in 12 disadvantaged provinces.
c) To support the five urban provinces with the highest rates of immigration in the scope of non-formal education.

The five components of SBEP were Quality of Education, Teacher Training, Non-Formal Education, Communication and Management and Organization, which support the "Reform at the Central Level" conducted by the Ministry of National Education. The reform project was implemented in nine selected pilot provinces and 120 schools. After the adoption of eight years compulsory primary education in 1997, the support was changed in nature, and was provided within the scope of curriculum development, material development and their piloting with the aim of supporting the Basic Education Reform. The support of experts was provided to the Board of Education in the 2004-2005 school years for the development of the primary education curriculum and the syllabus for Mathematics, Social Studies, Science and Technology, Turkish and Life Skills. In addition, all kinds of support for the 120 schools in nine pilot provinces, where the piloting was implemented, was provided including training, guidance and materials, resources, etc. As a result of the monitoring and evaluation activities conducted in the scope of the SBEP, the Grade 1-5 curriculums began to be implemented nationwide in the 2005-2006 school year. Four main subjects at the Grade 6 level were also piloted in 120 schools in nine pilot provinces in the year 2005-2006 and this curriculum was also implemented nationwide in the 2006-2007 school years (SBEP, 2007, pp. 4-8).

Although the SBEP is planned and initiated by the central government at a national level, it has critically aimed to increase potentiality and capacity of local school organizations by improving the skills of teachers, school facilities, equipments and materials of schools and program modules and textbooks. In addition, this project has provided a flexibility and initiative to change the curriculum depending on local features and necessities.

## PROS AND CONS OF REFORM EFFORTS

There have been no comprehensive reports evaluating the aforementioned educational reforms and proposals. However, observations and opinions of team leaders and leading international experts taking part in the project shed light on the performance of the project. For this reason the author conducted a qualitative research based on a case study (Turan, 2008). Research findings indicate that the reform realized in 1998-2007 constructed a necessary infrastructure for amelioration of educational processes and contributed to the national education system of Turkey. The centralized organizational culture has created some obstacles for implementation of the proposed procedures. Project team leaders and international consultants of the EU underline the paradigm shift in the Ministry of National

Education and the ambitions of the administrative and teaching staff as catalyzers. On the other hand, they point to the highly centralized political system and the low level of organizational commitment of the teaching staff as the main obstacles for the implementation of the project. According to the team leaders and international consultants of the national reform project, a number of issues are core catalyzers or obstacles that have impeded the reform efforts and the empowerment of schools to facilitate nationwide reform.

For instance, recognition of a desire for change as the country moved towards greater European integration is a catalyst, as the government was committed to change so that the different Ministries were obliged to institute new strategies to reflect a more forward way of thinking. A greater number of educationalists in the country recognized the need for a full review of education in the light of recent international research. The way adults and children learn and acquire knowledge led these educationalists to consider what was happening in schools across the country. Within the body of school principals there was a greater desire to see appointments made dependent upon competence. However, the involvement of provincial teams in training activities was seen to play an important contribution to school development. The principals also recognized the importance of involving local communities in the activities of their schools. The school principals also recognized that there was a need for greater opportunities for personal professional development, and that this should include classroom teachers as well. "Active Learning" as part of SBEP Project training could be used to "interpret" the new curriculum into activities in the classroom. These were related to learner centered approaches, classroom and schoolyard arrangements. In addition, English Language Training (ELT) provided much needed help and practical tools for teachers.

Training on Special Needs related issues may have made schooling easier for children with special needs. Also training in communicating with parents, Muchtars (elected village heads) and imams (prayer leaders) about the new approaches as well as the importance of sending all children, especially girls, and children at risk to school was a catalyst.

Head Teacher training provided useful tools and ideas to school managers and Project Cycle Management training provided administrators and teachers with tools for planning and implementing small scale school development projects.

Among the obstacles, the heavily centralized political system was seen as a hindrance to the appointment of school principals based on their professional competence. Principals and teachers were concerned with how they would be inspected once changes had been introduced. In addition, a large number of the current cadre of school principals was ill-equipped to become change agents in their schools.

Since the teaching force was employed for life, breaking the more traditional teaching styles would be a challenge. Many teachers were content with their positions and their teaching approach, knowing that they could not be easily moved. Principals were concerned with school budgets and the fact that they were centrally controlled. This impacted directly on what new initiatives could be started at the school level.

Many principals voiced a reluctance to share ideas with their peers, but on the other hand many voiced their support for some sort of national accreditation system for principals. This was a reflection of how the Ministry of National Education treated them as a whole, and the concept of developing a network of school principals working together at district and provincial level was most probably not encouraged.

Inspectors and other education administrators and officials did not often participate in the same training as teachers and did not necessarily understand the changes and, therefore, were likely to obstruct the development if they felt insecure about rules and regulations.

Many education authorities did not seem to appreciate the training arrangement approaches initiated by the project. This particularly hampered some of the training in the trainers' programs where workshop approaches and timetables were abruptly changed without consideration for the primary organizers. Even low level officials from the MoNE came in and disturbed and interrupted ongoing training without any respect for the programs.

The "process approach" (same participants come back after a certain period of time in their schools for reflection and additional refresher training) was not understood or accepted by education authorities or project decision-makers and stakeholders. Innovative ideas brought up by schools/teachers/head teachers were usually snubbed and therefore local enthusiasm was often quashed before it began. Participants in training or teachers and children who were waiting for visitors in their classrooms were kept waiting while officials had endless discussions "over tea" in the principal's office, completely neglecting other people who had prepared themselves for the opening of a workshop or visits to classrooms, certainly an obstacle to progress.

## CONCLUSION

A plethora of academic studies have been carried out on the restructuring of Turkish education in order to reinforce local school and teacher empowerment. However, those studies have been limited to academic concern due to fact that there is an institutional gap between results and implication of academic studies and official feasibility endeavors towards realization of teacher and school empowerment policies. Besides, governments have always aimed to implement public administration reforms. Nevertheless, due to financial problems and concerns, these reforms have not been put into practice. Turkish governmental institutions are centrally organized, which is the main obstacle in decentralization efforts. In reality, this is a paradigm conflict. The centralized administrative system has been creating obstacles for improvement of empowerment of school and teachers in spite of the fact that national governments have declared the strengthening of local administrative decision making structures in political programs and official reports. Besides, it has been claimed and discussed for some ten years that official state ideology could be another parameter which has blocked the development of local initiatives because of political agendas in Turkish society. That could be a so-called hidden agenda of Turkish state ideology. A sort of culture of fear exists at almost every level of society in Turkey, and a pessimistic point of view towards the citizens and especially civil servants prevails in public administration culture. Such a point of view emerges as one of the most significant hindrances confronting empowerment of the lower rank officials. The political structure in Turkey does not encourage citizens to participate in decision-making processes at any level. As for education, Turkey ranks high in OECD countries whose administration system is centrally organized. Privatization in education is very slow and behind by European standards. The State is seen as organizer, controller, planner and evaluator of everything. The State itself is aware of the disadvantages of such an administrative structure. Turkish citizens have a culture of expectation that the

State will provide services and meet all sorts of needs. In traditional Turkish culture, the State is like "an authoritarian father." Hence, above all, in educational and public reform efforts, what should be done at the very beginning are as follows:

a) Traditional State perceptions should undergo change.
b) The State should encourage initiatives of citizens.
c) The State and the Ministry of Education should assume the role of standards-setter and organizer.
d) Civil rights and freedoms should be reinforced and democratization in education should be promoted together with democratization in general.
e) Citizens should be granted to right to participate in school administration.
f) Expectations and demands of the citizens should be considered in determining the aims and contents of education.

Following these important points, there are some steps to be taken into consideration in the transition period to decentralization of education in Turkey. First of all, it is necessary to determine through which of the two ways it will be implemented – administrative or politics - and determine the decision subjects which will be delegated to local authorities. Also it should be necessary to express this as a policy. Besides, it is necessary to determine the aims and principles of decentralization in advance and these aims should be expressed in written reports. Then, the partners and people involved in the decentralization process should be educated and instructed comprehensively. After that, a method concerning how the school sources will be distributed, especially for each school, must be determined, as should a foundation of a planning process on the school budget. How the schools will be responsible for the decisions should be clarified. Then, a regional pilot study should be implemented at least for two years. Finally, all the new roles of the partners in the school administration must be clearly explained.

It is difficult to solve the problems of the educational system in Turkey by a centralist approach as the Ministry of Education has become a place where substantial bureaucracy is creating serious problems in education. The Ministry has an ungovernable and unchangeable, ponderous bureaucratic structure. In parallel to the arguments on downsizing the State and redefining its functions, it is argued that the Ministry should have a more functional structure, that authority should be delegated to local administrations, that problems should be detected and solved locally, and that there should be large-scale participation of society in the educational administration and problem-solving process. The Ministry in Turkey has been trying to apply some models and projects based upon the approaches and models of education in several developed countries. School Development Model, Total Quality Management Model, School Regions are among such models. Although these attempts are based on good intentions, they will not be concluded with expected results unless there is a sound logic at their core. In decentralization of education, it is necessary to define the roles, duties, authority and responsibility of directories of Ministry of National Education in provinces and towns. Also, it is necessary to make clear the relations and coordination among them. Redefining the duties, authority and responsibilities of the regions established in the provinces and of the boards in these provinces and allowing these boards a more autonomous structure in terms of administration and finances will accelerate the decentralization process of education.

In sum, control and domination are two central concepts that have defined the general nature of the Turkish administration of education since 1923. Dewey warned against the danger of centralization and the removal of local control in education (Turan, 2000). He pointed out that centralized systems can "prevent local communities taking the responsibilities which they should take; and produce too uniform a system of education, not flexibly adapted to the varying needs of different localities, urban, rural, maritime, and to different types of rural communities, different environments and different industries" (Dewey, 1983a, p. 280). Furthermore, he noted that: "there is also danger that any centralized system will become bureaucratic, arbitrary and tyrannical in action, and given to useless and perfunctory mechanical work in making useless records, requiring and filing useless reports from others, and in general what is termed in French 'papasserie' and in English 'red-tape'" (Dewey, 1983a, p. 281). According to Dewey (1939, 1983b), the functions of the Ministry should be intellectual and moral leadership and inspiration, rather than detailed administrative supervision and executive management. Nothing has been changed in terms of decentralization and management of education since Dewey's Report and Recommendations upon Turkish Education in the early years of the Republic.

The public administration system in Turkey was constructed on the centralized French Bonapartist public administration tradition of the 1920s. Although from the 1950s Turkey has turned its face to the US and its decentralized administration tradition, it has become increasingly difficult to break from its founding tradition. Though from the beginning of the 1990s, central governments have initiated many restructuring processes in public administration through empowerment of local public organizations including educational organizations, the most effective projects have come about through joint projects of Turkey and the EU. In this sense, teacher and school empowerment has become a critical issue in the last decade in those projects. Paradoxically even though central governments have tried to restructure the administrative system through decentralization and empowerment of schools and teachers, the efforts have failed mainly because of paradigm inconsistency between policy-makers and bureaucratic elites. Bureaucratic strictness, failure in dissemination of the idea of empowerment in the minds of Ministry bureaucrats and the lack of necessary and complementary laws and regulations necessary for putting empowerment into practice and disturbing perceptions that empowerment is a sham have emerged as the difficulties and obstacles that have not permitted empowerment efforts to succeed.

## REFERENCES

Akbaba-Altun, S. (2007). Harmonious texture of cultural values and democracy: Patterns of success. In S. Donahoo and R. C. Hunter (Eds.), Teaching Leaders to Lead Teachers: Educational Administration in the Era of Constant Crisis. Amsterdam: Elsevier (pp. 77-97).

Akyuz, Y. (2007). Turk Egitim Tarihi [Turkish Education History] Ankara: Pegem Akademi.

Aytac, T. (2000). *Okul merkezli yönetim [School-based management]*. Ankara: Nobel.

Basic Law of National Education Law No.: 1739 Date of Acceptance: 5/11/1973, Official Gazette: 42.6.1973/14574.

Cınkır, S. (2002). Egitim yonetiminde yerellesmenin ustunlukleri ve sakıncaları [Advantages and disadvantages of decentralization in educational administration]. Egitim Arastırmları (Educational Studies), 8, 101-110.

Coker, Z. (1995). Merkezden yonetim, il sistemi ve yerel yonetim reformu [Centralization, provincial system and public administration reform]. Yeni Turkiye (New Turkey), 4, 3-8.

Dewey, J. (1939). *Turk Maarifine Dair Rapor [Report and recommendations upon Turkish Education]*. Ankara: Ministry of National Education Press.

Dewey, J. (1983a). Report and recommendations upon Turkish Education. *In J. A. Boydston* (Ed.), *John Dewey: The middle works, 1899–1924,* Vol. 15: 1923–1924. Carbondale, Ill.: Southern Illinois University Press (pp. 273-297).

Dewey, J. (1983b). Preliminary report. In J. A. Boydston (Ed.), *John Dewey: The middle works, 1899–1924,* Vol. 15: 1923–1924. Carbondale, Ill.: Southern Illinois University Press (pp. 301–307).

Erdogan, İ. (1996). Okula dayalı eğitim [School-based education]. *Yasadıkca Egitim (Education As We Live), 49*, 24-29.

Eryılmaz, B. (1995). Kamu yonetimi [Public administration]. Izmir: Akademi Press.

European Commission. (2006/07). The educational system in Turkey. Brussels: Directorate General for Education and Culture.

Kıran, H. (2001). Milli egitim bakanlığı tasra orgutu yoneticilerinin egitimde yerinden yonetime iliskin tutumları [Local educational administrators' attitudes towards decentralization]. Pamukkale Egitim Fakultesi Dergisi *[Pamukkale Journal of Education],* 9, 1-9.

Kurt, T. (2006). Egitim yonetiminde yerellesme egilimi [Decentralization in education]. Kastamonu Egitim Dergisi *(Kastamonu Journal of Education)*, 14 (1), 61-72.

MoNe. (2003). Primary education in Turkey: Past, present and future. Ankara: Ministry of National Education Press.

MoNe. (2006a). National education statistics, 2004-2005. Ankara: Ministry of National Education Press.

MoNE. (2006b). *Report on fiscal year budget.* Ankara: Ministry of National Education Press.

MoNE. (2007a). 2007 budget report. Ankara: Ministry of National Education Press.

MoNe. (2007b). National education statistics, 2006-2007. Ankara: Ministry of National Education Press.

Prime Ministry of Turkish Republic. (2007). 59th and 60th Cabinet Program. Ankara: Basbakanlik.

SBEP. (2007). Support to basic education programme. Ankara: Ministry of National Education Press.

Turan, S. (2000). John Dewey's report on Turkish educational system revisited. *History of Education, 29*(6), 543–555.

Turan, S. (2008). Rethinking and revaluating reform proposals of education institutions. Unpublished manuscript, Eskisehir Osmangazi University, Eskisehir.

Wissler, D. F., and Ortiz, F. I. (1986). The decentralization process of school systems: A review of the literature. *Urban Education, 21*(3), 280–294.

Weiler, H. N. (1990). Comparative perspectives on educational decentralization: An exercise in contradiction. *Educational Evaluation and Policy Analysis, 12*(4), 433–448.

In: Centralization and School Empowerment...
Editor: Adam Nir

ISBN 978-1-60692-730-4
© 2009 Nova Science Publishers, Inc.

*Chapter 5*

# DEVELOPING AUTONOMY: THE CASE OF THE ISRAELI SCHOOL SYSTEM

### *Dan E. Inbar*

The Hebrew University of Jerusalem, Israel

## INTRODUCTION

The following discussion focuses on a basic dilemma: How can school autonomy be developed in a highly centralized elementary school system? This is a dialectic analysis which emphasizes the contradictory forces simultaneously pulling in two opposing directions: the desire to actualize autonomy and the volition to keep centralized authoritative control. In the Israeli case, the picture is more complicated. Enabling school autonomy is a declared policy of the Ministry of Education and Culture, but school principals are, for various reasons which will be discussed later, hesitant to undertake it. The central authorities are promoting autonomy and, at the same time, trying to retain a strong centralized control system in operation. School principals are reluctant to assume what they perceive to be a bounded autonomy, but at the same time try to actualize professional autonomy.

We divide our discussion into five parts. First, in order to clarify the complicated phenomenon of the autonomization process on the Israeli scene, some background of the Israeli school system will be presented, emphasizing three basic components: the way the educational system is organized, its size, and the type of value system under which it operates. Second, the complicated concept of decentralization will be discussed. Third, the long journey in the development of school autonomy, differentiated into two stages, will be analyzed and illustrated. Fourth, the current situation where autonomy is being confronted head-on and the school principal's reaction to it will be discussed, revealing the interdependencies between the drive toward autonomy and the process of school privatization. And finally, the second cycle, twenty years later, the introduction of School-Based management will be discussed, speculating whether anything has changed. Because of the basic differences between the secondary and the elementary educational system, the analysis will be focused on the latter.

# THE ELEMENTARY SCHOOL SYSTEM: BASIC FEATURES OF CENTRALIZATION

Let us start with some basic historic figures about the Israeli educational system. The State of Israel is a small country (20,770 sq. km.) with primarily an industrial and service-oriented economy (96.5%). The population of 6.8 million is composed of two primary ethnic groups: 81.5% Jewish and 18.5% Arabs who hold Israeli citizenship and are either Muslims or Christians (Bassok, August 24, 2004). Druze and Bedouin are two additional ethnic groups affiliated with the Arab sector. Israel boasts a high literacy rate of 95% among those over the age of 15. There are four primary religions represented in the country: Judaism (81.5%), Islam (14.6%) (predominantly Sunni Muslim), Christianity (2.1%) and the Druze (1.8%). Within this relatively small, yet densely populated country one can find a veritable mosaic of demography, ideologies and histories.

The State of Israel was founded in 1948, based on the Zionist movement, which called for the establishment of a Jewish national and religious homeland in the biblical Land of Israel. The major challenge in becoming a viable and stable Jewish state was the need to create a Jewish majority in Palestine where none had existed for 2000 years.

The first act enacted by the *Knesset* (the unicameral parliament) within minutes of declaring independence for the State of Israel in 1948 was the opening of all borders to unrestricted Jewish immigration. No other modern nation has seen its population grow more than almost six-fold in 50 years, and the number of pupils enrolled in the educational system increase by more than 16-fold from 108,131 pupils in 1948 to 1,804,410 pupils in 1998. With the passage of the Compulsory Education Law in 1949 and the massive entrance of children into public education, in an attempt to promote equality, the emerging national educational system featured a high degree of central control to ensure unity and uniformity in promoting and providing educational services. This change shifted the emphasis from the pedagogical and politically-oriented educational sub-systems, which characterized the administration of schools before 1948, to a more centralized and homogenous orientation.

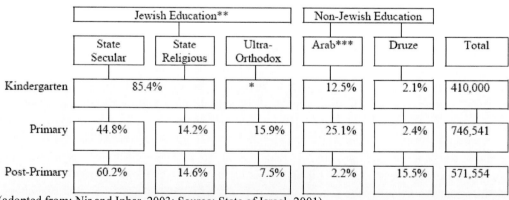

|  | Jewish Education** | | | Non-Jewish Education | | |
|---|---|---|---|---|---|---|
|  | State Secular | State Religious | Ultra-Orthodox | Arab*** | Druze | Total |
| Kindergarten | 85.4% | | * | 12.5% | 2.1% | 410,000 |
| Primary | 44.8% | 14.2% | 15.9% | 25.1% | 2.4% | 746,541 |
| Post-Primary | 60.2% | 14.6% | 7.5% | 2.2% | 15.5% | 571,554 |

(adopted from: Nir and Inbar, 2003; Source: State of Israel, 2001)
* No data available for ultra-Orthodox sector
** Data includes pupils enrolled in special education schools.
*** Data includes pupils in Israeli-Arab, Bedouin, Muslim, and Christian schools

Figure 1. A breakdown of Jewish and non-Jewish education by type of school.

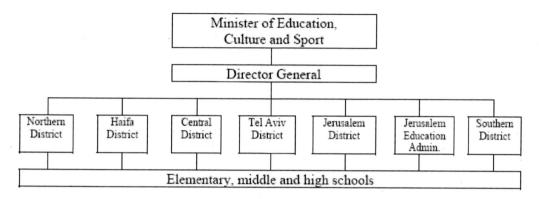

Figure 2. A schematic of the centralized bureaucratic control of the Israeli educational system.

By and large, the Israeli educational system can be characterized as being highly centralized. The Ministry of Education in fact controls the whole educational system for the entire population, Jewish and Arab. All educational laws and by-laws, such as it being free and compulsory education, apply to both sectors.

As shown in Figure 2, the educational system is divided geographically into six districts (the Jerusalem district is divided into the periphery of Jerusalem and the city of Jerusalem), which supervise and monitor the educational processes conducted by schools to ensure the compatibility of these processes with central policies (Zucker, 1985).

Seven main centralization features of the Israeli elementary school system having direct bearing on the autonomy question will be exemplified. First, there is a strong bureaucratized administration, located in Jerusalem at the Ministry of Education, headed by the Minister and run by the Director General, with a central budgetary and planning unit. The Director General circulates to all schools on a regular basis the Director General's Memorandum, which is a fundamental device for transferring decisions and policy orientations. It is intended to be the educational system's operative guideline.

Second, there is a tight, operative network of an authoritative control system through the superintendency and supervisory system. There are six district superintendents who are the interim echelon between schools and the central authorities in Jerusalem and who operate a tight, well organized supervisory network. Third, in the Ministry of Education, a Pedagogical Secretariat intended to be the focus of pedagogical thinking and the development of pedagogical policy-making exists parallel to the Director General. It is responsible for all educational matters. Fourth, under the Pedagogical Secretariat, a strong department of curriculum planning provides the main core of syllabuses and curricula for the educational system. Furthermore, formally, at least, the Ministry of Education has the authority to prescribe a uniform and obligatory basic curriculum (Kleinberger, 1969).

Fifth, in the elementary school system, all major inputs are centralized, allocated and controlled, the most important relating to teachers, principals and supervisors. All elementary school teachers, principals and supervisors are state employees and all salaries are paid centrally, according to one nationwide scale. In addition, all appointments, assignments to particular schools, and dismissals are controlled by the Ministry of Education through the district superintendents and the supervisory network.

Sixth, there is a centralized allocation of teaching hours, termed school standard, which in practice determines the amount of teaching hours for each class level in every school.

Seventh, there is a tendency toward the development of an objective process of evaluation through a diagnostic tool intended to serve teachers and school principals in the process of learning, teaching and other school-level activities. In its current form, this type of feedback is known as the Measure of School Effectiveness and Growth (*Meitzav*) (Gumpel and Nir, 2006).

## Small Size

In order to clarify the full meaning of the centralization of the educational system it has to be viewed through its relationships with two other main characteristics of the country — its size and its democratic nature. Without a doubt, in terms of national educational systems, the Israeli system can be considered small. Nearly all of the 3,600 elementary and secondary schools comprising the system are between two to three hours drive from Jerusalem. Hence, there is the feeling that one can comprehend the whole system, or at least a large segment of it. Familiarity with the system, where the central educational figures are acquainted with all the superintendents, most of the supervisors, many of the secondary school principals (probably all those heading big schools), and numerous elementary school principals and teachers, gives them the impression of controllability. Additionally, and this might be even more important, it strengthens the perception of the school-level staff of the centralized power of the Ministry of Education, often far beyond its real power.

## Democracy

The democratic value system and political orientation of the country seems to be of major importance in understanding the development of educational autonomy in Israel. Small size and centralization by themselves would tend to be closely coupled with a highly structured, authoritative system. However, combined with democracy, the same characteristics take a different orientation, bringing about an interesting process to the development of autonomy.

For the purpose of this discussion, two features of the democratic nature of the Israeli state will be emphasized. First, although Israel is considered a country of Jewish immigration attempting to crystallize a unified nation (Adler, 1969), maintaining its *pluralistic* nature, culturally and politically, is seen as one of its major social goals (Gumpel and Nir, 2006). This dual trend, of unification, inherent in any centralized system, and pluralism, yields one of the more interesting features of the elementary educational system and is of major importance to the development of the phenomenon of autonomy.

A State Educational Law, passed in 1953, was intended to unify the system by abolishing the unwholesome linkage of pedagogical and organized political trends in education (Bashi, 1985). However, the dual trend of pluralism and unification brought about the various Jewish religious educational sectors, the Arab sector, and the relatively autonomous kibbutz school system. A provision for supplementary programs which could comprise 25% of the total school program was also incorporated into the law, thus offering individual schools, parents and their local communities some freedom of choice. As will be discussed later, this provision — the well-known 25% — served as a springboard to autonomy.

The second democratic feature relevant to our discussion is the openness of the structure of communication. People have the right and the ability to communicate with top officials at various levels of the government in general and the educational system in particular. Hence, the combination of the centralized system, its small size and its democratic nature creates a unique situation (Inbar, 1986). Under these circumstances the central authorities are open to continuous pressure from schools, on the one hand, and are continuously involved in endless burning local issues, on the other.

The combination of the three characteristics — centrality, small size and democracy — sets the necessary foundation for the following discussion of the autonomy phenomenon.

## Decentralization: What does it Mean?

The term *decentralization* refers to the transfer or delegation of constitutional or political powers—from the central government and/or its agencies to subordinate units of government, semi-autonomous political organizations, local authorities, and private or volunteer nongovernmental organizations—to plan, manage, raise funds, make decisions, and run public functions.

Centralization and decentralization are organizational concepts that can be examined on various levels of administration or organizational systems. But despite the basic distinction between the two structural systems, they are not mutually exclusive. Every organization and every level contains arrangements characteristic of both concepts. They differ in the guiding principle behind the distribution of powers, the weight given to each concept, and their organizational profile; in each organization the human aspect must be integrated with the structural and qualitative aspects (Kruisinga 1954).

We can differentiate among four degrees of decentralization (Rondinelli 1983; Winkler 1989).

*Deconcentration* is a process in which some administrative power or responsibility is transferred to lower levels within the central government (government ministries, subunits or agencies). It represents the lowest level of decentralization.

*Delegation* is a process in which decision-making powers are transferred to agencies under the indirect control of central government offices and/or to autonomous public entities. At this level of decentralization, broad powers to plan and carry out decisions regarding specific activities—or a variety of activities—are delegated to or created for someone who can implement them technically and administratively.

*Devolution* of decision-making to local authorities is a process in which governmental subunits that are largely not under central government control are created or reinforced (financially or constitutionally).

*Privatization* is the most extreme form of decentralization. Some governments have completely divested themselves of responsibility for various functions and transferred it to volunteer or private organizations.

A different concept is expressed by Lauglo (1995), who distinguishes between the numerous meanings of different forms of decentralization. According to his distinction, the alternatives to bureaucratic centralization may indicate a *liberal political* concept that is manifested in local power, professional autonomy or market forces that operate on the system; a concept of *federalism,* which involves cooperation among regions and a relatively weak central government; a concept of *populist localism*, in which the power is held by local political forces; or a concept of *participatory democracy*, which is based on collective decision-making and a relatively flat administrative structure.

What is interesting about these conceptual distinctions is that similar decentralization alternatives can be reached from completely different points of departure. Based on quality and effectiveness, for example, Lauglo (1995) suggests four alternatives: *Professional autonomy:* In the case of education, the power is held by the teachers and principals, control is collegial, and the principles of action are professional. *Local administration*: Power is held by the school administration, and there are indicators to compare quality and budgetary standards. The *market mechanism* is based on competition, customer demands, outside accreditation and local administrative power. The last approach is *deconcentration*, aimed at easing the pressure in the center and trying to streamline the system by creating strong regions, i.e., turning the central hierarchical pyramid into a hierarchical pyramid constructed from several regional hierarchical pyramids.

To sum up, decentralization may be manifested in various situations, ranging from one in which the center opens local branches to one in which power is transferred to nongovernmental local units. What the entire spectrum has in common is that, in practice, some decisions are not made in the center, although the center is still held publicly accountable for the results (Bloomer, 1991). The question, then, is not simply whether there should be decentralization, but more importantly, what kind of decentralization there should be.

# THE PROCESS TOWARD SCHOOL AUTONOMY

## Autonomy and Authority

Based on the unique Israeli background, it would not seem too paradoxical to see that the main initiative and drive toward school autonomy springs from the central authorities, i.e., the Ministry of Education. When a centralized source initiates the idea of promoting local autonomy it will always be manifested, at least at the beginning, by allocating authority. However, there is a clear conceptual difference between allocating authority and undertaking autonomy, although they are interrelated. Without expanding the discussion in this direction, which has been done extensively elsewhere (Dearden, [1972] 1975, 1975; Gibbs, 1979; Nash, 1966; Peters, 1973; Telfer, 1975), some attention has to be given to this since it is central to the understanding of the Israeli case of school autonomization.

Delegating authority is a necessary condition for school autonomy; but, it is not a sufficient condition. Without authority a school cannot actualize autonomy. However, being delegated authority does not ensure autonomous behavior. Authority is a state of power relations; autonomy is a state of mind. Autonomy as a state of mind implying the right to freedom depends first of all on the ability and will of the delegated to behave autonomously (Ben Baruch and Shane, 1982). In order to be autonomous one has to actualize authority not only as a legitimate base of power, but also as one's right of behavior in the search for freedom. The process of delegating authority implies some dependency on the delegating power sources which, of course, can also restrain or prevent the authority from being delegated. The more conditioned the delegated authority is, the more it is followed by centralized control and evaluation processes; the more dependency on the central authorities, the less opportunity for the development of real school autonomy. Indeed, this dualistic feature of centralized delegation of authority is behind the autonomization process in the Israeli elementary school system.

As will be shown, the very delegation of authority by the Ministry of Education to schools has not developed autonomous behavior at the school level. To reach a better insight to the link between decentralization and autonomy, let us look into the concept of decentralization.

## Educational Initiation

The effort to promote autonomy started in the early 1970s. Provoked by the recognition that a rigidly centralized educational system does not answer the needs of a pluralistic society with a diversity of needs and professional responsibilities (Ministry of Education and Culture, 1979), by professional demands for organizational and structural reforms (Minkowich and Bashi, 1973; Peled, 1976), and international advocacy of more localized control (Fantini and Gittell, 1973; Levin, 1970), the Israeli Ministry of Education declared its intention to move toward more decentralization, on the one hand, and teachers' autonomy, on the other. This has been its ongoing aim through various different stages. The first traceable stage can be seen in the 1972 educational initiation idea. This was a centralized effort toward autonomization. In 1971 the Ministry of Education appointed two committees, one for the elementary and one for the secondary educational system, to confront the phenomenon of what was later termed "teacher burnout." The main recommendations centered on the idea of creating certain autonomy through educational initiatives. Why educational initiatives? In the Elementary Committee's words: "There cannot be any escape from tiredness, apathy and bitterness if the teacher will not be autonomous in certain aspects. Encouraging teachers' and principals' initiatives to promote autonomy is the elixir of life for renewal" (Committee on Educational Initiative Encouragement, 1972, p. 4).

From the structural side, the committees suggested establishing centers for educational initiative encouragement to allow each teacher three hours a week for initiating special activities and meeting with a supervisor for special educational-initiatives. The basic idea was that teachers should be more active, develop educational projects, and take more responsibility in school affairs. On the school level, the noted 25% provision was mentioned again. School principals were encouraged to develop specially initiated projects, up to 25% of the total school hours.

However, since the source of the process was the central authorities, it is not surprising that in fact the whole idea was kept under close control. Teachers and schools did not receive teaching hours (time) and other resources automatically. Schools and teachers had to submit their initiated projects for approval to the central authorities through the district inspector. It was a long, bureaucratized procedure and a process which could not really promote creative and nonconventional thinking.

Although there were schools and teachers who took advantage of the possibilities and introduced new projects into schools, mainly enrichment projects, the whole program fell short of developing real school autonomy. Initiation is more than bounded possibilities and autonomy is more than controlled initiative (Inbar, 1974).


## Flexibility

Toward the beginning of the 1973 academic year a new program was elaborated by the Ministry of Education which can be seen as a natural continuation of the initiative stage. The fundamental idea under this program was to allow schools more flexibility in the use of standard hours (in practice this means teaching hours) allocated to schools. It has to be remembered that in the centralized system, as discussed above, all elementary schools follow a suggested pattern of teaching hours (standard hours) utilization according to class level and subject matter.

Under the new program each school could make flexible use of — again— up to 25% of the total standard hours allocated to the school (Ministry of Education, 1972). The main goals of this program flexibility were to enable schools to initiate pedagogical projects in order to increase the pace and level of learning in certain subject matters, or in certain classes, to operate special individualized programs, and to advance cultural and social activities in schools (ibid., Article 161, p. 2).

The program, which can be seen as a step forward in the long process of autonomization, enabled more initiative with less dependency on the central authorities in approving each suggested project. Still, the inherent tension between real autonomy and the centralized system is clearly reflected in the Director General's announcement. It included no less than eight limiting principles. For example: opening new classes or dividing existing classes cannot be part of program flexibility; no subject matter can be abolished for more than two years; the general supervisor will be involved in any changes (ibid., Article 161, pp. 2-3). Furthermore, two suggested examples, one for the State Education System and the other for the Religious State Education system, were included in the Director General's announcement which in practice did not leave much degree of freedom for real change (ibid., pp. 4-6).

By the 1974 academic year, a special Director General's announcement was published, repeating the principles of program flexibility. It again encouraged elementary school principals to deviate from the binding teaching schedule and submit suggestions on flexibility intended to devote 25% of the teaching hours to subjects with special value to local school needs (Ministry of Education, 1973). Again, examples of programs with detailed teaching hour schedules for each subject matter for each class were attached. Nevertheless, in a highly centralized system, the very idea of flexibility, although as yet highly bounded, implies a basic attitudinal change. It legitimized the idea of locally based decisions for change.


## Democratization

Another centralized effort to promote school autonomy began in 1976, again through the Director General's announcement (Ministry of Education, 1976). And again there was a call for school autonomy, although at the end of the announcement there was a special note clearly stating that any autonomy to be delegated to schools would by no means subtract from the authority of the Ministry of Education to supervise the school (ibid., Article 1.3, p. 9).

However, in this announcement the idea of school autonomy was expanded beyond the usual call for developing new educational programs, promoting initiative, and advancing unique, localized programs. It stated that autonomy should not be interpreted only as autonomy of the school principal, but that the principal should, together with the school pedagogical council, develop new structural and procedural regulations to let teacher teams as well as individual teachers benefit from more autonomy. Furthermore, the Director General's announcement indicated that students' opinions and request should be heard and that the student body should be given the opportunity to initiate and plan learning projects (ibid., Article 1, p. 9). In fact, school autonomy has been interpreted as school democratization.

Indeed, since then a great effort has been made to encourage more school democratization. Although "the principal is the first among equals, it is more important to establish a management team close to the principal to help in monitoring and control" (Danilov, 1986, p. 84). In practice these ideas took the shape of nationwide in-service training programs for elementary school principals and for school teams geared to promoting team management and more authority for school pedagogical councils. By team management is meant that school principals would develop a small group of teachers who would receive special hours for management. These teachers, generally three or four in number, together with the school principal, become the managerial unit working as a management team. In each school there exists a pedagogical council which formally should discuss and decide on school policy. In many cases, however, these councils meet very rarely and when they do meet it is more of a ritual than a part of the school policy-making process. Making these pedagogical councils meaningful school bodies was thus considered to be a desired objective.

This interpretation of school autonomy was disclosed in a survey which included 500 schools in the Jewish sector. Only 12% answered that any autonomous activities existed in their schools. The main areas which were mentioned as indicators of school autonomy were educational initiatives, team work, community connections and the existence of team management (Danilov, 1986). For many school principals, autonomy **of** schools was mainly perceived as autonomy **in** schools; thus, from their standpoint, it meant a more democratized style of management.

## Professionalization

The relationship between autonomy and professionalization of teachers and school principals was perceived as a vehicle to "promote the teacher's self-image, to bring the teacher to creativity in his or her work, and to open for the teacher a whole spectrum of internal personal advancement. Autonomy is space for spontaneous innovative growth" (Peled, 1976, p. 90). A similar approach was taken by the State Committee on the Teacher and Teaching Professionals' Status. The need for pedagogical independence was related to the ability to develop and promote the teachers' and teaching professionals' status (Ministry of Education, 1979, Ch. 4, Art. 2.4). If, in this approach, professionalization was perceived as the dependent variable of autonomy, in the second approach the relationships are reversed. Here a relatively high level of professionalization was perceived to be a precondition to the development of school autonomy. This approach can clearly be seen in the planning team of the Pedagogical Secretariat's analysis of the possibilities and implementational principles of educational autonomy. "The success of the new policy [school autonomy] is conditioned first of all on the training of the teacher" (Reshef, 1984, p. 12). In addition, the teacher must be brought up to the same level of other professional roles, able to act as a specialist in his or her domain. Teachers and principals should be prepared and trained toward autonomy. Furthermore, a principal training program for the "school of the future" has been developed by Tel Aviv University and proposed by the Pedagogical Secretariat of the Ministry of Education (Danilov, 1986, p. 88).

Indeed, these ideas were reflected in nationwide in-service training courses for teachers as well as for principals. Since 1980 an academic training program for elementary school principals was developed and has been implemented in all universities in Israel, which implies mainly an educational up-grading of school principals (Ministry of Education, 1985).

## Participation

Complementary to democratization, participation has been considered as one of the main processes, even a necessary process of school autonomy. Beyond teachers' participation in school policy and in decision-making processes, participation in school autonomy has to expand beyond the school boundaries to include the parents and the communities. This was clearly expressed in the proposed plan, "Israeli Education for the Eighties," submitted by the Director General to the Minister of Education and to public debate (Peled, 1976). Growth of autonomy is here directly related to the involvement and participation of all concerned. The plan calls for the development of "educational communities" which will be run by "community councils" (Peled, 1976, pp. 103-118).

Years later, the special planning team of the Ministry of Education's Pedagogical Secretariat has clearly advocated community participation as part of school autonomy. On the national level it advocated the establishment of "organizational frames to develop educational policies with the participation of parents and the community" (Planning Committee, 1984, pp. 17-18). On the local level the committee advocated the "establishment of community educational councils composed of teachers, parents, community members, local municipal authorities and Ministry of Education representatives (Planning Committee, 1984, p. 18).

Without assuming a causal relationship, but with the implication of a supportive setting, in 1978 an experiment began which was aimed at creating "community schools." The basic philosophy of the community school was to make education part of community life. Hence, the operative principle of the schools was participation and involvement. Teachers', parents', and other community members' participation and involvement were seen as a precondition for community school operation (Harpaz, 1985). In each community a directorate of community councils was to be established, oriented to working together with the school staff (Sarlov, 1985). Such councils could develop unique programs and, again, the noted 25% of the learning curriculum was open to change (Sarlov, 1985, p. 10). In 1985, when about 40 community schools were in operation, it was decided that the experiment had been completed and the idea of community schools would be disseminated into the whole educational system.

In practice, these schools have a higher degree of community and parental involvement in school affairs, the 25% provision is exploited to a greater degree, but by and large they have not developed the status of an autonomous school. In all centralized regulations, supervision and manpower, and budget allocations, they are treated the same as all other elementary schools in the country.

## Autonomy — Head-on

Since the 1982 academic year, school autonomy has been approached head-on with a direct effort to almost force principals to assume it. It is possible to look at this year as a turning point in the Ministry of Education's attitude toward school autonomy: no more program flexibility, but rather a direct drive to promote autonomy. This can be seen in the Director General's announcement which clearly proclaimed school autonomy as a major educational goal (Ministry of Education, 1981a). This announcement clarifies that the "elementary school will benefit from more pedagogical independence, and its authority and responsibility will be extended. The school could increase initiative, planning and implementation — independently — of teaching and educational programs" (ibid., Section 276a, p. 18).

What kind of structural and procedural changes were attached to the head-on drive toward school autonomy? In referring to the seven criteria as elaborated above, the major changes are focused on the use of school standard (allocating teaching hours) and the curriculum. However, even this has several restrictions attached to it, as is revealed in the following.

The basic strong, centralized administration has not changed. The supervisory system remains centralized. All elementary school teaching staff continues to be appointed, assigned to particular schools, and dismissed through the central office and the district superintendents. As far as the allocation of teaching hours to each school is concerned, the centralized procedure continues, but with a major change. In the new approach, each school will receive a basic and a complementary standard and will be free to use it in any way it decides on condition that schooling for all students cannot cease before noon (ibid., pp. 18-19). The dramatic change is that the 25% provision has disappeared and schools are formally authorized to use *all* allocated teaching hours (school standard) according to their needs, and not only 25% of them. In a continuing memorandum of the Department of Educational Administration, and this seems to be of utmost importance, it was stated that teaching hours could be converted to finance the acquisition of educational equipment and special activities (Ministry of Education, 1981b, Section 14, p. 3).

Undoubtedly, in the last analysis, the real test of the freedom to use the school standard lies in the status of the curriculum, i.e., in the relationships between it and teaching. Up to now, a centralized, obligatory fundamental curriculum was the basis for school teaching in Israel. After the 1981 Director General announcement cited above, a change was pronounced also.

In the 1982 Director General's announcement, the curriculum status question was approached directly (Ministry of Education, 1982). It was declared that "in order to grant the school more pedagogical independence and to expand its authority and responsibility boundaries...school curriculum will be divided into three sections (of subjects): compulsory — learning according to a compulsory curriculum; choice — choosing from a given list; and optional — any subject or teaching approved by the Pedagogical Secretariat" (ibid., Article 344, pp. 33-34).

The dialectic tension inherent in the centralized drive for local school autonomy is clearly revealed. First, the main core of teaching subjects remains compulsory. Second, even those subjects which are optional have to be approved by the central authorities. Nevertheless, for all practical purposes these steps are clearly a new stage toward school autonomy.

In a centralized system the declared freedom of choice in using allocated teaching hours and the ability to transform them into money, in spite of all the attached restrictions, are significant signs with long-range implications. These intentions were reflected, for instance, in the special team which was assigned to draft a proposal for organizing autonomous schools with clear operative implications (Planning Committee, 1982, 1984). Furthermore, the Ministry of Education is now promoting an experiment, with a special budget, involving 30 schools to be specially nurtured toward autonomous management.

## Autonomy: Option without Possibility

Another drive toward school autonomy was related to budget cuts, which meant reduction in the number of teaching hours allocated to schools. The educational budget was directly affected by the nationwide effort to overcome the frightening trend toward 800% inflation. During the years 1980-1986 the number of pupils in the elementary school system grew about 12.9%, and by 1985 the number of teachers had followed suit, although at a slower pace, and grew about 7.7%, but has been reduced again since 1985 by 7.9%. From 1978-79 to 1985-86 the national educational expenditure as a percentage of the GNP was reduced by 1.3% (Ministry of Education and Culture, 1987).

This affected the system in various ways. The total number of teaching hours at the primary level was reduced during 1981-1986 by 28.5%, and after closing small schools, making a great effort to increase the number of pupils per class, and improving administrative efficiency by cutting administrative employees, the average number of weekly teaching hours was reduced in the elementary schools — except for the first and second grades — by 11.6% (ibid., 1987). Teachers' assistants were abolished, classes became more crowded, and many of the programs in art, music and natural sciences were drastically reduced.

School principals felt that the central authorities in fact had shifted the burden of budgetary cuts onto their shoulders. As one principal argued: "The only degree of freedom we received from the autonomy plan is the freedom to choose what cuts should be 'executed.'" Autonomy is conceived to be a ritual behavior without real content. Consequently, school principals resist implementing the idea, although supporting it in principle.

For several years little really occurred. The elementary school principals were caught in this dualistic situation where theoretically they could assume some autonomy but practically it meant being responsible for one-directional changes — cuts. Hence, it is not surprising that by and large elementary school principals were reluctant to accept the autonomy option and even resented it, arguing mainly that now they had the option for autonomy but did not have the possibility of actualizing it.

## Autonomy and Privatization

In the years 1985-1987 an interesting change started to occur and which is gaining momentum today — a process toward school privatization (Inbar, 1987).

The severe constraints put upon schools has accelerated the privatization process in two complementary ways. First, they really depreciated educational quality to a degree that parents felt it immediately as children began to return home from school at an earlier hour.

Thus parents' general uneasiness about school quality turned to clear frustration. Second, it served as a real justification and a convenient rationalization for parents to pursue the changes and for the Ministry of Education to approve them, although it was conscious of the possible inequalities and implication of segregation.

This trend led to the opening of "special" schools focusing on special contextual issues, and the development of special in-school programs in the regular schools. Major examples of the "special" schools are the art elementary school and the natural/science-oriented elementary school. Beyond the emphasis on certain contents, these schools have several notable aspects related to autonomy. First, they do not have bounded registration zones; students can enroll to this type of school from all over the city. Enrollment is based on two major criteria: parental choice and entrance tests. Both criteria are a meaningful departure from regular public elementary school practice, implying a new source of power for the school. In addition, if all public elementary schools offer free education, in these schools special payment, although relatively moderate, is required, adding an independent source of resources.

Another interesting characteristic of these schools is that students who do not measure up to school requirements, either in general scholastic achievement, behavior or talent in special programs (music, drama, art, crafts, etc.) may be asked to return to their original neighborhood elementary school. Although the number of such cases is small, the very idea is significant. The school gains the power to decide upon the structure of its student body.

Finally, one of the prerequisites of these schools is a high degree of parental involvement. Parents are required to participate in school programs, such as trips in the natural/science programs or working with students in workshops in arts and crafts programs. These programs are planned and controlled by the school with almost no central involvement. All of these are basic factors of school autonomy.

The most fascinating development in this direction is the in-school programs. Here schools, through direct parental participation, develop and offer special programs to students. The domain of these programs includes topics such as arts, crafts, ceramics, drawing, dancing, music, theater, drama, etc. However, beyond these relatively traditional extracurricular programs, programs such as history-through-museums, storytelling, logic, mathematical games, natural science, and computers have been introduced. These programs are very closely related to the central core of education beyond classical enrichment programs.

The programs are implemented mainly in two versions. First, after condensing all regular school activities into five days by adding one hour to each one of them, the sixth day is devoted entirely to the special programs. (The school week in Israel is six days, as is the work week.) Second, the special programs are provided in one or two days by extending the school day.

In most cases a group of parents' representatives, with the principal, form a steering committee which decides upon contents and which runs the programs. The programs are financed directly by the parents and the fee is decided upon by the steering committee and covers all expenses, meaning a totally independent budget. Teachers for the various subjects are specially hired by the steering committee and are paid by the parents in various ways, but of course not at any time by the Ministry of Education. Salaries are in many cases negotiated and are relatively high, far beyond what might be paid by the central educational authorities.

The special teachers can be replaced if their work does not meet expectations without involving the supervisors or any other centralized procedures.

After some hesitation, school principals have started to encourage the introduction of such special programs, and these types of programs are now spreading very rapidly around the country, mainly in the big cities, Tel Aviv, Haifa and Jerusalem, and their surrounding small towns. The whole phenomenon is quite new and without any central organization, and therefore no systematic information has been gathered on the subject. The central authorities of the Ministry of Education are aware of this phenomenon. However, since these programs derive their legitimation from the general trend toward autonomy, from the specific provision that parents and schools have the right to develop 25% of school programs, and because of the drastic budget cuts, they silently condone them, although it hardly resembles the type of autonomy they had conceived.

Watching this phenomenon through the perspective of autonomy, a change in the elementary school principal's role has begun to occur. School principals are now engaged in direct curriculum planning and policy development whereas in the past they perceived this as something they rarely had the opportunity to do because of their overwhelming administrative responsibilities (Goldstein, 1973; Inbar, 1977). Principals are starting to realize that parental involvement might increase their professional autonomy. With local financing, many school programs can be developed independent of the central authorities' control. Furthermore, the new situation now enables principals to initiate programs and ideas and thus assume much more autonomy than suggested by the central authorities. Schools may now develop programs with fiscal independence from the Ministry of Education, and may hire and fire certain teachers, an unheard of situation before. Instead of bounded autonomy in all school activities, schools are developing full autonomy in part of the school activities.

# THE SECOND CYCLE, TWENTY YEARS LATER: SCHOOL-BASED MANAGEMENT

In line with the inclination to increase school decision-making power that is sweeping educational systems around the world, the recent trend to introduce school-based management (SBM) has found its way into the Israeli educational system. In 1992, the Minister of Education commissioned a steering committee to explore the possibility of extending the scope of school autonomy and introducing SBM into the Israeli school system.

This initiative reflects a radical policy change, especially in light of the assumed contribution of centralization for ensuring equal educational services in a highly diversified and multi-ethnic society comprised of religious and non-religious Jews, Muslim and Christian Arabs, Druze and Bedouin citizens (Gumpel and Nir, 2006). Social diversity, however, was the very reason for attempts being made in the last couple of decades towards decentralization, following liberal voices that called for flexibility and pluralism and for better congruity between educational services and local needs (Nir and Eyal, 2003).

Decentralization has long been recognized as creating a fundamental dilemma for centralized governments to choose between the responsibility for the quality of education and the desire to increase school autonomy (Weiler, 1990).

Simply stated, SBM refers to the increase of authority at the school site (Clune and White, 1988), and emphasizes maximum delegation of decision-making power to the operational level (i.e., school level) within a centrally coordinated framework (Boyd, 1990, p. 90). SBM is not merely passing the central authority to the principal. Rather, it is an attempt to make it possible for the school head to work out the school policies and programs in collaboration with his professional staff and the community (Nir, 2006).

SBM is based on the assumption that decisions made closer to the clients are better decisions (Conley, 1991; David, 1989). Therefore, promoting school autonomy and decision-making power is likely to improve school outcomes and the accountability of school-level educators (Caldwell, 1990, p. 17). In this sense, SBM implies a revolution in the structure of power that has traditionally characterized centralized educational systems, shifting authority from higher to lower levels of the educational hierarchy (Nir and Eyal, 2003).

The emerging restructuring initiatives that call for decentralization and for increasing school-level control through school-based decision-making processes suggest a primary change in the process of external school control. The introduction of SBM in the Israeli educational system presented a contradiction between rhetoric and praxis in terms of the role responsibilities of the school superintendents. SBM proposes to increase school-level authority and autonomy and, therefore, to change the structure of external supervision on schools, in practice, the formal definition of superintendents' role duties was never changed. The tension between maintaining and loosening external control over schools by allowing for school autonomy to develop turns out to be an immanent feature in centralized systems.

SBM emphasizes school autonomy and flexibility and, at the same time, the accountability and responsibility of school principals for school outcomes. This explains why school principals are more attentive to their need to maintain control over the entire school enterprise than to increasing teachers' participation in school-management processes. Hence, one can argue that if increase of autonomy of schools in SBM in centralized systems is still questionable, the decrease of autonomy in schools is quite evident. This is particularly true when considering principals who have served for many years under a centralized structure, in which control, supervision and unity were emphasized rather than pedagogical autonomy and genuine initiatives and who experienced the failure of past decentralization attempts in the Israeli educational system. These failures led to skepticism of school heads about the intentions of the Ministry of Education officials, since no significant and long-lasting changes occurred in the actual autonomy of schools. It is less likely, therefore, that principals under SBM will change their managerial behavior if they will not be fully convinced regarding the sincerity of intentions of policy-makers (Nir, 2000). As one school principal explained: "Before, we were marionettes operated by strings, and now we are operated by remote control."

## SUMMARY

The democratic value system of Israel, its pluralistic nature and openness to outside influence, to local and professional demands and pressure, and dissatisfaction with the educational outcomes, might by themselves drive the educational system toward more school autonomy. However, the strong centralized structure, combined with the small size of the country, will tend to keep and even strengthen the highly centralized characteristics of the system. The combination of all three seems to yield quite a unique situation where SBM or school autonomy is promoted centrally and, nearly, enforced, reaching the paradoxical situation of "institutionalized" autonomy. This process, though, is in an ongoing struggle with two contradictory forces, the centripetal and the centrifugal forces; under these contradictory forces, the development of the idea of school autonomy took a long multi-stage journey which essentially reflects some of the basic features of autonomy.

Initiation, flexibility, democracy, professionalization and participation are indeed basic elements of autonomy. However, basing autonomy mainly on one of them will fall short in actualizing real autonomy. It seems that when autonomy is related to scarcity, school principals are reluctant to assume it: They would rather have the higher authorities make decisions on cuts (Nir, 2007). Last, it is not surprising that, at the current stage, there is an interaction between autonomy and the school privatization phenomenon. They share a broad common denominator: In a centralized system the two processes represent the weakening of the centralized authoritative control and the strengthening of school independence, increasing sectorial and local control on educational affairs. Being influenced by the neo-liberal ideas of competition and privatization might of course bring about what can be termed "privatized autonomy."

The future agenda calls for a close watch on how the three forces — the drive to school autonomy, the bureaucratized power of the centralized system, and the marketing pressure toward school privatization — will balance.

Interestingly, in the Israeli case the power of the centralized system is the main force in shaping schools. The fascinating example is the latest attempt to employ a comprehensive educational reform (Inbar, 2006), by a special national task force, a top-down committee appointed by the Minister of Education. Incidentally, teachers' union resistance put reform on hold which implies that in education the central authorities have enough power to prevent or slow down development, but are too weak to initiate and implement new development without the professional support of teachers.

## REFERENCES

Adler, C. (1969). Education and the integration of immigrants in Israel. *International Migration Review*, 3, 3-19.

Bashi, J. (1985). The primary education. In: W. Ackerman, A. Carmon, and D. Zucker (Eds.), *Education in an evolving society*. Jerusalem, Israel: Van Leer.

Bassok, M. (August 24, 2004). On eve of 5765, population stands at 6.8m. *Haaretz*, p. 1.

Ben Baruch, E., and Shane, P. (1982). Autonomy and delegation of authority. In: E. Ben Baruch and Y. Neuman (Eds.), *Educational administration and policy-making* (pp. 71-84). Herzliya, Israel: Unipress.

Bloomer, K. (1991). Decentralizing the educational system. Paper presented at the Commonwealth Secreteriat, Kadoma: April-May. Teacher Management Discussion Paper, Commonwealth Secreteriat (September).

Boyd, W.L. (1990). Balancing control and autonomy in school reform: The politics of Perestroika. In: J. Murphy (Ed.), *The educational reform movement of the 1980's,* Berkeley, Cal.: McCutchan Pub. Co.

Caldwell, B. (1990). SBM and management: International developments. In: J. D. Chapman (Ed.), *School based decision making and management* (pp. 3-38). London: The Falmer Press.

Clune, W.H., and White, P.A. (1988). *School based management: Institutional variation, implementation and issues for further research.* Center for Policy Research in Education, Rutgers University, New Brunswick, N.J.

Committee on Educational Initiative Encouragement (1972). Jerusalem, Israel: Ministry of Education and Culture.

Conley, S. (1991). Review of research on teacher participation in school decision-making. *Review of Research in Education,* Vol. 17, pp. 225-6.

Danilov, J. (1986). The pedagogical independence of the school. In: *Central Educational Issues in the Educational System, 1976-1986.* Jerusalem, Israel: Ministry of Education and Culture, The Pedagogical Secretariat.

David, J. L. (1989). Synthesis of research on school-based management, *Educational Leadership,* 46 (8), 45-53.

Dearden, R.F. ([1972] 1975). Autonomy and education. In: R.F. Dearden, P.H. Hirst, and R.S. Peters (Eds.), *Education and the development of reason* (pp. 58-75). London: Routledge and Kegan Paul.

Dearden, R.F. (1975). Autonomy as an educational ideal. In: S.C. Brown (Ed.), *Philosophers discuss education* (pp. 3-19). London: McMillan.

Fantini, M. D. and Gittell, M. (1973). *Decentralization and achieving reform.* New York: Praeger Publications.

Gibbs, B. (1979). Autonomy and authority in education. *Journal of Philosophy of Education,* 13, pp. 119-132.

Goldstein, J. (1973). School system personnel's attitudes towards the elementary school principal in Israel. *Studies in Educational Administration and Organization,.* 1,(1), pp. 61-101.

Gumpel, T. P., and Nir A. E. (2006). The Israeli educational system: Blending dreams with constraints In: K. Mazuerk and M. A. Winzer (Eds.), *Schooling around the world: Debates, challenges and practices* (pp. 149 - 167). N.Y.: Allyn and Bacon.

Harpaz, Y. ([1982] 1985). *Community schools: The development of an idea.* Jerusalem, Israel: The Israel Association of Community Centers.

Inbar, D. E. (1974). Educational initiative – planning, plans and implementation. *Studies in Education,* no. 2, pp. 149-156.

Inbar, D. E. (1977). Perceived authority and responsibility of elementary school principals in Israel. *Journal of Educational Administration,* vol. XV, (1), 80-91.

Inbar, D. E. (1986). Educational policy-making and planning in a small centralized democracy. *Comparative Education,* vol. 22, (3), 271-281.

Inbar, D. E. (1987). A backdoor process of school privatization: The case of Israel. In: W. L. Boyd and J. G. Cibulka (Eds.), *Private schools and public policy: International perspectives* (pp. 269-283). London: The Falmer Press.

Inbar, D.E. (Ed.), (2006). *Towards educational revolution?* The Van Leer Jerusalem Institute and Hakibbutz Hameuchad Publishing House, Tel Aviv.

Kleinberger, F. A. (1969). *Society, schools and progress in Israel*. London: Pergamon Press.

Kruisinga, H. J. (Ed.) (1954). *The balance between centralization and decentralization in managerial control*. Leiden: H. E. Stenferd Jrose .

Lauglo, J. (1995). Forms of decentralization and implication for education. *Comparative Education*, 31 (1), 5-29.

Levin, H. M. (ed.) (1970). *Community control of schools*. Washington, D.C.: The Brookings Institute.

Ministry of Education and Culture (1972). *Director General Announcement*. No. 32/10. Jerusalem, Israel.

Ministry of Education and Culture (1973). *Director General Announcement*. Special announcement No. 4, Jerusalem, Israel.

Ministry of Education and Culture (1976). *Director General Special Announcement,* No. 1. Jerusalem, Israel.

Ministry of Education and Culture (1979). *Special Director General Announcement: State Committee Report on the Teacher and Teaching Profession Status*. Jerusalem, Israel.

Ministry of Education and Culture (1981a). *Director General Announcement,* No. 41/8, April, Jerusalem, Israel.

Ministry of Education and Culture (1981b). *Educational Administration Announcement*, No. 159, Article 178. March 19, 1981, Jerusalem, Israel.

Ministry of Education and Culture (1982). *Director General Announcement,* No. 42/10, Article 344, June 1982, Jerusalem, Israel.

Ministry of Education and Culture (1985). The Department of Training and Advancement of Senior Staff. *The Curriculum of Academic School Principals' Training Program*. Jerusalem, Israel.

Ministry of Education and Culture (1987). *The Ministry of Education and Culture*. February, 1987, Jerusalem, Israel.

Minkowich, A., and Bashi, J. (1973). *A reform proposal of the inspectory and supervisory structure*. Submitted to the Ministry of Education and Culture, April, 1973, Jerusalem, Israel.

Nash, P. (1966). *Authority and freedom in education*. New York: John Wiley.

Nir, A. E. (2000). The annual plans of School-Based Management schools operating in a centralized educational system: Planning for ambiguity, *Educational Planning,* 12 (4), 19-38.

Nir, A. E. (2006). Maintaining or delegating authority? Contradictory policy messages and the prospects of school-based management to promote school autonomy. *Educational Planning*, 15 (1), 27 –38.

Nir, A. E. (2007). The effect of school based management on schools' culture of consumption. *International Journal of Leadership in Education*, 10 (4), 421-436.

Nir, A. E., and Eyal, O. (2003). School-based management and the role conflict of the school superintendent. *Journal of Educational Administration,* 41 (5), 547 – 564.

Nir, A. E., and Inbar, D. (2003). School principals in the Israeli Educational system: From headteachers to professional leaders. In: Watson, L. E. (Ed.) *Selecting and developing heads of schools: Twenty-two European perspectives* (pp. 137-148). Sheffield: Sheffield Hallam University Press, The European Forum on Educational Administration.

Peled, E. (1976). *Education in Israel for the 1980s*. The Ministry of Education and Culture, Jerusalem, Israel.

Peters, R.S. ([1959] 1973). *Authority, responsibility, and education*. London: George Allen and Unwin (revised edition).

Planning Committee of the Pedagogical Secretariat (1982). *Working paper: The meaning of school autonomy*. Tel Aviv, Israel: Tel Aviv University, School of Education, November.

Planning Committee of the Pedagogical Secretariat (1984). *Educational autonomy -- meaning and application*. Ministry of Education and Culture, May, Jerusalem, Israel.

Reshef, S. (1984). *Autonomy in education – background, possibilities and implementational principles*. Planning Committee of the Pedagogical Secretariat, Ministry of Education and Culture, Jerusalem, Israel.

Rondinelli, D. (1983). Implementation decentralization programs in Asia: A comparative analysis. *Public Administration and Development*, 3, 181-207.

Sarlov, Y. (1985). *Guidelines for the community school public council members*. Jerusalem, Israel: Ministry of Education and Culture and the Israel Association of Community Centers.

Telfer, E. ([1972] 1975). Autonomy as an educational ideal, II. In: S.C. Brown (Ed.). *Philosophers deiscuss education* (pp. 19-42). London: Macmillan.

Weiler, H.N. (1990) Comparative perspectives on educational decentralization: an exercise in contradiction? *Educational Evaluation and Policy Analysis*, 12 (4), 433-448.

Winkler, R. D. (1989). Decentralization in education: An economic perspective. The World Bank working paper, Population of Human Resourcs Department, WPS 143.

Zucker, D. (1985). The Israeli educational system: structure, organization, financing and patterns of action [in Hebrew]. In W. Ackerman, A. Carmon and D. Zucker (Eds.), *Education in an evolving society: Schooling in Israel*. Jerusalem: The Van Leer Institute.

In: Centralization and School Empowerment...
Editor: Adam Nir

ISBN 978-1-60692-730-4
© 2009 Nova Science Publishers, Inc.

*Chaper 6*

# SCHOOL EMPOWERMENT AND AUTONOMY IN THE ITALIAN SCHOOL SYSTEM

*Cesare Scurati[1] and Angelo Paletta[2]*
1. Catholic University, Milano, Italy
2. University of Bologna, Italy

## THE CONTEXT: HISTORY AND STRUCTURES

The Italian education system has traditionally been based on a strongly centralized model. The content of the curricula was nationally prescribed; the school personnel (teachers and principals) was recruited through national selections and enrolled on the lists of state employees (civil servants); pupils obtained national certifications at the end of the various levels of their school career; salaries were the same throughout the system; the heads were mainly seen as administrators in the bureaucratic chain of the Ministry of Education.

A first significant change was introduced in 1974 with the Collegial Boards for school governance (*Organi collegiali per il governo della scuola*) at the school, provincial and national level. These boards were set up in an attempt to distribute certain tasks or decisions to decentralized elected democratic boards composed of representatives of school personnel and of social groups as well. The participatory system introduced by the legislation of 1974 has been severely criticized for its inconsistencies, like the ongoing conflict with the ministerial bureaucratic powers, the purely ritualistic approach to the elective procedures, the useless and misleading ideologization of issues, the lack of a consistent range of influential decisions that produced an increasing disaffection of the various parts involved (i.e., parents, social agencies, teachers themselves), and that must be modified. Nonetheless, it paved the way to the further important step of school autonomy and made explicit the need for a totally different approach to the problems of school headship. Nowadays we are still waiting for a general reordering of participation.

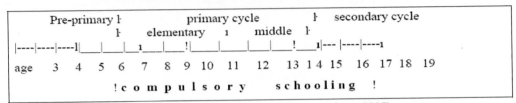

Source: The Ministry of Education (Ministero della Pubblica Istruzione, 2007).

Figure 1. The Italian system

In the second half of the last decade a wide spectrum of reforms was introduced (*riordino dei cicli*: reorder of the school levels) with the objective of moving towards a stronger modernization both on the structural and the professional level.

The school system has been reshaped and subdivided in two broad sections: the primary cycle (*ciclo primario*) from 6 to 14, and the secondary cycle *(ciclo secondario)* from 14 to 19.

Compulsory education (*istruzione obbligatoria*) has been extended from 8 to 10 years and now it includes elementary (from 6 to 11) plus middle (middle or low secondary or junior from 11 to 14) school and the first two years (from 14 to 16) of upper secondary school. The ages from 3 to 6 are not included in any requirement but noncompulsory attendance in preschool education (*scuola materna*) is very common (around 95% of the interested population). Attendance in the last three years of upper secondary education (from 16 to 19) is also not compulsory.

Access to compulsory (and noncompulsory) education is open to everybody with no restrictions as to gender, religious, ideological, ethnic or racial. Compulsory education is not intended to provide options but rather to promote the whole development of moral, intellectual and social qualities of the pupils and to help the pupils' orientation towards their future choices. The integration of children with special problems is prescribed together with the development of programs of ethnic and cultural integration.

Let us now look at the general system, referred to as the state schools, that is, the schools directly established, financed and administered on a nationwide basis by the Ministry of Education.

## Table 1: Basic figures of the Italian educational system

|  | Pre-primary | Elementary | Middle | Secondary | Total |
|---|---|---|---|---|---|
| Number of schools | 13,361 | 16,1120 | 7,149 | 5,107 | 42,007 |
| Number of pupils | 961,872 | 2,566,436 | 1,615,266 | 2,598,720 | 7,742,294 |
| Number of classes | 42,116 | 137,598 | 77,110 | 118,097 | 374,921 |
| Number of teachers* | 84,886 | 249,181 | 167,251 | 230,694 | 732,012 |
| Number of *support* *teachers* ** | 4,181 8.6% | 19,688 40.4% | 17,055 35% | 7,769 16% | 48,693 |
| Number of pupils per class | 22.8 | 18.7 | 20.9 | 22.0 | 20.7 |

Source: The Ministry of Education (Ministero della Pubblica Istruzione, 2007).

* Including the *support teachers*

** *Support teachers* (teachers devoted to the integration of handicapped or disadvantaged pupils in the normal classes).

The reorganization of the system has been accompanied by the revision of the nationally prescribed curricula (*programmi*) and by the redistribution of the classes in 10,759 school units (*unità scolastiche*) or school institutions (*istituzioni scolastiche)*. The school personnel include teachers (73%), clerical staff (25.3%), principals (25.3%), and other educators (0.2%). In July 2007 the Minister of Education issued the National Guidelines for Curriculum (*Indicazioni Nazionali per il curricolo*) to be tested and evaluated by the schools within two years.

## IN SEARCH OF A NEW QUALITY: SCHOOL AUTONOMY

Law n. 59 of March 15, 1997, concerning the Public Administration Reform, introduced the idea of autonomy of schools, conferring upon them a "juridical" character with powers and prerogatives that had been previously exclusive to the central authorities. The Law states that autonomy includes two basic aspects, that is organizational autonomy - freedom to make independent decisions about the best way to avail themselves of resources, to shape the school timetable, to introduce innovative technologies, etc. – and didactic-methodological autonomy – freedom to make independent decisions about the opportunities for enriching curricular provisions and to adopt more effective teaching methods and approaches. This secures for school personnel real powers of influencing and making decisions concerning school matters.

The Presidential Decree March 8, 1999, n. 275, regulates the operational framework and adds to the previous ones the notion of autonomy to experiment and to promote research. The relevance of this Decree is due to the fact that it extends the borders of the autonomy granted to the schools and fixes specific indications concerning contents and its forms.

Up to now school autonomy has been ruled and directed by this Decree (Falanga, 2001). The Decree prescribes that every year faculties must elaborate, implement and evaluate the Educational Plan (*Piano dell'offerta formativa*). Moreover, the schools may cooperate to establish various networks, and they are allowed to determine roughly 20% of the curriculum content on their own. Didactic autonomy requires the educational programs to be based on: specific and clearly outlined learning goals to be achieved by the pupils over a specified period of time; teaching timetables for each school subject to be determined by the schools, while respecting the teaching hours fixed by the central authorities; educational schedules, programs and activities to be organized by the schools; curricula to be enriched through the introduction of particular disciplines/activities, decided upon in agreement with local agencies; timetables of each subject to be established on a yearly basis rather than stipulated on a rigid weekly one; and criteria and procedures of students' evaluation in order to assess their learning outcomes to be identified by schools.

For example, schools may articulate the duration of subject teaching and learning activities in modules, define learning units not necessarily corresponding to one hour of teaching in a class, aggregate disciplines in different areas and domains, and activate original educational processes, organize groups of students coming from the same or from different classes or from different years, etc.

Information about the success of the realization and implementation of school autonomy shows a certain level of progress, even if differences among schools still remain, and the staff members of a number of schools are still unable to detach themselves from the attitude of waiting for the decisions to be made by central or peripheral employees of the Ministry of Education instead of making their own decisions and taking their own responsibility.

The conclusions of research completed after the first endeavors of the new model give us a pertinent picture. The main aims of the reform – the authors say – intended "to extricate the educational processes from the rigidity of the administrative procedures and to entrust them to the structures where they effectively take place" (Rescalli and Visalberghi, 1994, p. 179). The general opinion is in favor of autonomy not only on the organizational, managerial and administrative level, but also on the didactic and curricular one, "in a national framework including suggestions rather than prescriptions" (p.183), since "the schools cannot reform by themselves but they can implement national outlines in an original, creative and contextually functional attitude" (p.184).

## GOVERNANCE AND MANAGEMENT OF THE SCHOOLS: NEW PRINCIPLES

The new model of governance is based on three concepts: every school enjoys the status of an autonomous institution; state and non-state schools are integrated into the national educational system; a plurality of instances involved in the development of educational activities is connected in a specific network of central and local agencies. While attempting to pursue the effective autonomy of the schools, a gap emerges between the juridical-formal model and the effective one.

*Public (state) and non-public (non-state):* The non-public sector (excluding early childhood institutions), refers only to 5% of the users, while the public sector refers to more than one million people (teachers, clerical staff and assistants). The Ministry itself employs about 10,000 administrative workers (80% of them in the regional and provincial offices); the inspectors amount only to 8.2% (a new recruitment has been initiated).

From that we can argue that the Italian educational system remains a centralized one that has been decentralized mainly from an administrative point of view.

*Mission and resources: A difficult balance.* The effective implementation of autonomy of a school does not merely rely on the content of the law. In fact, the conditions for a harmonious balance among all the components of the school are not yet completely satisfied, since the capabilities of the schools are limited in terms of management of human resources: The selection, the recruitment and the careers of the personnel are in the hands of the administration, and teachers' salaries, with or without tenure, are not directly managed by the schools and their amount is the same all over the country except possible very low incentives dependent on the principals. As to financial management, the School Boards may give meaning to their autonomy, raising and utilizing financial resources with no constraint (Paletta, 2006).

In order to redress the matter, the Financial Law of 2007 introduced some measures that simplify the crediting of funds. In particular, school financing procedures have been simplified with the introduction of only two funds (*capitoli*). Resources allocated through these two funds may be distributed to a specific school with reference to objective criteria and measures, such as the number of the students enrolled, the number of the students with particular needs, a fixed quota related to the numbers of teachers and clerical staff, etc. The new funding system contributes to a more transparent financing process and eliminates the involvement of regional and provincial offices that were once the reference points for each school.

*New governance on a regional basis.* As mentioned before, the new structure of the Constitution foresees a "networked organization," based on the following principles: the State fixes norms for education, defines contents and national directions for programs, standards of services and essential levels of performance, institutes a national system of evaluation, issues medium- and long-term programs for teacher preparation, and establishes financial resources; and the national norms also plan the human and financial resources of the networks acknowledged by the Ministry of Education (Crema and Pollini, 1989).

Following a multicenter model of decision-making that charges the State with general tasks and powers of direction for evaluation, the new institutional approach diffuses within the system the regional governance, attributing new and important roles to provincial and municipal authorities, which become responsible for defining educational policies, while the local administrator's job is devoted to providing the services needed by the educational institutions within the local area. The cooperation to be realized among schools, municipalities, provinces and regions may become an institutional factor that influences the effectiveness of the school and of the local educational system (Bezzina, Paletta and Vidoni, 2006).

## SCHOOL HEADS: A NEW PROFILE

Participatory government (1974) and school autonomy (1997, 1999) played a paramount role in promoting a substantial change in the traditional profile of the school principals and heads (Fischer and Masuelli, 1998).

Both the heads and principals of the elementary schools (*direttori didattici*) and of the secondary schools (*presidi*) received an enhanced status, and new rules were promulgated as to their recruitment (Legislative Decree, March 6, 1998, n. 59), their employment and their career development. Nowadays they are generally considered *"capi d'istituto"* (following the French terminology: *chefs d'establissement scolaire).*

The reason for this development can be found in the conception of the school head as the basic change agent within the school, whose professionalism no longer reflects the traditional bureaucratic-administrative style but rather is modelled on the features that distinguish and qualify the characters of managers and leaders of complex human enterprises (Scurati and Ceriani, 1994).

*Empowerment* – with all its nuances: innovation, change, quality implementation, continuous development, production of meanings – becomes the watchword of the new trend. The leading concept is that if you want school heads to be able to promote the empowerment of their institutions, you must empower them to promote their preparation and reinforce their position (Artini, 2004).

In fact, all aspects of a process of empowerment to be introduced in a school – bettering the quality of the interrelationships, being functionally efficient, developing the continuous professional growth of the teaching and administrative personnel, projecting original curriculum plans, meeting the demands of the pupils, the parents, the social environment: the idea of "autonomy" includes all these meanings – find their meeting point in the personal and professional qualities (attitudes, competencies, styles) of the principal/head (Damiano, 1993).

In light of this new philosophy, the roles and the functions of the school principals have been redefined, establishing a new profile where they are required to promote and coordinate the activities that the School Board deliberates to undertake, are responsible for the functioning of the school and, therefore, are in charge of putting into effect all the decisions taken by the Collegial Boards. Furthermore, principals are called upon to promote and coordinate innovations and initiatives, to take care of the continuing professional development of the staff and to act as the linking agent between the school and the community. The emphasis has been moved from respecting the rules to responsibility for human and functional resources. Again, the principals are considered less as bureaucrats and more as managers.

The Legislative Decree of 1998 on "the managerial qualifications of school principals" introduced the concept that they are awarded "autonomous powers of leading, coordinating and empowering human resources" with a specific reference to the organization of the activities of the schools in an efficient and effectual way. They can also delegate some tasks to designated teachers.

Regarding the empowerment process as such, the role and the functions of school principals can be summarized as follows: orienting and monitoring discussions and debates during decision-making, putting forward the decisions taken by the faculties and the boards, providing the resources necessary to implement projects and initiatives, suggesting possible new ways of doing things, sustaining and enhancing the morale of groups, facilitating sound, objective and comprehensive evaluation activities (Paletta and Vidoni, 2006).

*Selection and recruitment* - In the former system, access to a position was open on the basis of years of service and selection consisted of written and oral exams with a nationwide perspective. No specific preparation (e.g., a masters degree or a diploma in educational management) and no specific career qualification (e.g., serving as a deputy or as a head of department or as a project coordinator) was required or taken into account. After five years of full-time teaching, every teacher could apply for selection (*concorso*). The selection was performed by a national commission (the same for all the applicants in the country) and assignment to a school depended on the last position occupied by those who succeeded.

The Legislative Decree 1988 included some important statements on this point: recruitment and selection will be effected on a regional and not on a national basis; the applicants must show a minimum of seven years full service and a graduate degree; the applicants are firstly selected on the basis of their professional curriculum (graduation, previous experience, career qualification, etc.) in order to be admitted to a written and oral exam; after having been approved they must follow a specific training course (four months) and prepare a written report, after which they are admitted to a final written and oral exam; those who succeed may undertake the position. The number of positions available is announced at the opening of the procedure.

*Initial and continuous preparation* - No specific pre-service preparation is formally required since up to now the Italian higher education system has not conferred any specific degree for this level, while study for masters' degrees (postgraduate courses) and/or advanced level courses (*corsi di perfezionamento*) has taken place only in the last years.

The above-mentioned shift from a bureaucratic to a managerial approach has led to the awareness that, in order to ensure a competent and progressive direction for a school, it was not possible to persist in relying only on personal goodwill and/or on formal observance of laws and regulations. Training of the school heads was expected to contribute to a better social interplay of the schools and their personnel with the social environment, to encourage a more conscious and active participation in the development of the qualitative growth of the schools, to pursue a higher level of goal attainment within the school, including the promotion of innovation and improvement of students' achievement and teachers' professional development.

The Ministry of Education itself understood the challenge and has been very active in promoting two national initiatives in order to update the school heads.

In 1992 all the elementary school principals participated in a national plan aimed at refreshing and updating their knowledge and their attitudes in order to ensure the best conditions for the application of the new organizational structure of this level of schooling. The implementation of the project was entrusted to the Regional Institutes for Experimentation and In-Service (IRRSAE) and lasted one school year.

An even greater effort has been made following the new regulations concerning autonomy. The Ministerial Decree of August 5, 1998, was devoted to the "institution, organization and implementation of courses in order to confer the new higher status of 'school heads' (*capi di istituto*)." Certified participation in the courses became the prerequisite to obtaining the new formal higher qualification of school head (*capo d'istituto*), that would also entail a substantial financial benefit.

The Decree issued a compulsory in-service national program of 300 hours with the aim of "furthering the acquirement and the strengthening of knowledge, the competencies and the skills necessary to guarantee the performing of the managerial functions connected to the experience of autonomy of the schools." A national panel of experts, administrators and representatives of the school personnel defined the contents and the methodological procedures of the plan; then all the possible interested agencies (universities, research groups, professional associations, private enterprises, etc.) were asked to present their projects to be classified in a national selective contest (Scurati, 2003).

No other national plan has been issued.

## NEW CHALLENGES: NEW REALITIES?

The agenda is almost entirely covered by problems of application in the field of all the innovations and the changes connected to the general process of school system reform. Many are doubtful about the effective developments of all the changes that have been initiated. The overall situation seems very promising, but still a great proportion of the heads is not entirely confident that all the beneficial implications of the reforms will really come into effect. As a matter of fact, most of the promises are still on the paper while a not unsubstantial percentage of the heads is confronted with the delicate problem of readapting themselves to new organizational situations and to difficult school populations.

Italian school heads can now be classified in two main categories: the "committed" (optimistic, in favor of change, professionally innovative) and the "awaiting" (uncertain, a bit skeptical, professionally prudent). Two different ideas can be found also in regard to the main corporate theories concerning the future of the profession. One vision inclines more in the direction of pursuing an even higher administrative position and status (reference model: the *grand commis* of the state administration), while the other one is more interested in looking at the successful top managers in the business field (Rubinacci, Gallegati and Quarantotto, 1999).

*School heads' evaluation*: A special case - The need of a formal evaluation of the school heads emerged when the reform, started in 1997-1999, defined a new profile for them. Point 5 of the Legislative Decree 286/99 (and Point 25 of the Legislative Decree 165/01) introduced the evaluation of the heads in an experimental way (SI.VA.DI.S model: Evaluation System of the School Managers). This reform was adopted during the school year 2005-2006 and acknowledged at Point 20 of the school managers' contract in 2006 (April 11th).

This evaluation includes two phases: The first one is operated by a Commission including an expert, an administrator and an educational professional with certified skills; the second is in charge of the chief of the Regional Educational Office (*Direttore Regionale*) and pertains to the results obtained and the skills demonstrated by the school heads.

The experiment does not imply any administrative or economic effect. In the present situation, the Sivadis Project is just testing a possible procedure. An evaluation of the Sivadis Project, carried out by the National Institute for the Evaluation of the Education System – INVALSI, 2006 (*Istituto Nazionale per la Valutazione del Sistema di Istruzione)*, expressed some criticism towards the methods and the contents of that evaluation. It is evident that the beginning of the systematic evaluation of school heads is not yet grounded on clear qualitative goals. It comes as no surprise that the dissatisfaction of the corporation with these solutions is substantial enough.

## CRITICAL ISSUES

Many of the evaluations of the current situation of the Italian school system incline to a more or less disguised pessimism. Reading of an "uncertain system" or of a "system in jeopardy" is quite frequent.

The political jeopardy of the country offers a number of arguments for that and, without any doubt, exerts a disruptive influence on the possibility of developing linear and cumulative processes of innovation and reform. It is enough to remember that every shift from one government to another halts some laws, introduces new curricular orientations that most probably will not be put into effect, starts provisions that can be modified, and so on.

The following remarks try to introduce some possible reflections about aspects and features that can be reasonably identified as sufficiently clear.

*Improving real autonomy?* - How is it possible to combine the timelines and the strategic effectiveness of the decision-making process with the need for a participative decision-making system?

We can take note of the failure of the ideal scenario, where the formal involvement of all actors satisfies the purpose of putting into effect the democratization of school life and where the task of implementing increased participation to its governance, is related to more effective management. If so, we need to rethink the governance of the school and we can do this by reviewing how schools are run and by introducing a balance of powers between the School Boards, the faculty and the school managers.

According to national objectives and directives, teachers are in charge of analyzing the outcomes of activities of the whole professional community of the school and the demands coming from students, families, public authorities and from the social, economic and cultural environment. They are expected to transform this analysis into a strategic plan to be operated within the school development plan. This plan needs to be approved by the faculty itself. An analysis of the outcomes of the plan and their communication to the students, the families and the community should be the final organizational step of an open educational process.

Moreover, if the schools become more and more autonomous even in the management of finances, educational choices and decisions cannot be separated from financial ones, and vice versa. That means that educational, financial and administrative decisions find their strategic location in the School Board, i.e., the pivotal agent of influence and control of a self-managing school.

Reinforcing management - The most important challenges relate to a more in-depth understanding of the external environment (economic, social, juridical and technological) in order to develop formal processes of strategic analysis and to evaluate the sustainability of the school's vision connected with the concrete means of operating. That means promoting structures and processes of decision-making focused on the students' interests and stimulating teamwork at all levels (governance, programs, teaching programs, projects management), developing an affordable evaluation system in terms of learning indicators and educational, organizational and contextual factors; moreover, it implies building a system of performance indicators that establishes the parameters to be used for the purpose of monitoring the strategic objectives pursued, supporting processes of monitoring, diffusing information, communicating and decision making within the school networks and among different organizations and institutions aimed at the creation of public value; and finally, encouraging processes that reinforce social equity through communication with the stakeholders of the results and the activities of the school that may bring about their involvement in the governance of the school (Susi, 2000).

Currently, Italian schools enjoy a limited autonomy on the statutory and normative side and a limited control over human, financial and material resources. These constraints must be considered together with the disaffection of the stakeholders towards the participation in the active governance of the school, since the innovative impulse for participative democracy of the 1970s lost its impetus and was not able to find new opportunities even when, at the end of the 1990s, the push in favor of decentralization and autonomy reached its peak.

The growth of school autonomy made the function of the teachers' faculty (*collegio dei docenti*) more untenable while allowing principals and their management teams to take on more responsibilities than those officially given them. And, since the system of external evaluation is still weak (and also can be seen as limiting the school principals' position), the balance of power and responsibility has not been reached as yet and, therefore, accountability at school level is still in a rudimentary stage.

# CONCLUSIONS

The empowerment process of the Italian school system – perhaps it would be better to talk of "empowerment processes" – concentrates on the issue of "school autonomy" that incorporates different kinds of values and purposes, extending from the administrative decentralization to the liberalization of the curricula to the self-managing powers of the schools, and so on. In other words, it tends to include all the aspirations and the expectations of inside innovation and outside success that the progressive part of the school population nurtures (Barzanò, 2002).

The process is still (the processes are still) not concluded, but the era of enthusiasm has gone, so that it is now possible to recognize the main obstacles and difficulties that have been met and will also be met in the near future:

- the general cultural, moral, political and economic situation of the country is not favorable: the diagnosis of "weakness of the system" is not inappropriate;
- the ideological confrontation is deeply rooted, and since the strategic decisions are taken on the political side this has a strong influence on the process itself: the centralistic point of view is still present and the supporters of autonomy often illustrate their positions in a too-aggressive way;
- it must be acknowledged that the first applications of autonomy showed too many examples of inefficacy, confusion, lack of quality, superficiality so that more and more people are becoming nostalgic for the past;
- generations of administrators, teachers and principals were not prepared, in light of the new notion and its implications, so that fear, cynical conformism and loss of orientation are not uncommon;
- empowering a school does not mean leaving it to its fate or simply allocating money: the right strategies and procedures of helping a school to empower itself without conditioning it are difficult to be found and to be applied so that very few of them have been concretely experienced.

Two substantial dilemmas have not been solved: Can the schools be allowed the authority to recruit their own teachers? Must the validity of the final certifications be connected to market competition or must it continue to depend on the formal guarantee of the state certifications?

There is much to do for a long time.

# REFERENCES

Artini, A.(2004). *I leader educativi*. Milan: F.Angeli.

Barzanò, G. (Ed.) (2002). *Management e leadership nella scuola*. Rome: Anicia.

Bezzina, C., Paletta, A., and Vidoni, D. (2006). Educational management and leadership: Making inroads within the Euro-Mediterranean context. *ISIDA*, 19.

Crema, F., and Pollini, G. (1989). *Scuola autonomia mutamento sociale*. Rome: Armando.

Damiano, E. (Ed.) (1993). *In cerca di identità.Storie di vita e professionalità del dirigente scolastico.* Bari: Laterza.

Falanga, M. (2001). *Il Regolamento dell'autonomia scolastica. Lettura e commento.* Brescia: La Scuola.

Fischer, L., and Masuelli, M. (1998). *I dirigenti e l'autonomia delle scuole.* Milano: F. Angeli.

Ministero della Pubblica Istruzione (2007). *Sedi, alunni, classi, dotazioni organiche del personale della scuola.* Anno scolastico 2007-2008, Rome.

Paletta, A. (2006). Il bilancio sociale nella scuola dell'autonomia. In: Paletta, A., and Tieghi, M. (Eds.). *Il bilancio sociale su base territoriale. Dalla comunicazione istituzionale alla Pubblica Governance.* Torino: Isedi.

Paletta, A., and Vidoni, D. (2006). Italian school managers: A complex identity. *International Studies in Educational Administration,* 34, (1), 46-70.

Rescalli, G., and Visalberghi, A. (1994). L'autonomia delle scuole: i risultati di una ricerca. *Scuola e Citta,* Firenze, n. 3/March, pp. 169-184.

Rubinacci, A., Gallegati, P., AND Quarantotto, F. (1999). *Dirigenza e dirigenti.* Brescia: La Scuola.

Scurati, C. (2003). The selection and development of headteachers in Italy. In: L.E.Watson (ed.). *Selecting and developing heads of schools: Twenty-three European perspectives.* (pp.149-158). Sheffield, England: Sheffield Hallam University - School of Education,.

Scurati, C., and Ceriani, A. (1994). *La dirigenza scolastica: vicende, sviluppi e prospettive.* Brescia: La Scuola.

Susi, F. (Ed.) (2000). *Il leader educativo.* Rome: Armando.

In: Centralization and School Empowerment...
Editor: Adam Nir

ISBN 978-1-60692-730-4
© 2009 Nova Science Publishers, Inc.

*Chapter 7*

# MALTA: EDUCATION ADMINISTRATION AND MANAGEMENT IN THE CENTER OF THE MEDITERRANEAN

### *Charles J. Farrugia*
University of Malta, Malta

## INTRODUCTION

Except for its land mass and population size, Malta shares many characteristics with its Mediterranean neighbors, whether it is in history and culture or in politics and economics. All these factors have had an impact on the various aspects of Maltese life, particularly so in the field of education. Education policies, management and administration have been heavily influenced by Malta's colonial past, by the Islands' history of dependence on larger and richer countries, and by traditions that stress centralized decision-making. They have been and are being shaped by the fact that the Maltese live on two small but densely populated islands constituting a close-knit, transparent society.

Since Independence in 1964 from Britain, Malta has endeavored to shed the negative remnants of its colonial baggage. It seeks to become self-reliant economically, and above all to develop its strongest national resource, namely its human capital. Education policies and delivery services play a crucial role in reaching these objectives. Over the years, educational services have improved to offer high standards from the kindergarten to the university level. Inevitably, this development has had a significant impact on people's lives. In turn, citizens' expectations are shaping the Islands' education policies and services. People-power has become stronger than ever before.

Through examples, the chapter illustrates how educational policy-makers and administrators continuously interact with the people at the receiving end, namely, the parents and the students. These in turn react according to their particular needs and their perceived gains or losses and accept or reject proposed policies accordingly. Because of the Islands' small size, citizens' feedback is almost instantaneous, and alternative or remedial action soon follows. Such phenomena can be regarded as peculiar to a small country; however, Malta's experiences can serve as a model not only to other small states, but also to small entities, such as regions or big cities in larger countries.


# BACKGROUND

   The Maltese archipelago consists of five small islands in the middle of the Mediterranean Sea. Two islands are uninhabited, one almost so. Just over 31,000 people live on Gozo, the rest live on the biggest island, Malta, with Valletta the capital. A total population of 405,000 living on a land area of 316 sq. km. make Malta one of the most densely populated countries (1,282/km.$^2$) on earth.

   The Islands lie 100 km. south of Italy, 280 km. north of Libya and Tunisia, and are almost equidistant from Greece to the east and Spain to the west.

   Malta's central position in the Mediterranean with its deep and sheltered harbors have, over the ages, attracted the dominant powers in the region to use the islands as a military or a trading base, often as both. Thus, in antiquity, the Romans and the Carthaginians fought over Malta in the Punic Wars. The Arabs drove out the Byzantines in the Middle Ages, with the former being replaced by the Normans 260 years later. The Muslim Turks unsuccessfully laid a long siege to the Christian Knights of St. John in 1565. Where the Turks failed, Napoleon Bonaparte succeeded when in 1798 he ousted the Knights. Britain helped the Maltese expel the French two years later, with the British staying on as colonizers until Malta's Independence in 1964. Malta played a prominent part in World War II as an Allied fortress, depriving the Axis powers of total dominance in the Mediterranean. Since political Independence, Malta has sought greater economic self-reliance, first through the development of tourism and light industries, and more recently through international servicing industries.

   The majority of Maltese are Roman Catholics, retaining their religious beliefs from 60AD when St. Paul converted the inhabitants to Christianity. The national language is Maltese, which is the only Semitic language written in Roman script. It is spoken by the inhabitants, the majority of whom also speak English, the second official language. Due to the proximity to Italy and the beaming of numerous television and radio stations from the nearby peninsula, many Maltese also speak Italian. Malta is a parliamentary democracy, which became a republic ten years after Independence. It is a member of the United Nations and its agencies, and of the British Commonwealth. Malta's most recent political development occurred in 2004 when the Islands joined the European Union (EU) and its euro economic zone in 2008.

   For centuries, the inhabitants of the Maltese Islands had been ruled by foreign powers, a factor that often impacts on their attitudes towards authority and self-determination. For example, in the debate leading to Independence in 1964, a significant number of Maltese (but not enough to win the referendum) were reluctant to opt out of the British colonial shield, which provided economic and military safeguards. At the same time, one notes that on several instances both ancient and modern, the Maltese rose against their colonial masters when they felt that political or economic decisions impinged intolerably on their civic or religious rights. The incongruent blend of seeking safety in an authoritarian cocoon coupled with a contrasting resistance to unilateral decision-making recur continuously in the Maltese political and social scene. As will be seen later, the mixture emerges continuously in the education management and administration sphere.

Any doubts the Maltese may have had about the benefits of Independence have since been dispelled. With independence, the Maltese were able to set their own political and economic policies rather than to have them dictated as was the case in colonial times. The Maltese, therefore, embarked on an industrialization drive aimed at generating national income from the exportation of locally manufactured goods and services instead of having to rely on the ever-decreasing funds paid by the British for using Malta as a military base. The major economic activities between the 1960s and 1990s were tourism, the textile industry, light but specialized manufacture of such items as electronic components, optics, precious stones, as well as printing and book binding.

Ship-building and ship-repair have remain the major employers in heavy industry; they also incur a heavy burden on the local economy since they need massive government subsidies to stay in business.

The building boom of the 1960s has never ceased, since it is closely linked to the flourishing tourist industry. The 1990s saw the loss of most manufacturing enterprises to cheaper producers in Asia and North Africa, and Malta has had once again to divert its economic base. Today, financial services, international banking, insurance, e-commerce, tourism and ICT have become the main employers and the major foreign currency earners. In 2007 Malta's GDP stood at €1,095.3m in real terms, GNI at market prices stood at €1,291.8m, while unemployment was 7.12 percent.

## EDUCATIONAL SYSTEM

Various forms of public and private education have been present in Malta since the 13th century, when the first mention of a public school was recorded in a 1460 notarial deed. Mass public education, however, was launched in the middle of the 19th century, while compulsory primary schooling attendance was introduced in the 1920s but fully enforced in 1946 at the end of World War II. Tuition-free secondary education became available in the early 1950s and compulsory schooling from years 5 to 16 came into force in 1974. The University of Malta has its origins in 1592 as a Jesuit College authorized to issue academic degrees, to become a fully-fledged tertiary institution in 1769 (Zammit, 1992). Students can follow the educational path from kindergarten to university as Diagram 1 indicates.

The Ministry of Education (usually with the addition of Youth and Culture, but currently with Employment replacing Culture) is responsible for the provision of schooling, with day-to-day management and administration delegated to the Education Division. Until recently the structure was very much a hierarchical, pyramidal one inherited from British colonial times (Farrugia, 1994). Indeed, public education trends in Malta still follow closely developments in Britain although membership in the EU benefits from the impact of diversity. For example, a major structural reorganization in the delivery and monitoring of the educational services occurred in 2007 when an Amendment to the Education Act transformed the Education Division into two new directorates (Diagram Two). The Directorate for Educational Services (DES) includes schools as the service providers; it also acts as the resources provider supplying schools with their human and material requirements. The Directorate for Quality and Standards in Education (DQSE) monitors the delivery of educational services to ensure best practice. Each directorate is headed by a Director General answerable to the Permanent Secretary and the Minister. For the purpose of this chapter, one should note that an important provision in the Amendment allows both Directorates (as well as schools) much greater freedom of operation than the old Division ever enjoyed (Malta, Policy Unit, 2005). As yet, few in and outside the educational sphere in Malta have realized what radical developments in autonomy and decision-making this change can bring about.

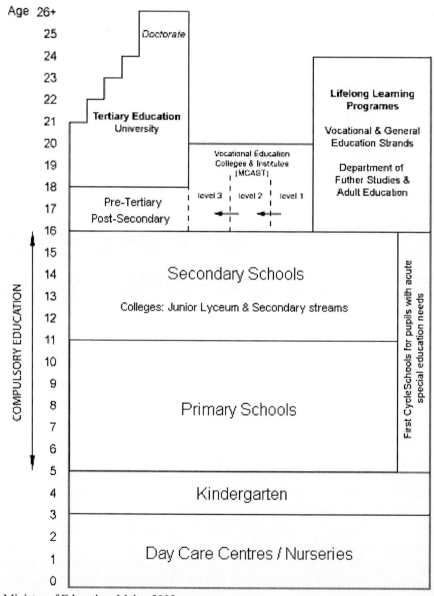

Source: Ministry of Education, Malta, 2008

Diagram 1. The Maltese Mainstream Education System

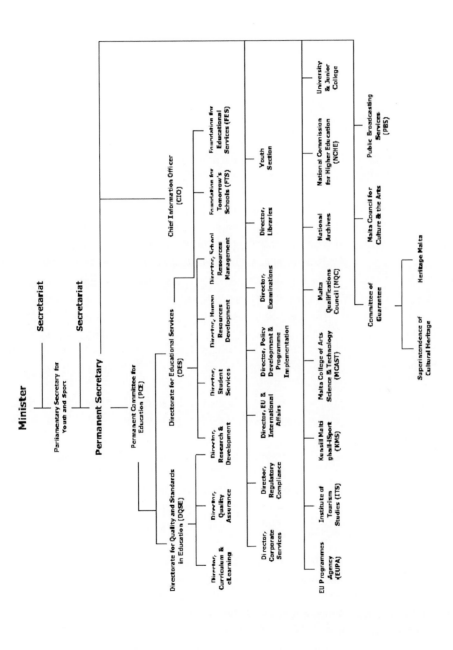

Source: Ministry of Education, Culture, Youth & Sports -2008

Diagram Two: Structure of the Ministry of Education, Culture, Youth and Sports

Currently, two-thirds of Malta's school population attend State schools; the majority of the rest go to Church schools, while a small minority are enrolled in Independent schools (Table One). All full-time state education from kindergarten to university is free of charge. The government heavily subsidizes Church schools; independent schools charge tuition fees, but parents can claim tax rebates. In 2008 the government budgeted eleven percent of its €2,498,463,000 national estimates to education. Such a high percentage, which reflects past practice, remains a clear indication of the high value that successive governments have placed on education by treating it as a major contributor to the nation's moral, social and economic well-being (Sultana, 1991).

## A Legacy of Central Control

Through the ages the Maltese have been accustomed to two major sources of central control, one consisting of military and colonial administrations, the other being the Catholic Church.

The typical and most recent colonial administrators were the British. For 164 years, governors appointed by the UK government in London, and their Colonial and War Office recruits, were primarily concerned with running a superb military base ever ready to meet any threat in the Mediterranean, whether the danger came from Napoleonic France, Fascist Italy, Nazi Germany or Communist Russia. Relations between colonialists and colonized ran smoothly as long as locally engaged personnel, especially those employed at the naval dry docks and the airfields, followed orders, and the rest of the population did not rock the boat. The former managed the island fortress efficiently; the latter enjoyed economic stability, social improvements especially in education and health, and military security. Local political leaders and their followers who questioned the *status quo* were exiled to the remoter parts of the British Empire.

As fervent Catholics, the Maltese have always had a high regard for their religious leaders, represented by the local Bishop and his Curia. Prior to the coming of the French in 1798, they had to deal with two additional sources of religious powers. One was the Grand Master, the head of an autocratic religious and military order, who was also the absolute civil ruler of the Islands. The third religious authority was the Inquisitor sent to Malta by the Pope to ensure everyone's adherence to Church doctrine. Obedience to the highly structured and strict hierarchy of Church authority was well embedded in the Maltese psyche. Rebels and doubters ended as prisoner-rowers on the Knights' galleys or in an Inquisitor's Palace prison cell, and in extreme cases, on the stake.

During their stay in Malta, the British absorbed well the lesson suffered by the French, who dared trim the authority of the Maltese church, and in the process instigated a nation-wide rebellion for their troubles. The British were cautious not to offend Maltese religious sentiments and to retain the most cordial relationship with the local church authorities.

The twin forces of military and church power have exerted tremendous influence on the attitude of the Maltese towards established authority. Employees, especially those engaged in the Civil Service, have been accustomed and conditioned to obey the rules, to follow established procedures, and to avoid making decisions. When difficulties arose they were instructed to refer them higher up to their superiors (Farrugia, 1992). Teaching personnel have not been immune to the above influences (Darmanin, 1990). Indeed, one can argue that they have been particularly exposed to the authoritarian tradition by having had - among others - two powerful and influential Directors of Education, namely Canon Paul Pullicino, a prominent priest in the local Catholic hierarchy, and Albert Laferla, an ex-army officer. The following case study demonstrates that the legacy of strict central control lingers on and influences educational decision-making and implementation.

## GREATER AUTONOMY FOR HEADS OF SCHOOLS

Until recently, the Education Division within the Ministry of Education regulated all scholastic and administrative procedures in schools to the extent that it set class timetables and all textbooks. Heads had even to seek permission from Head Office to take students on school outings and educational visits. In 1995, the Division issued directives allowing heads of school a measure of autonomy in deciding purely localized issues without the need to refer to the Head Office in Valletta. The most noteworthy liberalizing measures were direct responsibility for the formulation of the school's development plan, routine school administration and the organization of school events. Heads have control over the expenditure of the school's modest annual financial allocation. State schools can raise funds through social and extra-curricular activities as long as students' participation and parents' contributions are strictly voluntary. State schools cannot charge fees or accept contributions for educational or school medical services. They can select their students' textbooks once these are paid for from school funds.

In fact the degree of autonomy in Government schools is still limited. For example, heads of State schools cannot hire or fire school personnel except for cleaning and maintenance staff, while all teachers and assistant heads of schools are deployed centrally from Head Office. Cases for disciplinary measures are referred to be decided centrally by the Public Service Commission if these are of a serious nature, by Head Office if not so serious.

Church and Independent schools have much more leeway. They can hire and fire all their staff including teachers and administrators, provided they do not breach local employment regulations. Independent schools charge tuition fees and can raise extra funds as they see fit. Although the State heavily subsidizes Church schools and technically they are not allowed to charge tuition fees, parents are asked to augment school funds for such projects as the improvement of buildings, the purchasing of equipment, the hiring of extra staff, etc., through voluntary contributions and the holding of fund raising events. All schools, State and non-State, are required to follow the Maltese National Curriculum and can lose their license if the State's education officers who inspect them consider them to be in serious breach of curricular or education provisions regulations. In reality no school is known to have lost its license since those found lacking are given sufficient warnings and time to remedy the shortcomings.

Initially, the novelty of heads of State schools having greater autonomy was met with much enthusiasm. Heads of school felt that they had finally gained some operational freedom which they deserved. Gradually the euphoria evaporated. Many head teachers began to complain that they were being asked to do Head Office's chores and to serve as accounts clerks. They grumbled that they were spending far too much time on administrative odd jobs rather than dealing with scholastic and academic responsibilities. Many confided to this writer that they preferred the old system, which simply required them to follow the rules or to obey orders. Heads of school realized also that it had been far more convenient, and less socially problematic, to convey to their subordinates unpopular administrative decisions taken by higher-ups in Valletta than to take such decisions themselves. Under the new conditions, school personnel expected their heads to elucidate on their initiatives and to justify their decisions.

Some head teachers felt so uncomfortable with their new-found freedom that they were reluctant to delegate some of the new responsibilities to their staff, to the extent that they took it upon themselves to engage in such chores as purchasing minor school equipment, teaching resources and maintenance materials. They were so concerned not to breach financial regulations that they would not entrust anyone else with the job. Consequently, they turned themselves into purchasing officers, accounts clerks and storekeepers rolled into one, and their other more important scholastic responsibilities suffered in the process.

In contrast, a few heads took to heart their new autonomy in order to develop a school ethos, adopt innovative school policies, and use financial allocations to generate and increase school funds. They took advantage of the unexpected affluence to buy school equipment, which some Head Office officials considered too exotic and extravagant. These head teachers were cautioned to curb their enthusiasm. They were reminded that their schools still formed part of the State's national system and, therefore, they should not deviate too much from the national norm. In a reversal of policy, they were also instructed to first seek approval from officials at the Education Division in Valletta before taking radical administrative decisions or undertaking extraordinary expenses.

It has taken time to change a mentality conditioned by highly centralized bureaucratic control. It is only now, more than a decade later, that heads of school have been trained to carry higher levels of responsibility, to establish senior management teams, to publish school handbooks, to take collective decisions with their staff, and to hone their entrepreneurial skills. At the same time, a new class of Education Officers actually encourages the diminution of their previously draconian powers. They are promoting greater administrative autonomy, initiatives and creativity in schools. In the process they are liberating themselves from restrictive administrative chores to devote more time to proper educational developments at the national level. The 2006 Amendments to the Education Act significantly give schools the autonomy to conduct their scholastic and administrative duties to almost the same high degree of operational freedom enjoyed by the autonomous Church and Independent schools. The legacy of highly centralized administration and control has been shattered because political goodwill coupled with improved training for heads of school provide them with the competences and the confidence to operate as educational leaders in their own right, not as underlings in a monolithic structure emanating from Head Office.

## PEOPLE'S POWER

The earlier sections of this chapter may have depicted the Maltese as a hopelessly docile and subdued race always ready to act or react according to the dictates of their colonial masters. Such a conclusion would be invalid. This is not the place to list the uprisings or rebellions initiated by the Maltese against the powers that ruled them when the Islanders felt that oppression was unwarranted or when administrative decisions went against their sense of right and wrong. Invariably, the people achieved their ends.

The following example illustrates that the spirit of opposition to the government's unjustified decisions has not waned, especially when people regard such decisions as detrimental to their children's educational progress.

· In theory, the Secondary Schools For All scheme introduced in 1971 opened up free secondary education to any Maltese student who wanted to pursue it. In reality, however, only some 10 percent of the secondary school student cohort was able to attend the elite, highly selective State "grammar" schools. The rest attended the newly-opened Area Secondary Schools or opted to attend the then fee-paying Church or Independent schools. This system went against the staunch Socialist beliefs of the government of the time, which decided to dismantle it. Instead, it established a Comprehensive System of Secondary Education whereby all students proceeded from Primary to Area Comprehensive Secondary schools according to the location where they lived. The new system removed any form of scholastic selection. Most people regarded the educational reform as ideologically desirable, as long as it did not affect adversely their own children's chances of the best possible schooling.

The reform was badly planned and hastily introduced. It was also accompanied by the extension of the compulsory school leaving age from fourteen to sixteen. The extension meant that a large number of teenagers, who had looked forward to the end of school and the start of a working, wage-earning life, were abruptly compelled to stay on at school for an additional two years. These reluctant students recorded their disgruntlement by continuous acts of vandalism and school violence. The boys at the Lyceums and the girls in their Grammar Schools who had been selected through a rigorous, highly competitive national examination were joined by numbers of scholastically weak or unmotivated students. To render matters even worse, the previously elite schools were located close to Malta's Inner Harbour Area, which housed some of the toughest and delinquent youngsters. The Comprehensive education mix became a catastrophe.

Teachers suffered too. Those accustomed to teaching stimulated, high-performing students were unprepared to deal with the new category of reluctant students. The result was a lose-lose situation. The parents of students attending the elite schools saw the institutions figuratively (and occasionally, literally) being wrecked before their eyes. Parents awaiting the day when their children would enter the Lyceums and Grammar Schools had their expectations dashed. Parents eagerly expecting an increase in the family income from their street-wise youngsters had to wait an additional two unappreciated and unwanted school years before additional funds would be forthcoming.

Parents who could afford to withdrew their children from State schools and enrolled them in fee-paying Church and Independent schools; those who could not became furious and rebellious. The vast majority sought to redress the situation. These included staunch government supporters and Malta Labour Party officials.

The pressure was so intense that the Government had to relent. The Comprehensive system was withdrawn and new Junior Lyceums (i.e., Grammar-type schools) for boys and girls were established. The nation-wide Junior Lyceum Entrance Examination was re-introduced on the same lines as its predecessor before the introduction of the Comprehensive school system. Candidates who failed the selection examination could attend "new" Area Secondary Schools.

The whole episode was not without some positive outcomes. First and foremost, it was a lesson for future governments not to tinker with education without first carrying out careful studies of the implications and their impact on the populace. Second, the State was forced to double the student intake for the new Junior Lyceums and to start the process of increasing acceptance into these schools, eventually to treble their previous intake. Third, the exodus of students from State to private schools radically changed the nature of the latter. They now catered for an unprecedented number of motivated students and enjoyed an influx of badly-needed funds to evolve into worthy competitors to State schools.

The first lesson was not well-heeded by the same Labour government, as the sequence to the above events illustrates. Once again, it was at the cost of the government's popularity, when people-power prevailed.

As explained above, the years following the Comprehensive Education debacle led to a moral and financial boost for private schools, particularly Church-run ones. While previously regarded as a second choice to State schools, now parents were competing to get their children in the limited places available. The demand was so great that the shortages continued in spite of the rapid expansion of both Church schools and Independents. State schools had lost their more motivated students as well as their standing in people's esteem, to the benefit of Church schools.

This state of affairs became an abomination to Socialist die-hards. They saw their aims for an egalitarian educational system shattered by the reintroduction of the elitist Junior Lyceums. This event was compounded by the unexpected and unprecedented expansion, rising academic kudos and financial returns of Church schools. To counteract this, the government introduced legislation forcing Church schools to provide free-of-charge schooling, knowing full well that it was economically impossible for them to do so. In October, 1984, Church schools were not allowed to reopen for the new scholastic year unless they agreed not to charge school fees. None gave such a commitment, with the result that one-third of the Maltese school population were forced to stay home. On a different pretext, but mainly in support of Church schools (where the vast majority of teachers sent their children), State-employed teachers went on strike. This action deprived the other two-thirds of students from attending school for seven weeks.

Once again people-power took over when parents combined forces with teachers to organize classes and lessons in private homes. Following eight weeks of such contrived schooling, the government came under intense pressure to withdraw the ruling through face-saving solutions allowing Church schools to reopen and the State school teachers to return to work. However, education remained a hot national issue and contributed significantly to the Malta Labour Party losing office in 1987.

## A QUESTION OF SIZE

Small countries are not down-sized versions of large countries: They have an ecology of their own. This is particularly true of a micro-state like Malta. Problems, whether they are educational, economic, health-related, environmental, and so on, which are taken in stride by larger countries, can constitute national emergencies in a tiny island-nation (Farrugia and Attard, 1989). For example, the contamination of two main beaches through an oil spill would ruin for decades the Islands' entire tourist industry. The closing down of a medium-sized factory, with a negative ripple in large countries, in Malta would easily raise the unemployment figure by 10 percent. A health epidemic would spread throughout the small overcrowded Island in a matter of days before remedial action could be put in motion. In the educational sphere, it is prohibitively expensive to print textbooks in Maltese when the print-runs are so tiny.

At the same time, small size can have its advantages: Problems that may loom large in small countries can be dealt with speedily and at reasonable expense. The following examples illustrate the point and show how this phenomenon influences positively and negatively educational administration and management in Malta (Farrugia,1993).

## TEACHERS OF FRENCH

In the late 1980s the State's Department of Education faced a severe shortage of teachers of French, the fourth most popular language taught in schools after Maltese, English and Italian. At the request of the Department, the Faculty of Education at the University of Malta embarked on a recruitment drive for student-teachers of French. Four years later, at the end of their Bachelor of Education course, seven of the recruited teachers were employed to teach French in State schools, two joined Church schools, and the remaining three were redeployed to teach another subject until vacancies in French were filled. Similar stories can be recounted in the teaching of Geography, German and Arabic. The scale or numbers are so small that pre-recruitment planning becomes practically impossible to apply: a spate of pregnancy leave in one subject area can easily create a serious vacuum in that subject; an unexpected drop in the number of students opting for another subject would create a glut in the latter. However, imaginative thinking and determined action often lead to practical and inexpensive solutions (Farrugia, 1996).

## COMPUTERIZATION DRIVE

Following the very successful drive to render all primary school children computer literate, the government decided to extend the benefits to secondary schools. By the end of 2008, every class in all secondary schools will have one computer for every four students, while every teacher will be supplied with a laptop computer for pedagogical and personal use. The innovation entails the purchase of 10,200 computers at a cost of €22 million. A bigger country would consider this a minute financial outlay. It is a considerable investment for Malta, but a necessary one in view of its ambitions to become the most computer-literate country in the Mediterranean.

## MALTA'S BRAIN DRAIN

The question of scale can create situations with advantages as well as disadvantages in other respects. The case of medical doctors illustrates the point. For centuries, Malta has had an excellent provision of medical education, first, due to the presence of the Hospitalar Knights of St. John, and later when the British converted the Islands into one huge hospital site following the disastrous military World War I campaign at Gallipoli. The quality of medical education improved further by the replicated experience during World War II. Following Independence, the Maltese Medical School retained its contacts with leading British counterparts, which provided external lecturers and examiners to ensure that local medical education remained at the cutting edge.

All very well for Malta, except that besides having a decidedly prestigious and a generously remunerated occupation at home, Maltese doctors are highly sought after abroad, especially in the English-speaking countries of the British Commonwealth and the USA. Thus, many are lured overseas by higher salaries and better research facilities. The brain drain means that Malta foots the bill for the expensive medical education for its young doctors while inhabitants in far richer countries benefit from the graduates' services. Remittances from overseas, if any, hardly compensate. A similar situation exists with accountants who are being recruited by international firms to work all over Europe when they are badly needed for the financial services rapidly developing on the Islands. The actual numbers are minute: 25 or 30 graduates per year in each category. These numbers, however, represent some 50 percent of medical and accountancy graduates each year. Such a brain drain, insignificant for larger countries, is a heavy price for tiny Malta.

## A TRANSPARENT, OPEN SOCIETY

The management and administration of education, like any other public service in Malta, is significantly influenced by the transparent and open nature of its society. It is hyperbole to say that "everyone knows everyone else," but one is not far off the mark to claim that everyone on the Island knows someone who knows someone who knows the person being referred to. The extended family system, the small tightly-knit population and the short distances involved ensure quick, easy and effective human communication systems. Again, these have sometimes positive, sometimes negative impacts (Farrugia, 1991).

Through these systems, legislators and administrators can maintain an accurate gauge of people's moods, wants and dislikes. While public opinion polls claim a scientific basis for their predictions, astute politicians rely more on feedback from visits to the local market, attendance at baptism and wedding receptions, and Sunday visits to the local party and band clubs. They make it a point to spend the evenings leading the annual local *festa,* mixing with the crowd and pressing flesh. In such instances, the issue of scale becomes an asset since the numbers involved are favorable. Malta has a House of Representatives member for every 5,000 adult citizens, and one can travel across the largest island in less than one hour.

The complex social communication system operates also in reverse. Anyone wishing an impromptu meeting with a deputy or a senior government official or an influential company director will make it her/his business to discover which church and at what time the targeted individual attends to ensure a "chance" encounter at the end of the service. Alternatively, one can find out which supermarket the officials frequent and "accidentally" meet them there on the weekly shopping spree. Senior or public officials become captive audiences for petitions, airing of complaints, and requests for favors at family festivities. Supplicants and petitioners can arrange to be invited to a wedding, engagement, baptism, anniversary or other family gatherings where they feel certain that the intended target will be present and in a very difficult position not to hear them out. Such a system becomes extremely demanding on the officials concerned, and it is no wonder that most take their vacations overseas. However, as pointed out earlier, the officials themselves do exploit and often encourage the system. In any event, it is a most efficient method for people in authority to keep in touch with their constituents and make the right decisions. When the decisions are disliked, policy-makers receive instant feedback and have a good opportunity to retract or alter decisions, as the case studies described earlier illustrate.

The social conditions of openness and transparency exert positive as well as negative influences on school administration. On the positive side, schools become easily and quickly aware of services or facilities that other schools offer and emulate them. For example, until fairly recently only Church and the bigger State secondary schools organized annual school plays or concerts. However, once the practice was adopted by a few smaller primary schools, the trend spread so that now all schools (primary, secondary, State and non-State) including those in the smallest villages hold the annual event. Some eight years ago, one entrepreneurial head of a small primary school came up with the idea of holding first a book fair and later a flower-plant sale. Since then, the initiative spread to all schools as a means of generating greater interest in books and raising school funds. When one school bought a color printer/photocopier, the rage caught on.

Such emulation extends to curricular matters with neighboring schools collaborating in developing pedagogical strategies and the setting the statuary half-yearly and annual examinations. They team up in running staff development courses and the setting of common school policies. One positive outcome is that parents find less cause to compare adversely scholastic and administrative practices in one school with its neighbors.

One negative aspect is that schools can become too conscious of and absorbed with their image, and compete in areas which contain more show than substance. Another negative feature is the danger of unwarranted interference by the parents in purely academic affairs. As Maltese parents become more literate, more exposed to the international media and consequently more knowledgeable about educational matters, some set themselves as educational experts ever-ready to interfere in or dictate what their children's schools should or should not do. To end on a positive note, however, this tendency, which irks heads of schools and their staff, also forces them to be on their toes, to think through and justify their policies on sound pedagogical and administrative practices. It obliges educators at the national level to study carefully educational policies before launching them in the knowledge that unquestioned acceptance of dictates issued from the Capital is a thing of the past.

## CONCLUSION

Forty-four years of political independence have still not enabled the Maltese to rid themselves completely of the negative effects of millennia of colonialism. Nor can they escape the social and economic conditions created by the Islands' physical features such as the small size of the land mass encompassing one of the most densely populated countries on earth. The Maltese cannot escape their location at the cross-roads of the Mediterranean, rendering the Islands highly desirable venues for visitors, whether tourists or those seeking commerce. The Islanders' culture, economics and way of life are invariably influenced by their position at the southernmost tip of Europe and just north of the African Mediterranean coastline. For example, the fact that Malta now forms part of the European Union renders it an ideal place for transshipment commerce between EU and non-EU countries, as well as a destination for illegal immigrants from sub-Saharan Africa.

The Maltese have to cope with these conditions, whether these are the remnants of a historic past or an inevitable development in the quest for a brighter future. Successive Maltese governments have looked on education as a primary service to overcome the Islands' handicaps and to exploit their assets. They have recognized the fact that human capital is Malta's major, if not the only, natural resource. Consequently, they have invested heavily in education for the purpose of developing the citizens' potential. Suffice it to say that educational services provided by the State and by the Church are tuition-free from the kindergarten level to full-time post-graduate courses. Furthermore, the State pays stipends to post-secondary and undergraduate students in order to spur them on to tertiary education and beyond (Charmers, 2004). Local and foreign pundits argue that such a heavy subsidy to public education is economically unsustainable. However, education policies, management and administrative procedures are geared to maintain this commitment. Fortunately, these policies are bearing fruit (Malta, MEYE, 2005).

Consider two unemployment crises. In the 1950s and 1960s, when the British drastically downsized Malta's military base, the only opening for the dismissed workers was mass emigration to Australia and Canada. The outcome depleted Malta of its most skilled craftsmen and wrought havoc in the tightly-knit family and social fabric. An analogous situation arose in the late 1990s when the entire textile and many other manufacturing industries moved to low-cost countries in North Africa and Asia. This time, however, the employees' level of education made it possible for them to be retrained and become absorbed in tourism and specialist industries such as diamond cutting, quality tailoring and electronics. Employees at the management levels moved to Malta's ICT software markets, international banking and financial services. Their manufacturing and managerial experience served to strengthen the emerging entrepreneurial niches.

The needs and mindset demanded by the new global and globalizing sectors in the Maltese economy oblige local educational policy-makers and administrators to re-evaluate past practices and, where required, to adopt new ones. The Maltese example demonstrates that a country with a long colonial history can shed its dependency syndrome. It also illustrates the fact that an education system that originated in colonial times need not obstruct or deter the introduction of innovative educational ideas and practices capable of coping with emerging needs (Grima, 2005). Education has given the Maltese not only knowledge and skills, but also an aptitude to deal with contrasting social conditions and to cope with man-made crises. Under local conditions, this talent provides them with the capacity to experiment. It also provides local education policy-makers, managers and administrators the possibility of taking quick remedial action if and when things go wrong.

# REFERENCES

Chalmers, R. (Chairperson) (2004): *State higher education funding.* Floriana, Malta: MEYE.

Darmanin, M. (1990). Maltese primary teachers' experience of centralised policies. *British Journal of Sociology of Education*, 11, 3, 306-308.

Farrugia, C. (Editor) (1988). *Education in Malta: A look to the future.* Paris: UNESCO.

Farrugia, C. (1991). Malta: Educational development in a small island state. *Prospects* (UNESCO), XXI, 4, 80.

Farrugia, C. (1992). Authority and control in the Maltese educational system. *International Review of Education,* 38, 2. 155-171.

Farrugia, C. (1993). The special working environment of senior administrators in small states. *World Development*, Spring Issue.21, (2), 221-226.

Farrugia, C. (Editor) (1994). *A new vision for primary schools.* Valletta, Malta: Malta Union of Teachers Publications.

Farrugia, C. (1996). *Teachers' professional development model. La Scienza della Formazzione: Prospettive di Ricerca nell' Area del Mediterraneo.* Vito Antonio Baldassare (Editor), Rome, Italy: Edizioni del Sud.

Farrugia, C. (in press). National systems of education: Malta. *International Encyclopaedia of Education.* Colin Power (Sectional Editor). Oxford, UK: Elsevier Publications.

Farrugia, C. (Chairperson) (2001). *Strategic plan 2001-5.* Msida, Malta: University of Malta, UOM Communications Office.

Farrugia, C., and Attard, P. A. (1989). *The multi-functional administrator.* London: Commonwealth Secretariat.

Grima, G. (Chairperson) (2005). *MATSEC: Strengthening a national examinations system.* Floriana, Malta: MEYE.

Malta, Ministry of Education, Youth and Employment, National Commission for Higher Education and Secretariat for Higher Education (2005). *The Future of Higher Education in Malta.* Floriana, Malta: MEYE.

Malta, Policy Unit (2005): *For all children to succeed: A new network organization for quality education in Malta.* Floriana, Malta: MEYE.

Malta, National Statistics Office (2007). *Official Statistics of Malta 2005- Education Statistics.* Valletta: Malta Government Press.

Sultana, R. (1991). *Themes in education: A Maltese reader.* Msida, Malta: Mireva Publications.

Zammit, M. J. (1992). *History of education in Malta.* Valletta: Studia Editions.

Websites

    Government of Malta portal: www.gov.mt

    Malta Church Schools: www.maltadiocese.org.mt

    Ministry of Education, Youth and Employment: www.education.edu.mt

    Malta Union of Teachers: www.mut.org.mt

    University of Malta: www.um.edu.mt

In: Centralization and School Empowerment...
Editor: Adam Nir

ISBN 978-1-60692-730-4
© 2009 Nova Science Publishers, Inc.

*Chapter 8*

# ATTEMPTS TO EMPOWER SCHOOLS IN THE GREEK EDUCATIONAL SYSTEM

## *Amalia A. Ifanti*
University of Patras, Greece

## INTRODUCTION

Control of educational processes varies from country to country. In Greece, the central government through its Ministry of Education and its departments formulates and adopts educational policy (Ifanti, 1995, 2007). On the other hand, a variety of interest groups (e.g., teachers' unions, government officials, school inspectors and chief education officers, political parties, the Church, etc.) are active in demanding to participate in the decision-making process. At a deeper level, however, it can be argued that politics in Greece is centralist and corporatist (Ifanti, 1995; Panich, 1980; Schmitter, 1977) so that groups outside the government share the same values about the necessity for national educational policies that emphasize unity rather than diversity.

Potential debate about government policies can come either through constitutional mechanisms of the parliamentary system or through specialized educational interest groups (Ifanti, 1994). The centralized, bureaucratic and authoritarian control over education in Greece can also be explained by the relatively recent establishment of the modern state (1828), the political conflict among parties and the political instability of the country (Ifanti, 1995, 2007). The educational system thus reflects the basic principles of corporatist state education as, for instance, a uniform curriculum, the status of teachers as civil servants and the control over any educational aspect (e.g., the standard number of teaching hours, the content of the school curriculum, the textbooks, etc.) (Ifanti, 1995, 2007; Lauglo and McLean, 1985; McLean, 1988).

Nevertheless, by the turn of the 21st century and in view of the rapidly expanded scientific and technological production system, education in the developed countries, Greece included, is facing pressing demands for changes formally expressed in governmental institutions. The attempts at school empowerment and improvement are frequently related to the changes for decentralization of education and for the modernization of the administration system (Astiz et al. 2002; Carnoy, 1999; Fullan, 1991). Despite differences among countries, decentralization policies in education encompass a dynamic which transforms educational changes into a sociopolitical process and activates interest groups (e.g., students, parents, local, regional and national representatives in education), aiming at the lessening of central power and control over school practice (Altrichter and Elliot, 2000; Bullock and Thomas, 1997; Lyons, 1985; Temple, 2003).

In Greece, the educational reforms that have been attempted from the beginning of the 20th century reveal the strength of the politics of education, although the lack of a strong tradition of educational planning together with the chronic instability of Greek internal policy-making has not helped the cause of long-term educational policies and radical reforms (Ifanti, 2007). In this chapter, the attempts at decentralization of primary and secondary Greek education will be presented since the mid-1980s, according to the laws which appeared in the period under consideration, and how much they contribute to school empowerment will be noted. With this aim in mind, the structure and the administration of the Greek educational system, the management of education and the recent decentralization policies in the school system will be examined, and, finally, the extent to which such attempts reflect actual decentralization policies will be discussed. Before going further, it is necessary to consider some demographic, political, economic and cultural aspects of Greece.

## A NATION IN CONTEXT

The population of Greece is 10,939,771, according to the 2001 census, of which less than 20% live in rural areas. With the growing number of immigrants, the country is becoming a multicultural society (Ministry of Press and Media, 2002, p. 90). A large proportion of the population is concentrated in the capital city, Athens, a situation tracing back to the 1950s and 60s when the rural population largely abandoned the countryside to seek better conditions of employment, education and living – mainly - in Athens. At present, although the migration flow from rural to urban areas is limited, young people still prefer the urban centers (Ifanti, 2007).

The Greek Republic is a Presidential Parliamentary Democracy, according to the 1975 Constitution; the Parliament is comprised of 300 members from various political parties (Right, Left, Socialist, etc.). Greek politics are formulated in relation to the political and economic aspects of a globalizing world and by the necessity to function in the European Union.

In fact, from 1974 onwards, after the demise of the seven-year dictatorship (1967-1974), the need for a European orientation for the country together with the efforts to modernize the political system were apparent, whereas the political parties became the main factors in the restoration of democracy. It is also widely accepted that EU membership contributed significantly to reinforcing political and democratic stability in Greece. In addition, since the country's official entry into the EU (initially EEC) in 1981, and especially after the Maastricht Agreement (1992), when the process of European integration was more effectively articulated (Ifanti, 2007, p. 102), Greece has been determined to participate actively in European development (Ifanti, 2007, pp. 57-58). Consequently, Greece has managed to establish a macroeconomic balance mainly attached to the European integration process. For example, throughout 1990s Greek governments focused on lowering the rate of inflation and public sector deficits, achieving thereby nominal convergence and the final entry into the euro-zone (January 1, 2001) (Ministry of Economic Development, 2001).

As regards the cultural characteristics of Greece, modern Greeks have been very conscious of their Hellenic and Byzantine origins. Despite their variable fortunes since the Golden Age of Pericles in ancient Athens, and despite four centuries of Ottoman rule and the emergence of the modern state in 1828, they feel themselves descendants of the Greeks of Antiquity (Ifanti, 1992, pp. 19-20). This helps to explain why they have adhered so strongly to teaching the Ancient Greek language and literature in secondary schools and why classical texts have played so dominant a part in the school curriculum (OECD, 1982, p. 8, as cited in Ifanti, 2007, p. 20).

Religion, which symbolizes the Byzantine tradition, also plays an important role in the life of Greece. The power of the Greek Orthodox Church goes back to the centuries of occupation, when the monasteries and the village priests were the focus of independence and the guardians of the traditional culture and values (Ifanti, 2007). This ideal, with a Hellenic-Christian background, is illustrated by a well-known spokesperson of humanism:

"The Greek civilization for us, the descendants, did not have as its major aim to satisfy our curiosity in historical matters, nor to increase our wisdom but to strengthen our historical memory and consciousness, to uplift our national unity and to develop in our souls faith towards man and love towards higher things" (Vourveres, 1950, p. 734, as cited in Ifanti, 2007, p. 20).

The history of the educational system, on the other hand, is marked by constant demands for reform of its content as well as of its administration. In this chapter the focus will be placed on the system of educational administration in an attempt to present current innovative policies for school empowerment.

## STRUCTURE AND ADMINISTRATION IN THE GREEK EDUCATIONAL SYSTEM

In Greece, the desire to make progress within the European Union has led to constant attempts at the democratization and modernization of the educational system. Education, in turn, appears as an open system which includes teachers, students, the curriculum and other elements that interact for the attainment of educational purposes (Saitis, 2005, p. 179).

In terms of the structure of the Greek educational system, this is divided into three levels: primary education, secondary education and tertiary education (see Diagram 1). Primary education includes nursery (4-6 years) and elementary schools (6-12 years). Secondary education (12-18 years) is divided into the first cycle (gymnasium: 12-15 years) and the second cycle of studies (lyceum: 15-18 years); it also contains the technical-vocational sector at the lyceum level (15-18 years).

The admission of students into the secondary education is free of exams. Compulsory education extends to nine years of studies (6-15 years: elementary school and gymnasium). Both primary and secondary education is offered by state and private schools. The majority of the students in Greece go to state schools (www.ypepth.gr). Finally, tertiary education includes the higher education institutions (AEI in Greek) and the technological education institutions (TEI in Greek). The entrance of students into tertiary education is by nation-wide exams at the end of each school year. State education in Greece is free and textbooks are offered to students with no charge (www.ypepth.gr).

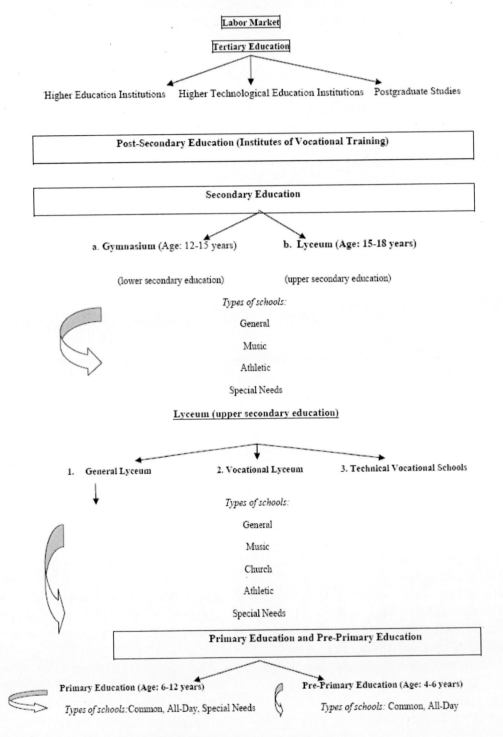

Diagram 1. The structure of the Greek educational system.

The educational administration system, in turn, is hierarchically structured. At the national level are the Minister of Education, two vice Ministers, the General Directorate, the National Educational Council and other Councils. At the regional level there are thirteen directorates of education; at the prefectural level there are the directorates and the offices of primary and secondary education, school advisers and prefectural committees of education. Lastly, at the local level are the school units, the local educational committees, the school committees, the school councils and the parents' unions (see Diagram 2).

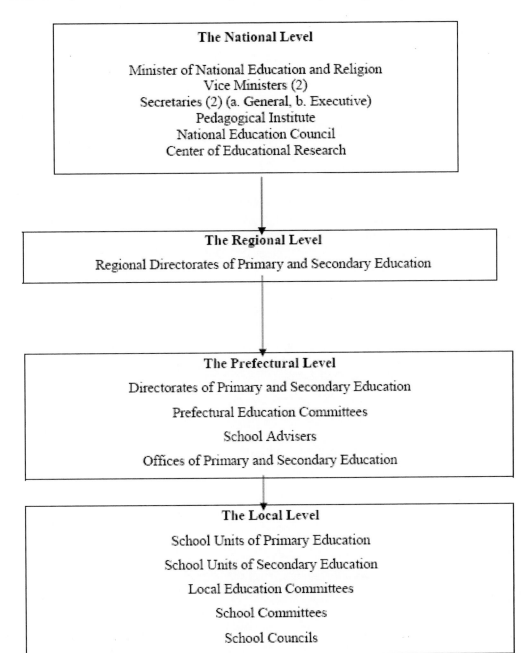

Diagram 2. The structure of the Greek educational administration system.

**Table 1. The total number of state schools, teachers and pupils in Greece (school year: 2003-2004)**

| School Levels | Schools (N) | Teachers (N) | Students (N) |
|---|---|---|---|
| Pre-Primary | 8,265 | 5,434 | 129,712 |
| Primary | 32,861 | 5,416 | 580,032 |
| First Cycle of Secondary Education: Gymnasium | 32,737 | 1,881 | 309,851 |
| Second Cycle of Secondary Education: Lyceum | 19,727 | 1,253 | 224,964 |
| Technical Vocational Sector | 13,868 | 462 | 112,921 |
| Total | 107,458 | 14,446 | 1,357,480 |

Source: Center of Educational Research, 2005.

School teachers - primary and secondary - hold university degrees and are appointed - after successfully passing specific national exams - by the Ministry of Education (www.ypepth.gr). Table 1 presents the total number of state schools, teachers and students, according to the most recent official data (Center of the Educational Research, 2005).

## EDUCATIONAL ADMINISTRATION IN THE SCHOOL SYSTEM

The school system in Greece is under a centralized and bureaucratic control. The Ministry of Education holds distinct authority and power and is unambiguously placed at the top of the educational administrative hierarchy. The educational administrative executives, on the other hand, who are perceived as "legitimized" interest groups (Kogan, 1975), function in a strict and bureaucratic context characterized by a top-down control (Ifanti, 1995; Saitis, 2005, 2007). To think through this issue the administrative system will be examined at its four levels: national, regional, prefectural and local.

### The National Level

The Ministry of Education and Religion is responsible for all educational activities in the country (e.g., the definition of the legal educational framework, financial control over any educational matter, design and development of the school curriculum, determination of educational aims and objectives, supervision of implementation of educational policies in schools, etc.). Only the higher education institutions are recognized as administratively autonomous and are legal public entities, according to the Greek Constitution (Greek Constitution, 1975, Article, 16). The Minister of Education is also assisted by two vice

Ministers: one responsible for the school system and the other for the higher education institutions (www.ypepth.gr).

The Ministry of Education comprises general directorates for the management of education under the control of the General Secretary. Additionally, the National Educational Council, which is a non-hierarchically structured pluralistic body (Kvavik, 1976) and is headed by the Minister of Education, has been legislated to contribute to the educational policy formation (Law 1566/1985, Article 18). Nevertheless, since its establishment, it has been rarely called by the Minister of Education. Another advisory body close to the Ministry of Education is the Pedagogical Institute, which is a self-administered organization charged with the development of school curriculum and the planning of teachers' training programs. It also keeps constant contact with the school advisers and the higher education institutions (www.p.i.gr).

Moreover, the Center of Educational Research, established in 1995 (Law 2327/1995), carries out research projects on educational issues, undertakes wider research educational programs and works in collaboration with international organizations (e.g., OECD, UNESCO, etc.) (www.kee.gr). It is administered by a seven member committee appointed by the Minister of Education. Finally, two other bodies contribute to the Ministry's activities: a) the Student Textbooks Editing Company (OEDB in Greek), which edits and delivers books to the state schools free of charge, and b) the School Buildings Organization (OSK in Greek), which is responsible for the school buildings (Ifanti, 1995). From 1998, the OSK became an anonymous company after a Ministerial Decision (www.osk.gr.index1.htm).

In general, the organizations mentioned above are controlled by the Minister of Education, who is not obliged by law to adopt their propositions; he/she can act autonomously of all groups, or cooperate with some groups, ignoring others. The centralized control of the Ministry of Education over primary and secondary education will be further revealed by examining the educational administration system at regional, prefectural and local level.

## The Regional Level

At this level, the Regional Directorates of Education (Primary and Secondary, total number: 13) was established by Law 2817/2000 and acts under the supervision of the Minister of Education, who determines the duties and commitments of the directors throughout the country's regions. These directors are school teachers and are appointed by the Minister of Education. They are charged with supervising school advisers as well as directors and heads of the educational offices of primary and secondary education in the prefectures. Some other councils also exist, such as the higher council of primary and secondary education respectively (APYSPE and APYSDE in Greek), and the regional council of administrative personnel (PYSDIP in Greek), which are constituted by the Minister of Education (Ifanti and Vozaitis, 2005; Saitis, 2005).

Additionally, the newly-established offices in each region for physical and environmental education, in-service teacher training, counseling, etc., represent a tendency to decentralize the central control of the system and to empower schools, although the system remained centralized (Law 2986/2002).

## The Prefectural Level

At this level, directors of education located in the 54 prefectures of the country, with the aid of the heads of the educational offices, administer primary and secondary education (Law 1304/1982). The education director is responsible for the coordination of the educational offices of education in the prefecture, the supervision of the heads of the schools, the distribution of funds to schools, the supervision of the school buildings and the allocation of the teachers to schools (Ifanti, 1995). The school advisor, on the other hand, is responsible only for the pedagogical guidance of teachers (Law 1304/1982).

Two other consultative bodies, the prefectural educational committee (headed by the Prefect) and the local educational committee (headed by the Mayor), have limited authority (Law 1566/1985) and are under the control of the Ministry of Education through the administration hierarchy.

## The Local Level

At this level, educational control is wielded by the head of the school, who is responsible for the implementation of the centrally designed educational policies in schools, for the activities developed at school and the supervision of the teaching staff. The teaching staff, in turn, instructs according to the national and unified curriculum and provides support to students where necessary.

In addition, two more bodies operate under the auspices of the local authorities, the school council and the school committee, which merely contribute to the function of the school (Ifanti, 1995, 2007). Finally, the students' communities undertake initiatives in schools, in line with the Ministry's regulations (Law 1566/1985).

## INITIATIVES TOWARDS SCHOOL EMPOWERMENT

It is widely accepted that decentralization policies are related to changes in school empowerment and improvement, mainly focusing on decision-making processes, school finances, curriculum planning, the professional status of teachers, educational opportunities and other issues (Altrichter and Elliot, 2000; Astiz et al. 2002; Ball, 2003; Bullock and Thomas, 1997; MacGilchrist, 2003). These attempts aim to activate education interest groups (e.g., parents, students, teachers, local, regional and national representatives, etc.) and to distribute the exclusive control of education from center to the periphery and to the local level.

In Greece, since mid-1980s some changes have taken place in the educational administration system at the primary and secondary level in order to be responsive to demands for modernization.

As mentioned earlier in this chapter, Law 1566/1985 introduced important changes in the system of educational policy formation (e.g., the establishment of a national education council, the introduction of prefectural, regional and community educational committees and of school councils), on the basis of the structure of the administration system at national, prefectural, regional and local level. Additionally, the handling of school affairs and the (re)construction of the school buildings went to the local authorities. Nevertheless, in practice, the national educational council has rarely been called by the Ministry of Education to contribute to policy formation, whereas the other educational bodies have been restricted to the development of local activities under the control of the Ministry of Education and their role approved to be merely advisory.

Moreover, the teachers' in-service training institutions have remained centrally controlled. The organization, administration and the curriculum of the institutions have been determined by specific Presidential Decrees. The Pedagogical Institute, on the other hand, was reestablished by Law 1566/1985, Article 23 (first established by Law 4379/1964 and then abolished by the dictatorship in 1967), and it is responsible for the development of the school curriculum, the development of teachers' training courses and for taking reports about the work in schools by the school advisers directly to the Minister of Education (Ifanti, 1995; Ifanti and Vozaitis, 2005).

In fact, the Law 1566/1985 attempted to establish a partnership between central government and the educational interest groups, but the formal institutions, which were located at the different levels of the administration system, appeared to be part of the complex system of decision-making process without changing the political context of schooling and its centralized control.

Later on, in the period 1990-1993, the then right-wing government tried to reform some of the measures legislated by their political predecessors (and opponents in that period) rather than to contribute to the decentralization of the system and to school improvement. For example, with the Presidential Decree No. 45/1993, although the Prefect undertook decisive responsibilities for educational matters in the area of his/her authority, however, he/she was not allowed to influence the educational policy formation.

In 1994, the Socialist political party in government criticized the bureaucratic, centralized system of administration and characterized educational politics of the previous period as ineffective for the betterment of schools (interview of the Minister of Education, *To Vema* Newspaper, March 1, 1995).

A few years later, Law 2525/1997 introduced the unified lyceum (upper secondary education) and a new system of university entrance exams. In the same legislative context, it is worth mentioning some innovative measures for school empowerment such as the establishment of all-day schools (pre-primary and primary) and of the second chance schools, the introduction of support teaching programs in schools as well as the establishment of 13 regional centers for educational planning (PEKESES in Greek, Article 29) which – unfortunately - did not work. Nevertheless, despite the Law's provisions for educational changes, the central control retained its well-known autocratic and bureaucratic features.

By the close of the 20th century, Law 2817/2000 aimed at the decentralization of the schools' administration system with the establishment of the Regional Education Directorates (Article 29, see also above). The Minister of Education retained his/her decisive role on the educational matters, taking into account the fact that the duties and the responsibilities of the directors were specifically defined by the Ministry, according to the Law. Some other consultative councils, established with the aforementioned Law (i.e., the higher council of primary education, the higher council of secondary education, the regional council of administrative personnel), function under central control.

Two years later, Law 2986/2002 tried to support the work at schools with the establishment of various centers at the regional level, for instance, centers of physical and environmental education, in-service teachers' training, students' diagnosis, assessment and support, youth counseling centers, etc. Nevertheless, despite attempts made for the administrative empowerment of schools with the appearance of these educational bodies, educational practices at schools did not change because the control system remained strictly centralized. Moreover, bureaucracy was further extended for the financial support of these centers (Ifanti and Vozaitis, 2005; Saiti, 2003; Saitis, 2007).

Additionally, this complex and multi-level system of administration with the Ministry of Education at the top of the hierarchy was not accompanied by other changes for the debureaucratization of the educational system. It was merely based on an earlier Law (Law 309/1976), according to which the country had been divided into 15 educational regions for primary and secondary education. It can thus be said that the decentralization of education cannot be attained by renewing past administrative policies and practices, but with the initiation of new measurements highlighting the need for cooperation between central government and peripheral bodies all aiming at school improvement.

Furthermore, according to Law 2986/2002 (Article 2), the Center of Educational Research together with the Pedagogical Institute became responsible for the assessment of teachers' work and for educational evaluation, with the aim to modernize education and society and consequently affect the bureaucratic character of the system, although the Minister of Education still retains the power to decide on any educational aspect. Equally, the organization for the education and training of in-service teachers (OEPEK in Greek) is always under ministerial control, because the head of the organization is appointed by the Minister of Education (Law 2986/2002, Article 6).

In this framework of Greek educational politics, some innovative activities were also developed. For example, the "Flexible Zone" (Ministerial Decisions: No. 73765/G1/14-07-2003, No. 74138/G2/15-07-2003) was a new measure which introduced an optional innovative educational program to the centrally designed curriculum of schools (primary and first cycle of secondary schools). In practice, although it did not release the central control of curriculum content, it nevertheless provided the opportunity for classroom interaction through an interdisciplinary approach to knowledge and for adoption of new teaching methods for four hours per week. The planning of this program was under the control of the school adviser.

Summing up, it becomes obvious that there is a gap between political discourse and educational practice; the Ministry of Education in Greece exercises control over the regional bodies of the educational administration system although, according to the relevant Law, he/she is expected to keep in contact the regional directorates of education (primary and secondary) and the school units and also to leave some room for the periphery to take initiatives. In addition, the attempts made to change everyday school practices were not facilitated by the appropriate administrative measurements and the necessary financial support. Thus, central control of the school system remained unchanged.

## Conclusion

It can be said that the politics of educational change in Greece is ultimately determined by the centralized control over the educational system. The Greek educational system is characterized by a hierarchical order in its organization and by a bureaucratic and centralized control over any educational aspect. Such power has also determined the long-term relationship between the Greek state and the educational sector.

Although the policies for educational decentralization in the administration system, which appeared over the last 20 years in Greece, aimed to improve schools and to develop innovative initiatives at the local, regional and prefectural level, the promise of the relevant legislation and of the rhetoric on the issue were found to be different from the practice. The central government remained powerful whereas some changes that occurred in the educational administration system were not followed up with the expected financial support needed to facilitate the implementation of the promised innovations.

An example easily comes from the Introductory Document to the Law 2986/2002. On the one hand, it underlines the need for modernization and decentralization of the educational administration system and, on the other hand, centralized policies penetrate the whole system without offering autonomy to schools and giving opportunities to teachers to participate in the educational decision-making process. Other changes also did not succeed in strengthening the school culture (Altrichter and Elliot, 2000) and consequently did not facilitate school empowerment or initiatives for autonomy at the periphery, mainly because they were not planned on the basis of the everyday school practices.

An explanation for the failure of the system to generate innovative initiatives in schools is provided by politics. The apparently contradictory phenomena of democratic institutions, innovative educational policies and strictly centralized politics have their origins in the dominant political structure in Greece, and special attention should be given to the communication, planning and control aspects of the Greek educational politics. In this perspective, centralism, corporatism and interest group politics are ways of describing the extent to which democratic decision making in Greece is undermined in practice. So, although corporatism emphasizes the role of the interest groups in policy formation (Lyons, 1985) the capacity of the state to shape interest groups is closely related to the structure of the state itself. The centralized bodies of the government (the Ministry of Education included) are revealed to be the main obstacles to educational reforms, whereas the administration system of education in Greece has contributed to the establishment of central and bureaucratic control over every educational aspect; this has been strengthened by the frequent changes of the Ministers of Education (Ifanti, 1992, p. 227). In this respect, W. Bacon's (1978) argument seems to underline the issue:

"The leaders of all welfare bureaucracies are forced to adopt a quasi-political role, in the sense that they do not operate within a social vacuum but must constantly pay heed to the consequences of their actions upon other competing groups and forces in society. Whatever specific interest they serve, be it education, welfare planning or recreation, they must consistently address themselves to three key and universal issues. Firstly, the need to maintain their authority. Secondly, the need to maintain the stability and security of their organization. Thirdly, the need to justify their continued claims upon the wider sources of society" (Bacon, 1978, pp. 179).

The Greek educational administration system needs thus to be re-examined in a new context of dissemination of power between the center and the periphery, in order to improve the whole system of education. Even central control becomes more effective for schools when it focuses on evaluation of educational practices and of school culture. Moreover, educational design and development demand cooperation among experts of various disciplines, who must be mobilized despite their ideological and political differences. Overall, education needs long-term plans and consent procedures, which exceed the possibilities of a political party in government.

## REFERENCES

Altrichter, H., and Elliot, J. (2000). *Images of educational change.* Buckingham: Open University Press (Chapters 3, 7).

Astiz, M.F., Viseman, A.W., and Baker, D.P. (2002). Slouching towards decentralization: Consequences of globalization for curricular control in national education systems. *Comparative Educational Review,* 46 (1), 66-88.

Bacon, W. (1978). *Public accountability and the schooling system.* London: Harper and Row.

Ball, St. (2003). *The more things change. Educational research, social class and "interlocking" inequalities.* London: University of London Institute of Education.

Bullock, A., and Thomas, H. (1997). *Schools at the centre? A study of decentralization.* London: Routledge.

Carnoy, M. (1999). *Globalization and educational reform: What planners need to know?* Paris: UNESCO (pp. 47-60).

Center of Educational Research (2005). *Recording the educational system at the school level.* Athens: Center of Educational Research (V. Koulaidis, Ed.), in Greek.

Fullan, M. G. (1991). *The new meaning of educational change.* London: Cassell.

Greek Constitution, 1975, Article, 16.

Ifanti, A.A. (1994). Education politics and the teachers' unions in Greece. *European Journal of Teacher Education,* 17 (3), 219-230.

Ifanti, A.A. (1995). Policy-making, politics and administration in Greece. *Educational Management and Administration,* 23 (4), 271-278.

Ifanti, A.A. (1992). *The politics of the secondary school curriculum in Greece.* Unpublished Ph.D. Thesis. London: University of London Institute of Education.

Ifanti, A.A., and Vozaitis, G. (2005). Attempts for decentralization of the educational control and school empowerment. *Administrative Science Review* (34) 3, 28-44 (in Greek).

Ifanti, A.A. (2007). Policy and curriculum development in Greece. The case of secondary school curriculum. *Pedagogy, Culture and Society* (15) 1, 71-81.

Kogan, M. (1975). *Educational policy-making.* London: George Allen and Unwin, Ltd.

Kvavik, R. (1976). *Interest groups in Norwegian politics.* Oslo: Universitesforlaget.

Lauglo, J., and McLean, M. (1985). *The control of education.* London: Heinemann Educational Books, Ltd.

Law 4379/1964 (1964). *On the organization and administration of general education* (in Greek).

Law 309/1976 (1976). *On the organization and the administration of general education (primary and secondary)* (in Greek).

Law 1304/1982 (1982). *On the pedagogical guidance of teachers* (in Greek).

Law 1566/1985 (1985). *On the structure and operation of primary and secondary education* (in Greek).

Law 2327/1995 (1995). *On the establishment of the Center of Educational Research* (K.E.E. in Greek).

Law 2525/1997 (1997). *Unified lyceum, entrance to the tertiary education, evaluation of the educational work and other legislations* (in Greek).

Law 2817/2000 (2000). *On the education for individuals with special educational needs and other legislations* (in Greek).

Law 2986/2002 (2002). *On the organization of the regional offices for primary and secondary education, on the educational evaluation, teachers' appraisal, in-service teachers' training and other legislations* (in Greek).

Lyons, R. (1985). Decentralized educational planning: Is it a contradiction? In: J.

Lauglo and M. McLean (Eds.). *The control of education.* London: Heinemann Educational Books, Ltd. (pp. 86-95).

MacGilchrist, B. (2003). *Has school improvement passed its sell-by date?* London: University of London Institute of Education.

McLean, M. (1988). The conservative education policy in comparative education: Return to an English golden age or harbinger of international policy change? *British Journal of Educational Studies* (36) 3, 200-217.

Ministerial Decisions: No. 73765/G1/14-07-2003, No. 74138/G2/15-07-2003.

Ministry of Economic Development (2001). *The competitiveness of the Greek economy.* Athens (in Greek).

Ministry of Press and Media (2002). *Greece in the European Union: The new role and the new agenda.* Athens.

Organization for Economic Cooperation and Development (OECD) (1982). *Reviews of national policies for education: Greece.* Paris: OECD.

Panich, L. (1980). Recent theorizations of corporatism: Reflections in a growth industry. *British Journal of Sociology* (31), 2, 159-187.

Presidential Decree No. 45/1993 (1993).

Saiti, A. (2003). The institution of the regional head of education and the administrative decentralization in education: Institutions in crisis? *Modern Education* (132), 75-84 (in Greek).

Saitis, Ch. (2005). *Organization and administration of education.* Athens: University of Athens (in Greek).

Saitis, Ch. (2007). *The head-teacher in the modern school.* Athens: University of Athens (in Greek) (pp. 273-275).

Schmitter, Ph. (1977). Modes of interest intermediation and models of social change in Western Europe. *Comparative Political Studies* (10), 7-38.

Temple, P. (2003). Educational research and policy-making: Findings from some transitional countries. *London Review of Education* 1 (3), 217-228.

*To Vema* Newspaper (1995). March 1, 1995.

Vourveres, K. (1950). Greek humanism. In: Encyclopaedeia *Helios*, Vol. 7, Athens (p. 734).

In: Centralization and School Empowerment...
Editor: Adam Nir

ISBN 978-1-60692-730-4
© 2009 Nova Science Publishers, Inc.

*Chapter 9*

# EDUCATIONAL ADMINISTRATION AND SCHOOL EMPOWERMENT IN PORTUGAL

*Natércio Afonso*
University of Lisbon, Portugal

## THE CONTEXT: SOCIAL, POLITICAL AND ECONOMIC CIRCUMSTANCES

Portugal is a European Union country made up of a continental territory (88,967.5 km2 in the western coast of the Iberian Peninsula, with about 10,040,000 inhabitants), and two archipelagos, Azores (nine islands, approximately 240,000 inhabitants) and Madeira (two islands, some 240,000 inhabitants), both in the Atlantic Ocean.

The Republic's political system was established by the 1976 Constitution. There are general parliamentary elections every four years. The President is also elected by popular vote, for a five-year term, and can be re-elected only once. The Atlantic islands have elected regional parliaments and autonomous governments.

At the local level the territory is divided into some 300 municipalities (including both big cities such as Lisbon, the country's capital, and many small villages with only a few thousands inhabitants) run by collegial bodies elected each four years. The current composition of the 230 member Parliament includes six political parties, but the two major parties (center left Socialists -121 and center right Social Democrats – 75) account for 196 seats (85%). The Socialists support the present government. The Socialist Party (PS) achieved an absolute majority in the 2005 elections. The President of the Republic, a former Social Democrat prime minister, was elected in 2006.

With a Gross Domestic Product (GDP) of around 141 billion Euros, in 2004, Portugal has the 20th largest absolute economy when compared with all 30 members of the OECD. Among the OECD countries, the relative position of Portugal falls to 24th when the indicator used is the GDP per capita, yet stays ahead of the Czech Republic, Hungary, Slovakia, Poland, Mexico and Turkey (2004 data) (OECD, 2008).

In recent years, after having attained a rate of real GDP growth of 4.7% in 1998, the Portuguese economy entered into a recessive stage with the consecutive decrease in growth rate reaching its lowest value (-1,2%). Nowadays a slow recovery is seen in the growth of economic activity, still clearly below the values needed to approach the average level of economic and social development of the European Union.

The structure of GDP shows an increase in proportional growth of services (occurring in government, health, education and other personal services) from 62.2% in 1990 to 70.99% in 2004. Agriculture, forestry and fishing saw their contribution to GDP fall from 8.0% to 3.5% during the same period. The remaining activities, of industry and construction, witnessed a fall in contribution towards GDP from 29.8% to 25.6% (OECD, 2008).

The evolution of the economic situation is reflected in the indicators relating to employment. The unemployment rate began to rise in 2001, from 3.9% to 6.7% in 2004, and reaching 7.8% in the last trimester of 2007 (INE: http://www.ine.pt/ accessed April 23, 2008). The worsening of the unemployment situation affects mainly women and the 15-24-year-old age segment of the workforce.

As for employment qualifications, there is an increase in the number of employees with academic qualifications equivalent to, or above, full secondary education.

In demographic terms, since the beginning of the 1990s, the resident population increased mainly due to the incoming migration.

Apart from the aging phenomena and spatial concentration in urban areas, immigration is currently, in Portugal, one of the most important demographic dynamics. The relative weight of the various nationalities that make up the foreign population has remained relatively stable, yet registering slight increases in the population coming from Portuguese-speaking African countries, Brazil and more recently from countries from Eastern Europe (INE, 2007a). In 2004, African people represented 41.8%, Brazilians around 11%, and the "miscellaneous" group, where Eastern Europeans predominate, at around 22.2%. This last group is the one which has shown the highest growth rates in recent years (9.1% in 2003 and 9.9% in 2004 [INE, 2007b).

|  | Age | Grade |
|---|---|---|
| Pre-school | 3 to 5 | |
| 1st cycle Basic School | 6 to 9 | 1 to 4 |
| 2nd cycle Basic School | 10 & 11 | 5 & 6 |
| 3rd cycle Basic School | 12 to 14 | 7 to 9 |
| Secondary School | 15 to 17 | 10 to 12 |
| 1st cycle H. Education | 18 to 20 | 1 to 3 |
| Master H. Education | 21 & 22 | 4 & 5 |
| Doctorate H. Education | 23 and over | 6 to 8 |

Diagram 1. A simplified structure of the Portuguese education system.

# EDUCATIONAL SYSTEM

This section presents a brief description of the Portuguese schooling system (for additional information, see Barcelos et al., 2002). The current structure of the schooling system was established by Parliamentary law nº46/86 in 1986, covering preschool education, basic education, secondary education and higher education (see Diagram 1).

Preschool education is a noncompulsory system addressed to children between 3 to 5 years of age. The public network of preschool education centers, under the control of the Ministry of Education, was established in 1977 and the statutory norms for preschool centers were approved in 1979. Until then, there was no formal education policy regarding preschool education. However, there were (and still are) many public preschool institutions under the supervision of other government departments, namely the Ministry of Labor and Welfare. The current norms for the curricular activities in preschool education were established in a public law of 1997, defining preschool education as the first step of basic education, within the lifelong learning process of each person.

In the 2006-2007 school year, there were 263,031 children enrolled in preschool centers, which corresponded to a schooling rate of about 78% of the age population.

About 52% were enrolled in public centers (137,979). Centers under the control of the Ministry of Education reached about 97% of the total number of children in public centers. On the contrary, in the private networks, only about 36% were under the control of the Ministry of Education.

In the 2006-2007 school year, there were 6,939 preschool centers, of which 4773 were public (circa 69%), corresponding to 52% of all children enrolled in preschool education. This corresponds to an average of about 29 children in each unity, against about 58 children per unit in the private sector.

In the same year (2006-2007), there were 16,996 preschool teachers working in those centers, of which 10,121 were in public centers (about 60%).

In sum, public preschool centers reached almost 70% of existing schools, hiring 60% of the working teachers and covering barely more than half of the demand (52% of children enrolled) (Portugal, Ministério da Educação, GEPE, 2007).

**Table 1. Number of pupils, schools and teachers (2006-2007 school year)**

| | Pupils | | Schools | | Teachers | |
|---|---|---|---|---|---|---|
| | Total | Public | Total | Public | Total | Public |
| Pre-school education | 263,031 | 137,979 | 6,939 | 4,773 | 16,996 | 10,121 |
| 1st cycle basic education | 498,971 | 446,870 | 6,818 | 6,298 | 33,944 | 31,209 |
| 2nd cycle basic education | 255,236 | 225,095 | 1,139 | 898 | 34,470 | 31,869 |
| 3rd cycle basic education | 398,592 | 350,856 | 1,514 | 1,200 | 88,280 | 79,998 |
| Secondary education | 356,711 | 289,714 | 919 | 546 | | |

Source: Portugal, Ministério da Educação, GEPE (2008). *Estatísticas da Educação 06/07.*

Preschool teachers must get a master's degree in preschool education to enter into the profession. However, as this requirement is quite recent (2006), the majority hold the traditional first level higher education degree in preschool education (3 or 4 years), from public or private schools of education.

Basic education corresponds with legal compulsory schooling (from 6 to 15 years of age), covers grades 1 to 9, and is divided into three cycles: 1st cycle (grades 1 to 4), 2nd cycle (grades 5 and 6) and 3rd cycle (grades 7 to 9). As a matter of a fact, basic education is a conglomerate of three very different schooling traditions: the primary school, the preparatory school, and the first comprehensive level of secondary education. The 1st cycle corresponds with the traditional elementary school where children are organized into grade level classes, each one with one classroom teacher. In small rural schools, classes are less homogeneous and may include children from two to more grades. There is a national curriculum defined by law focusing on reading, writings and maths, but including other areas such as music, visual arts and physical education. Since 2005, English is also mandatory for 3rd and 4th graders, as a complementary subject with specialized teachers.

The public network of primary schools is extremely diversified. Rural schools are one-classroom buildings with scarce teaching materials and poor equipment. In the late 1970s, more than 50% of all primary schools were small rural schools. During the last decades, the growing concentration of the population in the urban areas reduced the number of these schools and the moving of many 1st to 4th graders into larger units ("integrated basic schools" or "school districts"). In contrast, in the urban areas, mainly in the periphery of the big cities, there are overcrowded primary schools with hundreds of children, with the occasional need to organize the school activities into a shift system (two classes sharing the same room, one during the morning and other during the afternoon). However, the decreasing number of children resulting from a lower birth rate tends to attenuate this problem. Actually, the number of children enrolled in the 1st cycle of basic schooling decreased dramatically over the last 30 years, from 874,262, in 1985-1986, to 498,971, in 2006-2007, which means a reduction of almost 50%. The enrollment rate reached 100% in the early 1980s.

In the same year (2006-2007) about 90% of the pupils were enrolled in the 6,298 existing public schools (92% of all schools offering the 1st cycle). There were 6,818 schools (including 519 private). There were 33,944 teachers in the 1st cycle; about 92% of them worked in public schools.

Elementary school teachers must get a master's degree in basic education to enter into the profession. However, as this requirement is quite recent (2006), the majority hold the traditional first level higher education degree in elementary education (3 or 4 years), from public or private schools of education (Portugal, Ministério da Educação, GEPE, 2007).

The 2nd cycle of basic education corresponds to the network of the old preparatory schools for secondary education created in the late 1960s of the last century to expand enrollment rates in secondary education. In the 2006-2007 school year, there were 255,236 pupils enrolled, in 1,139 schools, with about 31,000 teachers. The public schools (78.8%) covered 88.2% of the demand with 92% of the teaching staff.

As with the 1st cycle, the total of pupils has been decreasing during the last 20 years, from 388,994, in the 1985-1986 school year, to 255,236, in 2006-2007, which means a decrease of about 35%. The enrollment rate remains at 86.4%.

There is a compulsory national curriculum, which includes detailed syllabi, subject programs and pupil evaluation norms. It follows the traditional subject approach of the old secondary education (Portuguese, maths, English, science, arts, music, history and geography, physical education, religion, civics, etc.). Each subject is taught by a specialized teacher, which means that each class has almost 10 teachers and a quite complex weekly schedule (Portugal, Ministério da Educação, GEPE, 2007).

Teachers must hold a first degree in the subject field, and a specific master's teaching degree to apply for a teaching position in public or private schools.

The 3rd cycle corresponds to a comprehensive approach to secondary education implemented in the late 1970s, resulting from the integration of the former existing two-track system (grammar schools and vocational schools). It is offered in basic schools jointly with the 2nd cycle, or in secondary schools as a preparation for secondary education. The curriculum is nationally mandated and follows the structure of the 2nd cycle, with a more detailed approach such as two foreign languages and specific science subjects (physics, chemistry and biology instead of integrated science). As in the 2nd cycle, there are detailed subject programs and pupil assessment norms and procedures to be followed nationally. Teachers tend to be more specialized and must hold a university subject matter degree and an additional master's degree in teaching. In the 2006-2007 school year, there were 398,428 pupils (350,841 in public schools) enrolled in 1,516 schools (basic, secondary or "integrated," from which 1,198 were public). The public schools (about 79%) covered 88% of the demand. The enrollment rate reaches 82.5%.

In the same year (2006-2007), at the secondary level (grades 10 to 12), there were 356,586 students enrolled (about 82% in public schools). There were 915 schools offering secondary education programs. About 60% were public schools. Many private secondary schools were small units offering specific vocational programs. The enrollment rate reached 59.8% and there is a high failure rate: about 50% of the students enrolled in secondary programs do not reach the end of 12th grade. Actually, secondary education is at the core of major current policy initiatives designed to improve enrollment and success rates. Most students follow more academic education programs leading to access to higher education institutions according to the core of the program such as science, humanities, social sciences, arts, and so on. What most public secondary schools and the majority of elitist private schools offer is based on these academic programs, designed along the traditional lines of the old grammar school curriculum. Thus, about 67% of all students attended classes in these programs, of which 81% were in public schools. About 13% of the secondary education students attended vocational programs, most of them (some 70%) in privately owned but publicly funded small vocational schools. The current policies aim at reinforcing the share of the vocational programs within secondary education, namely through the implementation of these programs in the traditional public secondary schools, in order to improve the enrollment and success rates (Portugal, Ministério da Educação, GEPE, 2007).

All schools are coeducational and formal selective procedures are not allowed. Schools must receive all pupils living in their neighborhoods, according to geographical regulations defined by the education authorities. However, there are schools believed to carry out informal (and illegal) procedures to select pupils according to academic ability, social class or ethnicity (Barroso, 2006).

# MAJOR RESTRUCTURING INITIATIVES TOWARDS SCHOOL EMPOWERMENT

According to the school administration law approved in 1998 (Decree-Law nr. 115-A/98, dated May 4th), the governance structure of each school or cluster of schools is based on a participatory governing body called School Assembly ("*Assembleia*") or Cluster Assembly. This body has between 6 and 20 elected members (depending on the size and level of the institution) representing teachers, parents, non-teaching staff, students (only in secondary schools), representatives from the municipal authorities and co-opted community leaders (optional). This Assembly meets a few times each school year and must approve broad school policies and discuss the strategic management documents such as the plan and the budget. The real governing body of the school, acting on a daily basis, is the Executive Council ("*Conselho Executivo*"), a team of three teachers elected from the teaching body of the school by an electoral college. This college includes all teaching and non-teaching staff, as well as parents and students representatives. The Ministry of Education must ratify the election of the Executive Council for each school or cluster, if the formal electoral procedures were respected.

For every purpose, the President of the Executive Council is recognized as the Headteacher of the school. The overall framework of the electoral process is defined by law through a government decree. Within that framework, each school or cluster of schools has the possibility to adopt specific organizational and administration rules, which must be clearly defined in the school regiment approved by the Assembly (Afonso and Viseu, 2001).

There are no local education authorities, as such. The municipal authorities have the formal responsibility to provide and take care of the facilities, equipment and food service for the 1st cycle schools, as well as free transportation for basic schooling as a whole, within their territory. However, the schools report hierarchically to one of the five regional directorates of education ("*direcções regionais de educação*") of the central Ministry of Education, in Lisbon (Afonso, 2004a). For detailed information about these directorates, see the Decree-Law nr. 213/2006 dated October 27th, which approves the current structure of the Ministry of Education.

The Executive Council is elected for a three-year period. The incumbent team can present itself for election in the subsequent periods, indefinitely. There is no formal performance evaluation procedure, besides the judgement implicit in the electoral process.

The candidates for the Executive Council elections must present themselves as a team and present some sort of an electoral program concerning their views about current issues and policies of the school. To be eligible, the candidates must have a tenured position as a teacher in the school (non-teaching staff people are not eligible), and some type of formal qualification in educational administration, or previous experience as a member of the Executive Council.

Actually, research has shown that the vast majority of the executive council members (more than 90%) do not have specific formal qualifications for the job, having been accepted for election on the basis of their previous professional experience as members of other executive councils, in their present schools or elsewhere (Afonso and Viseu, 2001).

The appointment of headteachers is therefore based on a political process carried out through voting procedures without the use of professional or technical selection procedures such as interviews, referees, curriculum vitae or psychometric tests. There is no formal performance appraisal procedure concerning the work of headteachers and other executive council members carried out by the inspectorate or any other Ministry department. There are evaluation and audit programs developed by the inspectorate of education and by the national budget authorities, but they are focused on institutional quality assurance requirements and do not concern the professional assessment of school administrators (Afonso, 2004a).

This framework means that there is no career of school administrator as such. Formally, school administrators are teachers temporarily performing that role, elected mainly by their peers. Most of them retain part of their teaching duties while serving as members of the executive councils. However, there are a significant number of teachers who remain as executive council members or presidents over several mandates, and it is not uncommon to find a president of an executive council serving in that position for 15 or 20 years without interruption. While in their management functions, teachers retain their teaching position and salary and advance in the teaching career like all other teachers. The material incentives for the job are the partial or full discharge of teaching responsibilities and extra remuneration (Afonso, 2003a).

There are in-service training programs on educational administration and school governance, most of them offered by a network of teacher training centers linked to associations of schools organized on a territorial basis and funded by the Ministry of Education with European Union monies. These are usually short programs of about 25 to 50 hours concerning specific topics like "school project management," "leadership," "discipline and violence in the school," "relationships between school and family," and so on. These programs are designed for headteachers as such since every teacher can apply and they do so because they provide needed credits for advancement in the teaching career, based on certified in-service training and seniority. There are also graduate programs (master and doctorate) in Educational Administration offered by the Higher Education institutions (Afonso, 2003a).

## RESTRUCTURING CONSTRAINTS AND CATALYSTS

Educational administration in Portugal is carried out within a framework of a centralized and highly regulated system. Centralization corresponds to a tradition common to the whole system of public administration, with deep roots in the specific historic development of the Portuguese state itself, a tradition stressed and reinforced during the almost five decades of dictatorship (1926-1974), for obvious ideological and political reasons. Indeed, after the 1926 military coup, the new authoritarian regime reinforced the centralization and control of educational administration. The new regime's educational policy focused on the inculcation of traditional values and on ideological indoctrination. School administrators were conceived as political commissars controlling the ideological purity of teaching and the political compliance of teachers and students, much more than the quality of education provided by the school (Formosinho, 1987). Therefore, decision-making was highly concentrated at the top political level of the Ministry of Education. This tradition of centralization is a key feature of the Portuguese school system, and remained unchanged after the fall of the dictatorship in 1974 (Afonso, 1993).

The provision of human and financial resources for the schools is an example of this centralized system. Thus, the hiring of teachers and other staff as well as personnel mobility from one school to another are carried out through yearly computer-controlled national competitions, run by a central Ministry department, without any kind of input from school management or local authorities. On the other hand, the annual budget of each school is strictly divided into discrete items centrally defined according to an incremental approach, without any concern about eventual strategic priorities defined by the schools.

Another key issue is the prescription of a mandated uniform national curriculum in elementary and secondary education, including not only the courses, their name, time allocation and sequence, but also the detailed content of each course, with objectives, topics, sequence and teaching methodologies. In spite of some recent attempts to implement experiments with some curriculum flexibility, the truth is that the uniform curriculum, "ready-made and single size," is still a major constitutive element of the Portuguese educational system.

Another major element of this tightly regulated and centralized system is the intensive organizational formatting, namely in the upper elementary and secondary schools. An outcome of the tensions between the needs of the Ministry's bureaucratic control and the self-management and corporate pressures of the teaching staff, this excessive regulation trend took over the daily management of schools, transforming the headteachers and principals into mere formal executives of norms and regulations, without any kind of project or strategic vision for the future of the school.

The system remains highly centralized, with a regulatory approach dominating relationships with schools. Within this logic, the school is conceived as a State service located at the periphery of the bureaucracy, a place where the policies decided centrally are supposed to be implemented, for the provision of the education public service (Afonso, 2004b).

In the early 1970s and the middle 1980s, the launching of large-scale educational reforms reinforced the centralized and bureaucratic nature of the Portuguese educational administration. Indeed, it was assumed in those reforms that educational change must be conceived and developed by experts and must be implemented on a top-down basis, according to the positivist approach of experimentation followed by generalization. This technocratic approach to educational change is based on the false assumption that all schools are similar and that what "works" during the experiment will "work" generally. Besides, such an approach is based on the naive belief that the mandated "reforms" are really implemented in each school, in full accordance with the exact way they were conceived and "experimented." It is believed that such full compliance can be achieved through the provision of adequate support and training, and the use of policy marketing operations based on such slogans as "Democratization of Schooling" or "Educational Reform." Finally, what is behind this educational technocracy is the idea that there is (or can be defined) one best way to teach the pupils and run the schools to be transmitted to the schools and to be fully adopted by them (Afonso, 1993).

Since the end of the 1960s, and with a significant delay after other European countries, Portugal went through a process of extreme expansion of mass schooling, above the traditional level of the old primary education (until fourth grade). Since then, this "explosion of schooling" became the central issue in educational policy-making.

From the quantitative viewpoint, the expansion of mass schooling produced a rapid growth in the number of pupils, schools and teachers in the intermediate sub-system between primary education and higher education. This was carried out with quite a contradictory "democratization" strategy based on the idea of making available, for all, the new "unified" secondary school, reconstructed according to the elitist and selective model of the old traditional grammar school.

On the qualitative side, the explosion of mass schooling at this intermediate level demanded a growing complexity in the educational services to be provided by the schools. Indeed, schools became more and more under pressure to multiply and diversify what they had to offer educationally, according to the diversity of these newly-enrolled masses of students: diversity based on locale, social and family background, as well as on ethnic and cultural background, given the rise of immigration, mainly after the mid-1980s.

In the centralized framework of the Portuguese public administration, this expansion and diversification of what education had to offer generated a rapid and uncontrolled growth of the educational administration structure. As significant countermeasures were not taken to neutralize it, this gigantic bureaucracy tended to make the school system practically ungovernable, thus reducing drastically the State's capacity to run it.

In addition, keeping the public schools under the direct administration of the State, through executive structures of the central government (the Ministry of Education), tends to produce, by the very nature and urgency of the decisions, the prevalence of daily administrative and management problems, over the strategic issues of policy making in the whole field of educational policy (including public and private schools). As a result, it became more and more difficult for the State to successfully launch new and innovative educational policies with significant impact on the quality of education provided in schools. Therefore, the overexpansion of the educational administration bureaucracy and the predominance of administrative concerns over policy issues came to be seen as the two major risks undermining the State's responsibilities in the field of education (by lack of capacity to act), leaving the educational policy-making processes under heavy pressure from interest groups and lobbies.

The awareness of this situation pressured the State to develop new strategies and models of policy-making, dropping the centralist and bureaucratic reform approach, and redefining the roles of the State's different levels in the administration of the school system. This new approach to policy-making presupposes a strategic perspective about the way schools work as organizations. They are conceived as "specific action systems" (Crozier and Friedberg, 1977), whose internal working logic contains strong "refraction" capacities concerning the normative inputs from the State's bureaucracy. Indeed, each individual school has its own way of working, organized into standard operational procedures and relationships, stabilized over time by the actors' power games and by the specific cooperative needs of the organizational tasks carried out for the provision of the education service.

Thus, the schools are "specific actions systems" with a large amount of organizational energy and "political" malleability, enabling them to manipulate internally the mandated "reforms," adapting or assimilating them to their own routines and practices, according to the internal struggles and balances of power, therefore reducing or even neutralizing the intended innovative potential of those reforms. On the other side, these same organizational features of the schools may develop into significant innovations with a potential for development, dissemination and relevant impact on the whole system, in a way that is unrelated to the mandated reforms or even contrary to them (Afonso, 2003b).

The recognition of this new perspective about school reform changed the strategies for policy-making and for administration of the system. Now, given the relative autonomy of the school as an organizational context, the central government tends to focus on approaches based on the actors' involvement in the decision-making processes. The new policies tend to stress the use of procedures based on negotiation, decentralization, contracts, differentiation and evaluation, with an agenda that presupposes the reconsideration of the State's role in the administration of the school system, namely in what concerns the balance of power between the central government and the local authorities.

That reconsideration implies the acceptance of school management autonomy and the provision of the needed support for its reinforcement, with a simultaneous effort to stress its responsiveness towards the community. This way, the school is no longer seen as a local extension of the State's bureaucracy. Instead, it is conceived as a community institution where the State's input must be restricted to the definition of a national legal framework of equity and consistency and to the provision of resources and external evaluation. In opposition to the "Educational Reform" of the 1980s, this new strategy focused on the idea of social collaboration and the identification of specific partners. The Minister of Education presented it in 1996 through a widely publicized booklet entitled, "Education Pact for the Future." Specific measures developed since then tried to put that strategy into practice. However, the success of such measures tends to be seen as modest and its impact on the system as a whole is mediocre.

One of these measures was the design and implementation of a school administration and management reform through a new law (Decree-Law nº 115-A/98), aimed at recognizing and expanding the autonomy of the schools in the daily management processes, and establishing participatory governance bodies with representatives from teachers, other school staff, students (in secondary schools), parents, local community agencies and local authorities. The reform appeared as being imposed on teachers who fully controlled the school management structure through the election of the principals among themselves in each school. According to the law, the principals and their assistants are still elected from among the teachers, but no longer by the teaching staff only. While teachers maintain the majority of the votes, parents, students and other school staff can also vote to select the school management team.

The reform and the whole new approach to educational policy initiated by the government in 1995 was denounced by some scholars and teachers' union leaders as the product of right-wing neo-liberal ideologies designed to undercut the responsibilities of the State in the provision of public services, therefore contributing to the privatization of schooling and the growth of inequalities in access to education.

Some indicators seem to point to a certain irrelevance of the reform effort. The intended changes tended to be assimilated by the ongoing standard operating procedures, as if the reform itself were in the process of being swallowed up and gradually attenuated by the combined pressures of the educational administration bureaucracy unwilling to alleviate its traditional grip on centralized rule-making, and the schools' self management culture dominated by teachers' collegiality. Therefore, the impact of the reform in the daily working of the schools was not very impressive. As is often the case in the history of educational reform, continuity prevailed over the change efforts.

In sum, the system remains strongly centralized and the changes introduced in the school administration structure did not touch the core features of the educational provision. Thus, the detailed and biding national curriculum remains unchanged. Teacher recruitment is still conducted by the Ministry's Human Resources Office. However, a few small steps have been taken towards school empowerment. Schools can now introduce minor changes in the curriculum, to gain some flexibility without changing the syllabi and the programs. Schools can now recruit teachers in specific situations (such as temporary substitute teachers).

Decentralization and school empowerment policies have rested on the political agenda since the early 1990s. Specific measures have been taken and some minor changes were achieved, but decentralization and school autonomy remain more rhetorical than real, and the failure to produce a major change is unquestionable. Most measures were taken within a top-down policy framework, with the naïve belief that what is legislated is actually implemented in the schools. Public schools are conceived by most people as State-owned institutions providing a public service nationwide. The sense of community ownership is weak. Therefore, there is not a significant public call for local empowerment. Besides, teachers are reticent, to say the least, about school autonomy and community empowerment, because central policy-making is easier to influence with strong union action. On the one hand, school autonomy reinforces the power of school heads and widens the professional gap between teachers and administrators. On the other hand, it favors accountability and social control over schools and their professionals, hindering the informal collegial autonomy and the peer-friendly climate of most schools (Barzanò, 2007). In sum the Portuguese system is moving away from centralism, but still has a long way to go.

## RECENT TRENDS AND A LOOK TOWARDS THE FUTURE

At the political level, the most relevant challenges for school leadership result from a growing pressure to perform the role of principal within the lines of a "managerial" perspective, in the sense defined by Gerwitz (2002). This implies more competencies and responsibilities in the management of the curriculum and other peripheral educational activities (study time, special projects), as well as in the domain of financial and human resource management, including the hiring and performance appraisal of teachers. This pressure contradicts the collegial culture prevailing in the vast majority of public schools.

As a teacher elected mainly by his or her peers, the principal rests symbolically and politically on an electoral legitimacy, in contradiction to the managerial logic of his/her role. The result is the development of management strategies based on ambiguity and ambivalence (Dinis, 1997, 2002). The Ministry of Education of the present government has enforced the implementation of unpopular school management measures within a policy framework conditioned by the State fiscal crisis and the urgent need to cut public spending. These measures indicate a heavier weekly workload for teachers, as well as changes in the statutory norms for the teaching career, undermining the old promotion rules based on seniority, and favoring progression and pay based on the quality of professional performance evident through scrupulous evaluation procedures (Pires, 2007; Rufino, 2007; Simões, 2007).

The implementation of these measures occurs within a climate of strong union unrest and loud dissatisfaction of the teaching profession. Therefore, most principals face a difficult dilemma, put in a position to choose between loyalty to the professional group to which they belong and the managerial logic implicit in the way they are required to run their schools (Ribeiro, 2007).

This contradiction becomes more and more relevant as the public demand for accountability keeps growing, fuelled by the increasing media attention and debate on education and schooling (Pina, 2007). Poor school results on national exams and international evaluation programs such as PISA get increasing media coverage. Criticism is fuelled also by the growing mistrust and lack of commitment of the middle classes with public mass schooling, with the equal opportunity ideology and with the myth of meritocracy (Afonso, 2004b; Ball, 2003). The legal framework for the regulation of school management is under reconsideration in order to open up the "black box" of the current collegial and teacher-friendly management procedures, in order to increase public scrutiny and social control.

To do so, several layers of legislation have forced the participation of municipal, community and parental representatives in the school administration boards previously reserved for teachers and other non-teaching staff representatives. In addition, specific strategic management instruments were made mandatory. This was the case of the school project, the curricular project for each school and for each class, and the school year planning document.

These measures opened the way for the current implementation of audit and school evaluation programs, both internal and external, focused on the assessment of goal achievement and the effective development of planned activities (Afonso, 2004a).

The ongoing changes in school administration structures respond also to efficiency concerns, focusing on measures that integrate schools into clusters defined on a territorial basis and including several schooling levels. The goal rests on improving efficiency in the management of available resources (closing small schools, requiring a more flexible use of teaching staff).

The new legislation on school autonomy and administration, approved in 2008, reinforces this managerial approach to the principal's role, highlighting his/her position as interlocutor of the government authorities.

An example of this policy trend is the recent establishment of a new consultative body within the structure of the Ministry of Education, made up of elected representatives from the schools' executive boards (the Schools' Council) (Decree-Law nr. 213/2006 dated October 27th). Another relevant example has been the novelty of organizing regular meetings involving the Ministry's political leadership, namely the Minister, and the presidents of the schools' executive boards.

The current practice of school management and leadership in the daily working of the public schools expresses tensions resulting from two conflicting logics of action:

The first is anchored in the routines of the professional bureaucracy resulting from the "historic compromise" between the educational administration hierarchy and the teaching profession, and built during the Keynesian era of mass schooling expansion.

The second presupposes a managerial approach implicit in the pressure of the recent government measures, and gets reinforced by the active and influential opinion-makers and the wide media coverage of their demands for "quality."

Ambiguity, tacit negotiation and passive resistance are among the strategies mobilized by the school leaders (the current presidents of the executive boards) to deal with these tensions. Ambiguity consists of management strategies that tend to avoid making clear decisions about controversial issues where and when relationships between teachers and the government are tense and conflictual. Tacit negotiation is a strategy focused on implicit transactions with teachers and with the educational administration bureaucracy that avoids or softens the collusion between government policies and teachers' interests in the daily working of the school. Passive resistence concerns the avoidance of taking active measures in the implementation of specific policy measures seen and controversial or expected to be opposed by teachers. Tactics of passive resistance comprise claiming that additional regulations must be produced, or that specific training programs must be implemented, or that additional resources must be provided, in order to implement a specific policy believed to produce unrest among teachers.

In the wider scope of civil society, there are no relevant expectations about the role of the public schools in the development of the communities to which they belong, what is commonly defined as community education. In general, schools are conceived by their professionals and by the surrounding communities as local instances of State bureaucracy for the provision of a specific service, that is, the delivery of public education for children and youth.

The ongoing policy measures concerning changes in school management are not carried out within the traditional logic of educational innovation. The rationale of these measures comes from the desire to change the nature of the principal's role as school manager, within the lines of wider policies on public administration modernization and rationalization.

The call for more decision-making autonomy for school leaders highlights the desire to implement what is called "the new public management" in the field of educational administration. At this level, the key management issue rests more on accountability for results and less on the compliance with norms and regulations. Therefore, the role of the principal and the configuration of school management remain deeply ambiguous and vague, in spite of the successive layers of legal restructuring. This ambiguity and the lack of clear definition of roles and relationships come from the very nature of the democratic state rebuilt in 1974 after the fall of the dictatorship.

Established in the Republic's Constitution as a key-structuring dimension of the new democratic regime, the political and administrative decentralization of the State has been postponed indefinitely and was explicitly rejected in a national referendum in the late 1990s. As a result, the traditional structure of a very centralized and routine-based State administration has remained unchanged over the last three decades. During the same period, however, successive layers of specific and atomistic measures were implemented establishing delegation and deconcentration of operational decentralization mechanisms of public administration services at regional and local levels, institutions and municipalities (Cruz, 2007).

The lack of clear policies to do with the evolution of the country's State administration structure and the reconfiguration of the central government has led to growing legitimacy and efficacy deficits. Contradictions are deepening between the ongoing routines of the government's bureaucracy, based on prescriptive norms and hierarchic compliance, and the discourse of many politicians and administration civil servants who, paradoxically, want to enforce autonomy, the spirit of initiative, "entrepreneurship," benchmarking and self-evaluation.

Along with the traditional mechanisms of bureaucratic regulation based on the imperative definition and control of norms and standard operational procedures, new models of management are implemented focusing on accountability for results, new policies are designed wrapped in a rhetoric of "flexibility," "innovation," "variable geometry" with promises of more efficacy and efficiency in the provision of public services.

At the same time, these changes take place while the young but prematurely debilitated and the Portuguese Welfare State suffers a fiscal crisis, with a large budget deficit, facing the growing gap between its unfulfilled promises and its more and more scarce resources. Thus, at different levels of State administration, namely in the municipalities and in the public schools, government policy discourse, focused on rationalization, flexibility, and administrative modernization, comes to the perception of "street-level bureaucrats" (Lipsky, 1980) as simple pretexts to reduce public spending, to impose heavier work loads and to dismantle and privatize public education. Naturally, the outcome has been the vehement rejection of these policies seen as products of the diabolized scapegoats: "neo-liberalism" or "globalization" (Charlot, 2007).

This way, a strong mechanism of mutual mistrust is building up between the government authorities and the educational administration bureaucracy on one side, and the local authorities and the teaching profession on the other side. In this situation, the position of school administrators becomes particularly fragile, given their role as gatekeepers in the relationship between the teaching profession and the government authorities. Their status has been always ambiguous and contradictory, resulting from the conflict between the collegial and teacher-friendly self-management tradition (an inheritance from the 1970s when the government-appointed principals were removed) and the inevitable exercise of hierarchic power within the State administration of public schools (Afonso, 1993).

It was possible to manage this conflict while the "historic compromise" between the State and the professional bureaucracies was kept alive, supported by a certain social consensus about the need to implement mass schooling, and by the belief in the Keynesian myth of equal opportunity. However, as new public policies define new competencies and responsibilities for school principals, stressing the managerial characteristics of their role, it has become more and more difficult to accommodate between two loyalties becoming increasingly antagonist.

On the other hand, during the last decade, and especially since the inauguration of the present government cabinet and the new team in the Ministry of Education, the policy-making and implementation processes went through deep changes regarding its legitimacy sources and strategies. Thus, there has been a growing use of mechanisms and instruments of policy regulation with reference to educational research and scientific knowledge, such as statistical data, quality indicators and "good practice" standards.

Meanwhile, there is a trend to downplay the traditional legitimating modes based on grand ideological reform principles and on the democratic authority of the "hard power" rule of law. The new public policies tend to be developed and implemented through "soft power" strategies using the scientific and technological knowledge as their sources of legitimacy, with an apparent neutralization of the values embedded in those policies.

Consensus building about specific policies tends no longer to develop around great principles (the equal opportunity ideal of the "European social model," "education for all" as a public good), but mainly around concrete policy mechanisms and instruments believed to produce the intended results (school autonomy, self-evaluation of schools, strategic planning, parental involvement, vouchers, rankings, teacher pay for performance, etc.). Submitted to a process of political "cooptation," school principals play an important role in the management of this soft power, as translators and gatekeepers during the reception and adaptation of policies in their schools. This amplifies the contradiction between their attachment to the teaching profession and their new identity built around the urgent needs of the daily managerial decisions, often conflicting with the interests and values of their peers.

The policy narratives of recent measures on teacher evaluation show that attachment to the profession is viewed in symbolic terms, as an added value in the management of their soft power. The present policy context is dominated by the recent approval of the new statutory legal framework for the organization and administration of public schools (Decree-Law nr.75/2008 dated April 22nd). The explicit goals of the reform focus on "reinforcing community and family participation in the school's strategic management and reinforcing the schools' leadership an autonomy."

The government argues that the achievement of these goals with be reached through three key changes in the organization and management of public schools. Firstly, formal parental and community participation in schools will be increased through a bigger percentage of their representatives on the school board (previously designated Assembly, now called General Council). With the new law, teachers and other school employees together will not have the possibility of holding the majority on the board, as previously could happen. In addition this body becomes more powerful because the recruitment and appointment of the principal becomes one of its major competencies. Previously, a specific electoral body elected the executive committee. Additionally, there is now the provision for a permanent commission of the council to supervise the current daily working of the school, while the Council, with its 21 members, meets only a few times each school year.

Secondly, there will be a principal or headteacher (a "director") instead of an executive committee. This is a major symbolic change. Since the mid-1970s, public schools have been run by teams made up of teachers elected mainly by their peers. Now, the principal will be selected by the school board from among the candidates applying for the position. The candidates can come from other schools or even from outside the public school system. In addition, the new principal will have stronger powers, if compared to the previous executive committee's president: He or she will be the head of the Pedagogic Council (previously elected among its members) and will appoint his/her deputies and the middle level management team (school and subject supervisors, previously elected by their peers).

Thirdly, there will be an enlargement of the discretionary power of each school authorities, namely the General Council, to design the internal organization of the school, according to the specific characteristics of its environment, and its educational project. Therefore, the law provides a more flexible and less detailed general framework for school management, leaving room for specific arrangements according to the local projects and circumstances. This is a relevant goal because the excessive formatting of school organization and management structures, coming from the law, from administrative norms, and the daily working of the educational administration bureaucracy, has been a powerful hinderance to the development of school leadership.

However, in itself, the new law under implementation will not represent a major change in the way public schools are run and will be run by their leaders in the near future. The relevance of the proposed changes results from their congruence with and adequacy in the wider policy context depicted above. It represents a window of opportunity for the consolidation of the managerial school, and the development of new identities for principals, away from the collegial teaching culture. Like other instances of public administration bureaucracies, though, public schools are solid systems of action (Friedberg, 1993) where national policies are reinterpreted, adapted, translated and, eventually, even ignored or discarded if need be and possible.

Therefore, it is not expected that the new policy on school autonomy and administration will produce dramatic changes. But it follows and stresses the trend to expand headship responsibilities and accountability within the "new public management" framework.

# REFERENCES

Afonso, N. (1993). The reform of school administraion in Portugal. A case study in organizational politics. Boston: Boston University School of Education (Ed.D. Thesis).

Afonso, N. (2003a). The situation in Portugal. In: L. Watson (Ed.), Selecting and developing heads of schools; twenty-three European perspectives. Sheffield England: School of Education of Sheffield Hallam University for the European Forum on Educational Administration (pp. 195-214).

Afonso, N. (2003b) A Regulação da Educação na Europa: do Estado Educador ao Controlo Social da Escola Pública. In: J. Barroso (org.), A Escola Pública, Regulação, Desregulação, Privatização. Porto: Asa (pp. 49-48).

Afonso, N. (2004a). Approaches to the evaluation of schools which provide compulsory education - Portugal. Brussels: Eurydice. (http://www.eurydice.org).

Afonso, N. (2004b). L'émergence des espaces intermédiaires de régulation dans l'administration de l'éducation au Portugal : le cas des directions régionales de l'éducation. Recherches Sociologiques, Vol. XXXV, n° 2, pp.121-140.

Afonso, N., and Viseu, S. (2001). Relatório Sectorial 4 – A reconfiguração da estrutura e gestão das escolas públicas dos ensinos básico e secundário: estudo extensivo. Lisboa: Centro de Estudos da Escola, Faculdade de Psicologia e de Ciências da Educação da Universidade de Lisboa.

Ball, S. (2003). Class strategies and the education market; the middle classes and social advantage. London: Routledge Falmer.

Barcelos, E., Bento, D., Brito, M. C., and Couto, P. (2002). Portugal – Outline of education system. In: Barzanò, G., and Clímaco, M. do C., and Jones J. (Eds.) (2002). School Management and Leadership – A comparative approach in Italy, Catalonia, England and Portugal. Roma: Anicia srl Editorem (pp. 119-137).

Barroso, J. (2006). La régulation de l'éducation comme processus composite: the cãs du Portugal. In: Maroy, C. (Ed.), École, régulation et marché; une comapraison de six espaces scolaires en Europe. Paris: PUF.

Barzanò, G. (2007). Headship and accountability in three European countries: England, Italy and Portugal. London: Institute of Education, University of London (PhD. Thesis).

Charlot, B. (2007). Education and globalisation: An attempt to bring order to the debate. Conference at the Faculty of Psychology and Educational Sciences of the University of Lisbon, June 14, 2007. Sísifo. *Educational Sciences Journal*, 04, pp. 127-134.

Crozier, M., and Friedberg, E. (1977). L'acteur et le système. Paris: Éditions du Seuil.

Cruz, C. (2007). Municipal Councils of Education: Educational policy and public action. Sísifo. *Educational Sciences Journal*, 04, pp. 65-74.

Dinis, L. L. (2002). O Presidente do Conselho Directivo: Dilemas do Profissional Docente enquanto Administrador. Administração Educacional. Revista do Fórum Português de Administração Educacional. N° 2, pp. 115-136.

Dinis, L. L. (1997). Presidente do Conselho Directivo: O Profissional como Administrador. Escolas do 2°/3° Ciclo do Ensino Básico. Dois Estudos de Caso. Dissertação de Mestrado. Lisboa: Universidade de Lisboa.

Formosinho, J. (1987). Educating for passivity. A study of Portuguese education (1926-1968). London: Institute of Education, University of London (PhD. Thesis).

Friedberg, E. (1993). Le pouvoir et la règle; dinamiques de l'action organiseé. Paris: Éditions du Seuil.

Gewirtz, S. (2002). The managerial school. Post-welfarism and social justice in Education. London: Routledge.

Lipsky, M. (1980). Street level bureaucrats: Dilemmas of the individual in public services. New York: Russel Sage.

OECD (2008). OECD FactBook 2008: Economic, environmental and social statistics.

Pina, A. (2007). The press and the mediatizing of educational policies. Sísifo. *Educational Sciences Journal,* 04, pp. 101-110.

Pires, C. (2007). The construction of meaning in educational policy: The full time school case. Sísifo. *Educational Sciences Journal,* 04, pp. 75-84.

Portugal, INE (2007a). Anuário Estatístico de Portugal, 2006. Lisboa: Instituto Nacional de Estatística

Portugal, INE (2007b). Indicadores Sociais 2006. Lisboa: Instituto Nacional de Estatística.

Portugal, Ministério da Educação, GEPE (2007). Séries Cronológicas, Alunos (1977-2006), Volumes I and II . Lisboa: GEPE-ME.

Portugal, Ministério da Educação, GEPE (2008). Estatísticas da Educação 06/07. Lisboa: GEPE-ME.

Ribeiro, J. C. (2007). The construction of the role of school head in the local regulation of educational public policies. Sísifo, *Educational Sciences Journal,* 04, pp. 57-64.

Rufino, C. (2007). Internal assessment of schools and circulation of public policies in a European educational space. Sísifo, *Educational Sciences Journal,* 04, pp. 29-38.

Simões, G. (2007). Self-assessment of schools and regulation of public action in education. Sísifo, *Educational Sciences Journal,* 04, pp. 39-46.

## LEGISLATION

Decree-Law nr. 769-A/76 dated October the 23rd – Democratic Management Regime;

Decree-Law nr. 43/89 dated February the 13th – Defines the concept and establishes broad guidelines for school autonomy;

Law nr. 46/86 dated October the 14th, which approves the Educational System Basis and establishes the General Board of the Educational System;

Decree-Law nr. 172/91 dated May the 10th – New regime of Administration and Management of educational establishments;

Decree-Law nr. 115-A/98, dated May the 4th. Approves the structure of autonomy, administration and management of pre-primary school, primary and secondary education state buildings, as well as related groupings;

Decree-Law nr. 355-A/98 dated November the 13th. Approves the rules governing the exercise of duties of the President of the Executive Council or director and vice-president of the same council, or assistant to the director of the administrative and management body of pre-primary, primary and secondary education state buildings, as well as related groupings;

Implementing Law nr. 10/99 dated July the 21st. Legalizes an autonomous framework, administration and management applicable to pre-primary education buildings and those of primary and secondary education approved by Decree-Law nr. 115-A/98, dated May the 4th, establishing the structures of educational guidelines as well as the co-ordination framework of those same structures;

Law nr. 24/99 dated April the 22nd. Proceeds to the first amendment, due to parliamentary approval of Decree-Law nr. 115-A/98, dated May the 4th which approved the autonomy, administration and management running of state buildings of pre-primary, primary and secondary education as well as related groupings;

Law nr. 159/99 dated September the 14th. Shows the creation of local education councils as a competent part of the municipal bodies;

Implementing Law nr. 12/2000 dated August the 29th. Establishes the necessary requirements for grouping buildings of pre-primary education and primary education, as well as the procedures relating to its creation and operation;

Decree-Law nr. 7/2003 dated January the 15th. Rules municipal councils of education and approves the process of elaboration of an education charter, transferring competences to local authorities;

Law nr. 49/2005 dated August the 30th. Proceeds to the second amendment to the Education Act;

Decree-Law nr. 213/2006 dated October the 27th. Approves New Structure of the Ministry of Education;

Decree-Law nr. 15/2007 dated January the 19th . Approves major changes to the teachers' career statutes, creating two separate categories (senior and junior), an exam to enter the profession and a set of performance appraisal requirements needed to gain seniority;

Regulatory Decree nr. 2/2008 dated January the 10th. Sets the norms to implement the teacher performance appraisal framework.

Regulatory Decree nr. 3/2008 dated January 21st. Sets the norms to implement the entry exam into the teaching profession.

Decree-Law nr. 75/2008 dated April 22nd. Approves a new regime for the management of public schools, reinforcing parent and community participation, and creating the role of principal ("director") to run the school, instead of the previous collegial "executive committee."

In: Centralization and School Empowerment...
Editor: Adam Nir

ISBN 978-1-60692-730-4
© 2009 Nova Science Publishers, Inc.

*Chapter 10*

# DECENTRALIZATION IN THE SPANISH EDUCATIONAL SYSTEM

## *Paulino Murillo Estepa and Carlos Marcelo García*
University of Sevilla, Spain

## THE CONTEXT: POLITICAL, ECONOMIC AND SOCIAL CIRCUMSTANCES IN SPAIN

Concern for the future of education, and for its present, involves considerable reflection, and gives a glimpse of different aspects (social, political, economic and educational), letting us know what we are faced with, where we are, and what we can do.

Today's vast amount of information (and the knowledge it generates), and the processes of technological re-conversion, demand another way to educate. Together with skills, the learning of values, procedures, codes and methods, and the development of attitudes and behavior favoring the education of citizens who are critical, caring and creative, must, more than ever, be foremost.

It also has to be taken into account that, as an effect of globalization and of the internationalization of education and training, individuals are no longer educated and trained to work exclusively in their own country. They can do so anywhere in the world, so governments must give greater attention to creating the conditions necessary to improve the quality of education at all levels, particularly with regard to its adaptation to the work environment. We are witnessing a series of changes in organizations, making them less hierarchical and centralized, reinforcing the necessary participation. Nevertheless, on both an institutional and local (and even worldwide) scale, inequalities are increasing.

The reform of the Spanish educational system in 1990 (LOGSE), which we will refer to later, recognizes this reality and perceives education as the best tool for progress in the struggle against discrimination and inequality. The steady integration of Spanish society into the European Community, particularly following the Constitution of 1978, partly explained the profound reform produced by the LOGSE, seeking not only that the Spanish educational system was adapted to the changes taking place, but that it would also be prepared for those who might come, based on an "improved structure, with better qualitative tools and a concept of greater participation and adaptation to its surroundings."

If we recognize that knowledge is the most important variable in explaining the new forms of social and economic organization, the basic resource for society and people is information, knowledge itself, and the ability to produce and process it.

In the 21st century, the school is at the core of any new proposal. Often, new functions are attributed (without reconsidering others), new messages assigned, and teaching in new subject areas is required – that is, new demands are made, the product of problems that society cannot resolve. Such demands are rarely accompanied by the granting of the means necessary for an adequate response. Despite this, in the future, the school will continue to be the most important tool society has to ensure a solid common foundation of values and skills, and to avoid the obstacles that will continue to crop up. It is no longer enough to say that the school continues to be dominated by an old-fashioned way of thinking, a traditional culture and out-of-date working methods. A way forward must be found. But the school, which is partly liable, is not responsible on its own – today's educational problems must be solved by cooperation between society and the school.

And in Spanish society, increasingly shaped as a society of knowledge, the different educational reforms have recognized the need for education to share with other social bodies the transmission of information and knowledge, and its capacity to position them critically.

The successive educational reforms in Spain from 1990 emphasized the advisability of a broad mission to ensure having sufficient means required to put them into practice — a political and social undertaking to be reflected in an economic report accompanying the regulation, and manifested in successive budgetary measures. But this has not always been the case, and ambitious changes in education, whose success depends on considerable spending, are not always sufficiently financed.

Educational policy has to take into account that public education is an institutional task, carried out by teams of professionals organized in schools, not by conglomerates or aggregates of individual teachers. It will be possible to improve the quality of education when the schools are strengthened as institutions with vision and initiative. They must be allotted attributions, capacities and the possibility of access to resources and support, depending on their own goals and projects. In exchange, schools must make defined commitments with their communities, and assume the responsibility of the processes they carry out, and their results. To complement this, a system has to be developed of national and autonomous attention to educational quality that is effective and reliable and yields information without any leeway for suspicion – and the considerable increase in the school population in recent times has not impacted on the levels of quality offered (Penalva, 2007).

Spain, despite traditionally having been centralized, is, according to Puelles (1993), a clear model of intermediate decentralization – it presents a considerable (though not total) administrative decentralization and a significant political decentralization. Nevertheless, this same author suggests there is a continuing temptation to centralize by both the central and autonomous governments, reproducing in their respective spheres the centralized models of state administration. The meager offer of participation to their own territorial communities – localism – at provincial, municipal level is one of the most important problems for education decentralization in Spain during recent years. Although educational decentralization has revolved around autonomous responsibility, some voices call attention to the increased educational control by certain regional authorities (Bolívar, 2004), which could mean that such localism falls victim to an arbitrary use of power.

## CURRENT STRUCTURE OF THE SPANISH EDUCATIONAL SYSTEM

The Spanish educational system is structured in stages, tracks, grades, academic years, and levels of teaching, ensuring the transition between and within them.

The teaching offered is shown in Figure 1, although we specify the most noteworthy characterization, arrangement and aims of only some.

*Pre-school education* is an educational stage with its own identity that serves girls and boys from birth to six years old. It is noncompulsory, and is arranged in two tracks. The first takes in those up to three years old, and the second from three to six. This stage is undertaken by suitably qualified teachers; its aim is to contribute to the physical, emotional, social and intellectual development of the children.

- Early education
- Basic education
- Primary education
    - Compulsory secondary education
- Post-compulsory secondary education
    - Higher secondary education
    - Intermediate professional training
    - Intermediate professional teaching in plastic arts and design
    - Intermediate physical education
- Higher education
- Higher professional training
    - Higher arts teaching
    - Higher professional teaching in plastic arts and design
    - Higher physical education
    - University education
- Language teaching
- Adult education

Figure 1. The Spanish educational system.

*Primary education* is compulsory and free. It comprises six academic years, from six to 12 years of age, organized in three tracks, of two years each, in areas with a global and integrationist nature. According to the Resolution 1513/2006, of 7 December, which sets out the teaching bases for primary education, its aim is to give all pupils an education that enables them to secure their personal and emotional development and welfare, acquire basic cultural abilities in oral expression and comprehension, in reading, in writing and in mathematics, and develop social abilities, habits of work and study, artistic sense and creativity. Section 4 of article 14 of the Resolution emphasizes that schools, in exercising their independence, may adopt experimentation, work plans, forms of organization, or extend the school timetable as determined by the educational authorities, but not, under any circumstance, call for contributions from the families or impose demands on the educational authorities.

Secondary education comprises the stages of compulsory secondary education, higher secondary education, and intermediate professional training.

Compulsory secondary education (ESO) is a compulsory, free educational stage that completes basic education. It is organized in accord with the principles of common education and with regard to the diversity of the students. It gives special attention to educational and professional guidance, its main aim being that all students acquire basic cultural elements, especially with regard to the humanities, art, science and technology.

Those who complete ESO, achieving a basic competence and the aims of the stage, get a certificate of graduate in compulsory secondary education, allowing them to go onto higher secondary education, intermediate professional training, intermediate professional teaching in plastic arts and design, intermediate physical education, or into the world of work.

Higher secondary education is the final stage of secondary education; it is voluntary and lasts two academic years, normally between 16 and 18 years of age. It has various categories (the arts, sciences, health, human and social sciences, and technology), giving specialized training to students (who have a choice of different paths within each category) for their incorporation into higher studies or into work activities. Its most important aim is to offer general training towards greater intellectual and personal maturity, and greater capacity to acquire a broad range of skills and abilities that will prepare the students for later studies, both university and professional training.

To obtain the certificate of high school matriculation, a positive evaluation is required in all the subjects of the category taken. The matriculation certificate opens the door to higher professional training and to university studies. In the latter case, it is necessary to pass an entry test, which, together with the grades achieved in higher secondary education, objectively evaluates the student's academic maturity and acquired knowledge. At the same time, it enables students to go on to higher levels and studies in the arts, after having passed the corresponding test.

Professional training within the educational system prepares a student to enter the various professions. Its aim is to train the students for activity in a professional field, providing diversified training enabling them to adapt to the changes in work that might take place throughout their lives.

Students who complete intermediate and higher specific professional training obtain specialist or higher specialist certification, respectively. The former gives access to higher secondary education, while the latter gives direct access, without the need for further testing, to a particular university course related to the professional studies undertaken, as set out in the relevant regulations.

With regard to the distribution of schools, teaching staff, and students in the various educational categories considered, the Data and Figures Report (*Datos y Cifras*) of the Spanish National Ministry of Education and Science for the academic year 2007-2008 gives a total of 23,678 schools of non-university general teaching, 2,052 special schools, and 74 universities, as follows:

**Table 1. Distribution of schools in the Spanish educational system**

|  | Total | Public teaching | Mixed and private teaching |
|---|---|---|---|
| Non-university general schools | 23,678 | 16,725 | 6,953 |
| Pre-school institutions | 4,745 | 2,291 | 2,454 |
| Pre-school and primary schools | 10,085 | 9,608 | 477 |
| Pre-school, primary, and compulsory secondary schools | 2,343 | 737 | 1,606 |
| Compulsory secondary schools /Higher secondary /Professional training schools | 4,675 | 3,843 | 832 |
| Others | 1,830 | 246 | 1,584 |
| Special schools (Schools of Art, Higher Plastic Arts and Design, Centers of Dance, Schools of Music and Dance, ...) | 2,052 | 1,277 | 775 |
| University | 74 | 50 | 24 |

Source: Spanish National Ministry of Education and Science, 2008

With regard to teaching staff, the figures for the academic year 2006/2007, and estimates for 2007/2008 are the following:

**Table 2. Teaching staff in the Spanish educational system**

|  | Year 2006/2007 | Estimates 2007/08 |
|---|---|---|
| Non-university teaching staff | 607,540 | 623,974 |
| Staff in public teaching | 43,470 | 455,130 |
| Primary teachers | 244,770 | 251,161 |
| Secondary teachers | 175,987 | 180,901 |
| Technical teachers in Professional training | 22,713 | 23,068 |
| Teaching staff in Mixed and Private | 164,070 | 168,84 |
| University teachers | 104,840 | 107,905 |

Source: Spanish National Ministry of Education and Science, 2008

With regard to students, the data for the academic year 2007/2008 are the following:

**Table 3: Student numbers in the Spanish educational system**

|  | Total | Public teaching | Mixed and private teaching |
|---|---|---|---|
| Total | 8,587,639 | 6,109,519 (67.6%) | 2,478,120 (32.4%) |
| Non-university education | 7,205,890 | 4,870,090 | 2,335,800 |
| Pre-school education | 1,620,515 | 1,041,426 | 579,089 |
| Primary education | 2,603,175 | 1,752,099 | 851,076 |
| Special education | 29,555 | 16,005 | 13,550 |
| Compulsory secondary education | 1,826,825 | 1,216,909 | 609,916 |
| High school education | 625,275 | 465,414 | 159,861 |

Table 3: (Continued)

|                       | Total     | Public teaching | Mixed and private teaching |
|-----------------------|-----------|-----------------|----------------------------|
| Professional training | 500,545   | 378,237         | 122,308                    |
| University education  | 1,381,749 | 1,239,429       | 142,320                    |

Source: Spanish National Ministry of Education and Science, 2008

There have been important changes in the student population and in the non-university teaching staff between the academic years 1997/98 and 2007/08: while the former decreased by some 4%, the latter increased by 24.2%. This resulted in a considerable reduction in the mean number of students per unit in pre-school education, primary education, and compulsory secondary education, which stabilized at somewhat fewer than 20 students per unit in pre-school education, around 21 in primary education, and fewer than 25 in compulsory secondary education.

Total public spending on education in Spain (excluding budgetary components, for a closer approach to the international indicators: OECD, EUROSTAT and UNESCO) in 2007 was 45,149.6 million euros, 4.32% of the GNP.

## TYPES OF SCHOOLS

The Education Statute 2/2006 of 3 May, in its Section IV, deals with the schools: their type, their legal situation, and the programming of the network of schools from the standpoint of education as a public service.

The schools are classified as private, private/mixed and public. Private schools are those pertaining to a "private" individual or body. Private/mixed schools are those adopting a mixed regime as legally framed, and public schools are those run by a public authority.

Given the level of decentralization in Spain, it is the different educational authorities that are responsible to guarantee the universal right to education, and the individual rights of students and families.

The private schools that offer free teaching and meet the needs of schooling can adopt the "mixed" regime under legally established terms, it being the responsibility of the autonomous communities to regulate their setting up, establishing reciprocal rights and obligations with regard to the financial management, duration, extension, and cancellation, the number of school units agreed, and other conditions. These are the private mixed schools.

## LAWS AND REGULATIONS PROMOTING DECENTRALIZATION

The Spanish education reform of 1990 (LOGSE) opted for decentralization as a guarantee to adapt the official programs to the nature of each social context, although this process of decentralization began with the enactment of the Spanish Constitution of 1978, which led to the creation of the Autonomies and to the division of responsibilities between them and the state with regard to education.

This process of decentralization was carried out in two stages, depending on the way autonomy was granted: first, responsibility for education was transferred to the so-called "fast track" autonomous communities (article 151 of the Constitution), and afterwards education was transferred to the "slow track" autonomous communities (article 143).

Responsibility for education was transferred in two blocks: non-university teaching and university education. In the case of the "fast-track" autonomous communities, non-university teaching was transferred first (between 1980 and 1983) to Catalonia, the Basque Country, Andalusia, Galicia, the Canaries, and the Valencian Community. In 1990 it was transferred to Navarre. The transfer of university education was not begun until 1985.

In contrast, the "slow-track" autonomous communities first attained responsibility for university education between 1995 and 1997, and non-university teaching later, between 1997 and 2000. Nevertheless, as a common denominator in the whole process of education decentralization to the autonomous communities, responsibility of the local bodies remained significantly reduced (Pérez and Morales, 2006).

The Spanish Education Reform of 1990 created numerous transformations necessary for the modernization of the country's educational system, according to Marchesi (2001). Of note were the changes in structure of education — as a result of compulsory education being extended to 16 years of age — and the greater independence of schools to prepare and develop their own projects, with more responsibility for the educational community.

We have to be careful when evaluating the decentralization promoted by the different reforms, because, as Touriñan (2000) warns, centralism should not be identified with "poor" education and decentralization with "good" education. The essential thing is that each system of education opts for the principle of equity, and that decentralization brings to life a model of reform guaranteeing this principle and avoiding social exclusion of the less advantaged, an aspect not always attained. Although international bodies such as the World Bank or the United Nations have for some time recommended policies of decentralization, these have conformed more to political strategies than to essentially technical decisions.

In the Spanish model of reform, the state is responsible for the basic elements of the curriculum. They are put into effect and developed initially by the autonomous communities, and subsequently by the schools. The Ministry of Education and Science determines the basic structure of the various educational stages and the corresponding certifications. Thus, although the Spanish reforms, as we have said, promote educational decentralization, the state retains the responsibility for determining the standard basic curriculum, the general structure of the educational system's arrangement, and the criteria for obtaining certification.

## THE TEACHERS AND THEIR PROFESSIONAL DEVELOPMENT

In order to understand the Spanish educational system from the centralization vs. decentralization standpoint, it is necessary to look at the teachers, their initial training, professional entry, working conditions, and professional development. The Education Statute (2006) emphasizes that the functions of teachers in Spain are programming and teaching, evaluation of the learning process, tutoring and guidance of the students, attention to intellectual, emotional, physical, and social development of the students, coordination of teaching activities, information to families, participation in the activities of the school, participation in plans of evaluation, together with research, experimental programs, and ongoing improvement.

Consistent with the organizational structure of the Spanish educational system that we have set out, the educational authority distinguishes among different types of teacher: early education, primary education, compulsory secondary education and higher secondary education, professional training, arts teaching, language teaching, physical education, and adult education.

In Spain there have been and continue to be two parallel systems of initial teacher training. One is directed at teachers of early and primary education, while there is a different one for the teachers of compulsory secondary education, higher secondary education and professional training. The initial training of teachers of early and primary education is the responsibility of the universities, and is carried out in the Faculties of Education Science, with a specific and professional curriculum depending on the skills to be acquired. This training used to last three years, but the reform required by the European Space of Higher Education has extended it to four years.

No single institution offers complete training for teachers of compulsory secondary education, higher secondary education, and professional training. There is a model of successive training by which candidates for teaching in secondary education must first attend university (five years), following the same course as any other professional (chemist, philologist, historian, etc.). Having graduated, those who wish to enter the teaching profession must follow a six-month course of psycho-pedagogical training. With the reform obliged by adaptation to the European Space of Higher Education, this course will be considered a Master of two years.

In Spain, as noted above, there are three types of schools: private, private/ mixed, and public. The entry into teaching of teachers in these schools depends on their category. In the case of private schools, which are maintained wholly by the fees paid by the parents, teachers are selected and paid by the school itself. In the case of the private/mixed schools, teachers are selected by the owner of the school, but the salary is paid by the state (the percentage of teachers in private and mixed schools in Spain is 27%). In the case of teachers of public schools, entry is by public examination ("*concurso-oposición*"). To enter the teaching profession in public schools, the candidate must pass an exam consisting of several tests. If successful, he or she can become a civil servant. Thus, in Spain, teachers in public schools (some 73%) are civil servants. They have tenure without being subjected again to any other competition. In contrast to the private and mixed schools, in which the administration of the schools selects the staff, in public schools there is no such capacity to select teachers. So how is the teaching staff organized? Each year there is an internal competition among the permanent teachers who, depending primarily on their years of teaching seniority, seek to form part of the staff of a particular school. This is a critical aspect of the independence of the schools in Spain, as, with extremely rare exceptions, the school community has no capacity to select teachers — the selection is imposed by the educational authority.

With regard to the working conditions of the teachers, in the early and primary school, the teachers must undertake 30 compulsory hours in the school – 25 in the classroom and 5 for complementary activities. They complete the 35 hours with other teaching activities and professional improvement, which may be outside the school. In the case of secondary education, the time the teachers must remain within the particular school is also 30 hours – 18 in the classroom, and the rest for complementary activities and training.

The student/teacher ratio is approximately 22 students per teacher in primary teaching, while in secondary it increases to an average of 25. Salaries, in the case of primary education, are 4.7% higher than the average in OECD countries, and for secondary education, 8.8% higher, according to an OECD report (2006).

The professional development of teachers in Spain has, since 1984, been organized by institutions designated Teachers' Centers (CEP). These institutions are run under the auspices of the educational authority, but are relatively independent regarding functioning and organization. The Teachers' Centers have a decentralized structure, with several in each province (depending on its area). They have a staff of advisors who carry out training tasks under different training models. The advisors are teachers who have participated in innovative educational projects and who leave teaching temporarily to become involved in the training. The universities do not take part formally in this training, which is managed by the teachers themselves.

One of the characteristics of professional teaching development in Spain is the variety of categories of training. Thus, together with the training courses, there is a growing variety of training related to innovative projects, work groups, training projects centered on the school, projects of school improvement, etc. In this category of professional development, it is the schools themselves and their teachers that decide on the topics of training or innovation, and that organize and participate in the projects, with the support of the advisors of the Teachers' Centers. As a result, the professional development of teachers in Spain is an attempt to approach teachers' needs, giving priority to initiatives that go beyond concrete activities in training courses, to seek training better connected to school improvement and innovation.

## INITIATIVES OF RESTRUCTURING AIMED AT THE INDEPENDENCE OF THE SCHOOLS: MOST IMPORTANT EFFECTS AND AREAS OF IMPACT

Before examining in greater detail the current Law of Education in Spain (LOE), we will briefly describe the most important laws of recent years, and their most significant effects.

After the Spanish Constitution (29/12/1978), and before the repeal of the General Law of Education of 1970 by the LOGSE (1990), the Spanish state recognized the right to education and to the participation of society in the educational system. The Statute 8/1985 of 3 July, on the right to education (LODE), had as its basic purpose the integrated development of the principles relating to education in the Constitution, and which guarantee, at the same time, educational pluralism and equity.

Five years later, the General Statute 1/1990 of 3 October, on the educational system (LOGSE), established a decentralized system of teaching in Spain, allowing the autonomous communities to manage their schools and to develop a substantial part of the curricular content. It extended compulsory education to 16 years, and structured higher secondary education as two academic years and four categories. It also incorporated arts teaching into the general system, and enabled the school councils in the schools to elect their principal. The faculty, as a professional body, lost some of its earlier responsibility. The lack of any provision of funding for development and the automatic promotion of students at certain stages are some of the most controversial points of the law.

The Statute 9/1995 of 20 November (LOPEG) reaffirmed the right to education for all, without discrimination, and consolidated the independence of the schools and the responsible participation of the various parts of the education community. It established an organizational framework for achieving the reform and improving the quality of teaching aimed at in the LOGSE.

Section I dealt with participation in governing the center, among other topics. At the same time, it regulated the independence of its management, the drawing up and publication of its education project, and independence in the managing of resources. Section II regulated the governing bodies of public teaching centers, establishing the procedure for the election of principals and setting out means of support for their operation.

Thus, we find ourselves with a law that established and secured basic responsibilities, and at that time instigated those of the autonomous communities with responsibilities in education. It gave them and the Minister of Education and Sciences both controls and responsibilities – not only in aspects related with improving the quality of teaching, but also in the statutory regulation and organization of school life. This law is a further encouragement to the participation and independence of the different sectors of the education community in school life.

The Statute 10/2002 of 23 December, on quality in education (LOCE), while recognizing the important role of the earlier reforms, clarified significant areas of deficiency that justified the enactment of new regulations. The law was structured around five central topics: a) the culture of effort and of personal endeavor as basic conditions in improving the quality of the educational system; b) a more open orientation of the educational system towards results; c) a significant reinforcement of opportunities of quality education for all; d) policies aimed at the teachers; and e) development of the independence of the school based on mutual trust and on shared responsibility between them and the authority.

However, this law remained virtually unapplied because of a change of government in Spain. A Resolution passed by the Council of Ministers on 28 May 2004 paralyzed the timetable. On 24 May 2006, it was repealed by the Statute 2/2006 of 3 May.

## THE EDUCATION STATUTE 2/2006 OF 3 MAY

The Education Statute 2/2006 of 3 May (LOE) was an attempt to simplify the laws relating to non-university education. It repealed the most significant laws from the first stage of the Socialist government — LOGSE and LOPEG — and the law representing the stage of the government of the Popular Party — the LOCE. It keeps in force the backbone of the LODE and the Statute 5/2002, of 19 June, on qualifications and professional training (LOCFP).

The regulatory development of the LOE in the state and regions, and the education laws that each region can draw up, are shaping a new legal framework based on the greatest possible consensus towards the stability of the needs of the educational system.

Of note among the educational principles on which the LOE is built is the relationship it establishes between equity and quality without giving up educational excellence, while reinforcing attention to diversity, equality of opportunity, and educational compensation of inequalities. It values both individual and shared effort, highlighting the importance of the coordinated labor of families, teachers, authorities, and other educational and social agents. No less significant are the independence of the public schools, the cooperation among authorities — with modest proposals for involving the local governments — and the concept of continuous education and that of adults as a life-long process. Lastly, the provision of funding in the law enables the new regulations to be applied under optimal conditions.

With regard to the topic under review, the LOE (actual Educational Law) considers the participation, independence and administration of the schools. Chapter I of the Law refers to participation of teachers and parents in the functioning and the administration of the schools. It is recognized that the schools will be independent regarding teaching, organization and management. This guarantees the independence sufficient for each school to be able to draw up, approve and carry out both its education project and management. The same applies to its rules of organization and functioning. In exercising their independence, the school can adopt experimental projects, work plans and forms of organization, or extend the school timetable under the terms established by the educational authorities, but not, under any circumstances, make demands for these or for contributions from the families.

We have to refer to the professional bodies of government and of coordination of teaching in the public schools. The school council is made up of representatives from all sectors of the education community, including the local authority. Among its responsibilities are the approval and evaluation of the annual general programming of the schools. It takes part in the selection of the principal and is active in deciding on the admission of students.

The principal is selected by competition among the tenured teachers of the school. It is a process in which the education community and the educational authority take part, and it meets the principles of equality, publicity, transparency, merit and ability. The rest of the management team (secretary and head of studies) is nominated by the principal from among the tenured teachers of the school and proposed to the educational authority after informing the faculty and the school council.

## THE EDUCATION INSPECTORATE AND ITS ROLE IN THE SYSTEM

According to Mayorga (1999), professional education inspection started in Spain in the mid-19th century (although there were antecedents from 1370), linked to primary, compulsory and free education. That author claimed that the professionalism and independence of its professionals has been, and must continue to be, what sustains the whole performance of the functions entrusted, which, according to some authors, has neither changed much nor will change in the future (González, 1999). Among these functions, control, assessment, and evaluation are always a common denominator. However, the essential thing, according to González (1999), is not so much the nature of the functions that the education inspectorate has to carry out, but the way and the context in which they are exercised.

Today, the inspection of the educational system in Spain is regulated by Section VII of the LOE, as a responsibility of the public authority. The inspecting function has to be carried out on all the elements and aspects of the educational system, and must guarantee the rights and obligations of all those taking part in the processes of teaching and learning. Distinction is made between the education inspectorate, which is the responsibility of each territorial community, and the Chief Inspectorate, the responsibility of the state.

Among the functions of the education inspectorate specified in article 151 of the LOE is supervision and control, from the pedagogic and organizational standpoint, of the functioning.

of the schools and the programs they affect. It is also responsible for the supervision of teaching practice and the management function, together with participation in the evaluation of the educational system and of the elements of which it is comprised.

It might be said that the functions of guidance and control entrusted to the education inspectorate materialize just when there is a change as a consequence of the new didactic and organizational approaches resulting from the process of decentralization. And real independence for the schools requires sufficient resources, along with equality and equity in their distribution. The inspectorate has to be scrupulous in carrying out this role of regulator and rectifier of inequalities.

Education inspection is carried out by the educational authorities via civil servants of the Education Inspectorate. These civil servants enter through public examination, open to professionals of the bodies concerned with public teaching who are appropriately qualified (PhD, graduate, or the equivalent) and with a minimum six years of tenure and teaching experience of the same length. The structure and functioning of the bodies responsible for conducting educational inspection in the respective territorial areas are regulated by the educational authorities.

The Chief Inspectorate is the responsibility of the state. It was created to guarantee the fulfillment of the powers related to the teaching matter and the observance of the constitutional principles and norms, and other basic norms described in article 27 of the Constitution. One of its most important functions is to check the completion of the requirements established by the state in the general arrangement of the educational system with regard to categories, stages, tracks and specialties of teaching, and the number of academic years in each case. It is also responsible for checking the inclusion of the basic aspects of the curriculum within the respective curricula, and that these are studied in accord with the corresponding state regulation. It also has responsibilities to check the fulfillment of the conditions for obtaining qualifications and of academic or professional effects.

The civil servants of the Chief Inspectorate wield the power of public authority. Its organization and staff are regulated by the national government, on which it depends in consultation with the autonomous communities as to its activities.

## PARTICIPATION OF THE EDUCATION COMMUNITY

By participation we mean a strategy of intervention in the school based on the improvement of the decisions taken and on the satisfaction of the staff involved; the staff, on being able to express its opinions, will have an increased commitment to the organization. However, caution is required in developing these strategies, as some of them, even when aimed at encouraging participation, can become mechanisms of exclusion (Sánchez Blanco, 1998). Participation — it is well understood — will contribute to the development of responsibility and of the capacity for dialogue, and to fostering an attitude of listening and of the processes of planning, evaluation, learning and teamwork.

In 1985, the Statute on the right to education was passed as an attempt to respond to the problem of school participation, among other reasons. It regulated the rights and obligations of all members of the education community. Ten years later, the LOPEG revisited and reinforced the importance of participation of the education community in the schools, and in the definition of their educational projects. Currently, the LOE, in its Section V, conceives and establishes participation as a basic value in the education of citizens who are independent, free, responsible and committed; hence, it is the responsibility of the educational authorities to guarantee the participation of the education community in the organization, administration, functioning and evaluation of the school. Particular attention is given — as we have seen — to the independence of the school, both in pedagogic matters, via the drawing up of their educational projects, and in the financial management of the resources and the fixing of their norms of organization and functioning.

With these assumptions, we can pose the following questions: Is there participation, in the broad sense of the term, of the components of the education community in the schools? Is there real and constructive participation, or is it relegated to formal and bureaucratic processes? Is the desired type of participation viable in today's reality? Would the reworking of certain forms of participation be appropriate? As suggested by Sánchez Blanco (1998: p. 12), "it is important not only to ask the families to participate, but also to develop in the school the most varied situations regarding such participation (...) without converting this participation into one more mechanism of exclusion or self-exclusion." This must be one of the great and continuous challenges: to attempt to generate ideal conditions contributing to the fostering of various situations that help to activate the process of participation in the school — understanding that decisions are richer when there are different points of view in the mix.

An analysis of the functioning of governing bodies of schools, initially created to encourage participation, shows that, after so many years in existence, none of the sectors involved has demonstrated particular enthusiasm for participation, resulting in a significant lack of commitment.

For a considerable time, the management function, despite the new conditions introduced by the LOPEG (early accreditation, prospects of professional development of the management of the schools, increased financial complements, etc.), which in theory contribute to changing the situation, continued to be affected by the limited motivation of teachers to participate. The lack of candidates for principals was such that the educational authorities had to designate an extraordinarily high percentage of them. To avoid this situation, the management function is today recognized in article 139 of the LOE, not only with the provision of a greater financial incentive, but making it possible to consolidate part of it, besides the opportunity of obtaining other personal and professional recognition.

With regard to the school councils as professional bodies with participation and representation from each and every stratum of the education community, their actual functioning also has to be considered. A burden of purely administrative and bureaucratic activities results in the apathy of the teachers, the indifference of the students, and – in the words of Santos Guerra (1999) – the non-participation of the families in fundamental aspects. The educational authority, concerned by low levels of participation, makes use of publicity campaigns to encourage families to participate in elections for school councils.

The creation of a culture of participation in the school has to be through increasing the involvement of families, improving the channels of communication, coordination and information, and offering real opportunities of access to fundamental questions that exceed the bounds of appearance and the superficial. However, we cannot disregard the fact that three sectors (families, students and teachers) come together in the schools, with different basic interests that may be an obstacle to understanding, but whose integration is equally important.

Thus, the search for alternatives aimed at strengthening active and systematic participation in every education community is a significant challenge in the current period of changes in which we live. It means that families, students and teachers are involved more actively in the life of the school, a policy of groups and teamwork is launched, and a management style is developed that encourages others to take part by considering the suggestions they might make, all within the current legal framework.

## ASPECTS HELPING OR HINDERING THE INDEPENDENCE OF THE SCHOOLS

To analyze the different aspects that can positively or negatively affect the independence of the schools in Spain we will focus on the levels at which, in our view, the institutional analysis operates — that is, the level of the organization itself, in all that is determined externally or internally and is specified in the formal structure: laws, regulations, building, resources, etc. We also have to focus on the processes taking place daily in the schools, and in the social system, with its structures of relationship and shared significance. All this, we believe, can have a great effect on the independence and mechanisms of participation in the school.

## THE STRUCTURE

Any organizational action takes place within the framework of a structure that establishes regulations and procedures, assigns roles to the subjects, flags aims, defines tasks, fixes lines of authority, controls and evaluates. The structure represents the more static aspects of an organization, and refers to a stable system that enables relating the different elements of a reality.

The formal structure of the educational organizations is a pattern of conduct common to all the schools of a country, region or province that does not exhaust the explanation of what happens within each one. Nonetheless, understanding it and using it properly is a condition for the good functioning of the educational institutions.

We can therefore say that the structure is the set of connected elements from which are executed the rules, regulations or procedures making an organization work. The structure implies assigning a series of specific tasks to individuals, roles or groups of the organization, and the coordination of such tasks with regard to broader goals. This means that the independence of the school can be facilitated, or not, by their structure, and by that of the educational system, given that the regulations and laws constitute an essential part of the latter. As we remarked at the beginning of this chapter, the reality of Spanish education is a clear example of a model of intermediate decentralization, and although the existence of statutes such as the LOE allows decentralization where the various autonomous communities can formulate their own regulations, including laws, it is true that in some cases there is a certain temptation to centralize, not offering real participation to smaller communities and increasing the control from national and/or autonomous bodies. We can thus come up against the paradox that at the same time that decentralization is promoted by specific regulations, it is inhibited by the control exercised by intermediate communities.

The proportions and nature of a school's structure, therefore, will be an important factor in determining its independence, especially the differentiation between its components (functions, posts, specializations, etc.) and the degree to which is laid down how and when the tasks should be performed and who should perform them. The analysis of the structure of an organization involves a quantitative study of its members, but also a study of the distribution and sharing out of tasks and functions, the areas and departments in which they are grouped, and the legal framework regulating the activity of the components that, depending on the interpretation made, can result in a greater or lesser degree of independence.

## THE INSTITUTIONAL PROCESSES

The institutional processes of the school have an organizational component and, at the same time, a social one, so that the combination of the two will be essential to the life of the school. These not only apply regulations, but also alter structures and patterns of relationship, establishing new values and systems of belief. Moreover, social conflicts and dynamics, examined in the next section, will flourish precisely in the development of the institutional processes, that are thereby converted into a field where the institutional identity is subjected to review, and in which new formulas are tried and new modes of behavior that the institution adopts to confront the disturbances are produced.

To speak of institutional processes is to speak of processes of coordination, planning, innovation and assessment, but also of other processes natural in the day-to-day life of any school, such as its management or the processes of evaluation carried out in it. Here, once again, although these processes are regulated, it is the interpretation made by the schools that can determine the extent of the development of their independence, and in this — as in so many other things — the management teams and the inspectorate will be important players.

The management teams, as important basic promoters of change in the school, have to understand the internal dynamics of the contexts in which they act, and in which they make others act, and for this they must take as a starting point the institutional identity and the fact of knowing how to interpret the regulations in the light of its interests, always given the leeway of flexibility permitted by the legal framework in force at that moment. Without such understanding and without the disposition to find a middle course, they cannot achieve their role as required in today's society, which is increasingly distant from that of the efficient manager of earlier times.

## SOCIAL DYNAMICS

As we said in the previous section, management activity is carried out in a specific context. However, it is also in a particular social system, shaped by communication among members of the organization and those of the education and social community in general. At the same time, the fact that we can find considerable variability in schools, even when the social structures are the same for all of them, leads us to think that such variability can be created by the social system of each school and by the relationship between it and its environment. The social dynamics of each school are thus formed, on one hand, by its own universe of meaning and, on the other, by a network of relationships. The concepts of culture and power will be equal ingredients in the social dynamics of the schools. The importance this has in the development of the independence of each school is somewhat transcendental. In the face of the enthusiasm for a particular decentralizing norm, how it is interpreted by each school is fundamental: eagerness for the opportunity to increase the level of participation is not the same as the interest of particular social groups for continuing to increase their area of power.

At the same time, the rituals, implicit norms, values, assumptions and beliefs inherent in the cultural content of each school, as a social construction, will direct organizational actions and responses to the difficulties and problems that crop up all the time. In this way, culture, as an area of significance more or less shared among the members of an organization, must also be understood as a structure relatively independent of the predominant social culture – which does not mean that it remains isolated from society.

However, as we also said, communication is based not only on shared symbols and significance, but also on a structure of relationships and on the ability to influence. Authority appears as a social construction that determines the present and the future of events in the life of the schools.

Culture and authority are intimately connected and mutually sustained, and this connection is a determinant in the responses that each school offers to the demands made of it or to the norms imposed on it.


## THE PROSPECT OF SCHOOL IMPROVEMENT


The school of the 21st century will have to change, to fit another shape, and to function in a manner different from earlier times. As Hopkins and Lagerweij (1997) suggest, the proposals of school improvement for educational change have the long-term goal of creating an ideal school that is self-renewing. They also refer to the centralization-decentralization paradox and to the pathology of educational change. They suggest that in most Western countries there are pressures, apparently contradictory, on one hand for centralizing, and on the other for decentralizing. This creates tension, contributing to making it difficult to put into practice changes aimed at altering the quality of teaching.

The International Project for School Improvement (ISIP), sponsored by the OECD, like later studies, has been stressing this proposal for some time, defining school improvement as *"a systematic and continuous effort aimed at changing the conditions of learning and other internal conditions associated in one or more schools with the ultimate aim of achieving educational goals more effectively"* (van Velzen et al., 1985). Therefore, as pointed out by Marcelo (1994), the concept of *school improvement* means a commitment by the members of the education community to undertake constant self-review processes, leading to the establishment of a culture of change that fosters greater integration and relationship between the teachers, and the development of a curriculum adapted to the needs and nature of the students and of the context.

From such assumptions and from the analysis and impact of the different educational reforms taking place in Spain in recent years, we agree with Marchesi (2001) about the initiatives that should be considered concerning the main obstacles and problems that have been generated. The thrust towards the independence of the schools and their teachers, the support for schools with the least-protected students, and inter-institutional cooperation could mean interesting responses that seek quality education for all, rather than conceiving organizational improvement and learning as an ideal situation of some schools that base quality on responsibility or on rigid organizational models.

If we want an education community to take on more responsibility, it has to be granted sufficient independence to be able to draw up its own projects, duly contextualized, and which can actually be put into practice. This does not mean that each school does whatever it wishes. Independence must be negotiated with the educational authorities, which have to establish specific basic norms giving coherence to the activity of the schools.

Teachers perceive little social recognition in the exercise of their profession and the performance of their functions. At the same time, there is a generalized sense that the reforms respond to a type of interest that rarely meets their real professional demands. The same mistrust exists regarding the decentralizing measures resulting from the different norms.

The professionalization of teachers and the participation of other actors in the school are demands commonly expressed in today's Spanish educational policy (although there are those who see them as contradictory) (Ortiz, 2007). But "proclamation" is one thing, and "action" another. Burdules and Densmore (1992a; 1992b) consider that professionalization is in conflict with the aims of democratic public control. They suggest that a too-rigorous admission into the teaching profession only lessens representation of the least-privileged sectors. Other authors take a different view, recognizing that a professional authority does not weaken democratic controls, rather the opposite, so that it should be reinforced in teachers (Snykes, 1992).

What is true is that it is increasingly necessary to introduce more flexible models of professionalization that use teachers' skills and make their leadership possible. Such policy could awaken the interest of the teaching profession and grant it the level of recognition it deserves, in order to attain the required quality and excellence. Equally important is to be able to create in the schools a professional culture that urges teachers' cooperation and involvement in the collective improvement of learning. Lastly, we must remember that schools are not islands. Today, more than ever, it is necessary to extend the forms of participation and cooperation of the different sectors of the education community, but also to incorporate new cooperating agents, such as former students, volunteers or members of non-government organizations, aimed at shaping real learning communities. At the same time, the configuration of networks among schools and teachers must be consolidated, thereby making possible new opportunities for improvement.

It is difficult to imagine schools that can develop their function without significant exchanges with others. In fact, rather than considering the "outside" as a threat, it is necessary to see others as providing room for growth and as sources of learning, interaction, and even sustaining of institutional life. A school that views itself as the only source of resources wastes its energy, demands too much of its members, and runs the risk of frustrating its components.

On such a stage, the construction of networks is a path by which the school and the projects it develops can be sustained, enriched and nurished, integrating all the social voices.

However, building new management models from networks is not a simple task. It has to be asked what new viewpoints and possibilities emerge from this concept, and to what extent are new terms being used to designate something that has in fact always existed.

In the educational sphere, networks mean new ways of organizing the work inside each school, and the type of exchanges made with the community. This necessarily involves the opening up of the school, not only so that the community can access it, but also for the school to include among its activities work with other organizations of the community. This means establishing relationships of intra- and inter-institutional interchange that reinforce the specific task of the school: teaching and learning.

Today, the teaching team and the management of the schools have a considerable degree of control over the management of the institution, over the topics taught, over the linking of certain courses with others, over the evaluation of the students, and over the relationships with their environment. The teaching team gives the work a particular orientation, depending on the principles, procedures and tools used in the management of the school or in the teaching/learning relationships within the classroom, in accord with the criteria set out in the institutional project. A managing or teaching professional usually enjoys more independence in his/her work than do other workers. This relative independence helps to create networks that foster cooperation among education institutions to work together in a common project, to share resources, and to achieve specific aims. Such opportunity must not be allowed to elude us.

## REFERENCES

Bolívar, A. (2004). La autonomía de centros escolares en España: entre declaraciones discursivas y prácticas sobrerreguladas. *Revista de Educación*, 333, 91-116.

Burdules, N., and Densmore, K. (1992a). La perspectiva del profesionalismo: es duro abrirse camino. *Educación y sociedad,* 11, 27–104.

Burdules, N., and Densmore, K. (1992b). Los límites de la profesionalización de la docencia. *Educación y sociedad*, 11, 67–83.

González, T. (1999). Sobre el futuro de la inspección educativa. Consideraciones en el umbral del siglo XXI. *Revista de Educación*, 320, 159-191.

Hopkins, D., and Lagerweij, N. (1997). La base de conocimientos de mejora de la escuela. In D. Reynolds, R. Bollen, B. Creemers and L. Stoll *Las escuelas eficaces. Claves para mejorar la enseñanza*. Madrid: Santillana, pp. 71-101.

Marcelo, C. (1994). *Formación del profesorado para el cambio educativo*. Barcelona: PPU.

Marchesi, A. (2001). Presente y futuro de la Reforma Educativa Española. *Revista Iberoamericana de Educación*, 27, 57-76.

Mayorga, A. (1999). La Inspección en el nivel de la Educación Primaria. Proceso histórico. *Revista de Educación*, 320, 11-38

OECD-CERI (2006). *Education at a glance. OECD Indicators - 2005 edition*. Paris: OECD.

Ortiz, B. (2007). Las demandas de profesionalización docente y de participación de otros actores en la escuela. Revista Iberoamericana de Educación, 43 (7), 1-9.

Penalva, J. (2007). La descentralización educativa: problemas de aplicación. *Revista Iberoamericana de Educación* (Edición Digital), 42/5- 25/04/2007.

Pérez, C., and Morales, S. (2006). La descentralización del gasto público en educación en España. Un análisis por comunidades autónomas. *Provincia*, 15, 11-40.

Puelles, M. de (1993). Estudio teórico sobre las experiencias de descentralización educativa. *Revista Iberoamericana de Educación*, 3, 13-40.

Sánchez Blanco, C. (1998). ¡Animarles a colaborar sí!, pero ¿cómo? Dilemas docentes sobre la participación de las familias en la Educación Infantil. *Kikirikí*, 50, 10-15.

Santos Guerra, M.A. (1999). *El crisol de la participación. Investigación sobre la participación en consejos escolares de centros*. Málaga: Aljibe

Snykes, G. (1992). En defensa del profesionalismo docente como una opción de política educativa. *Educación y sociedad*, 11, pp. 85–96.

Touriñan, J.M. (2000). Globalidad y educación. Nuevas perspectivas para el debate "enseñanza pública-enseñanza privada" en el marco de la society de la información. *Revista de Educación*, 322, 189-210.

van Velzen, W., Miles, M. , Ekholm, M., Hameyer, U., and Robin, D (1985). *Making school improvement work*. Leuven: ACOO.

In: Centralization and School Empowerment...
Editor: Adam Nir

ISBN 978-1-60692-730-4
© 2009 Nova Science Publishers, Inc.

*Chapter 11*

# CENTRALIZATION AND SCHOOL EMPOWERMENT: THEORETICAL ASSUMPTIONS REVISITED

## *Adam E. Nir*

Hebrew University of Jerusalem, Israel

## THE CONTEXT OF PUBLIC SCHOOLING

Public schools, social institutions responsible for the socialization and the preparation of children for life as adults, are protected institutions in the sense that the state ensures their existence and continuity even when their effectiveness and outcomes are questionable. As we gradually move into the 21st century, the context of public schooling in many Western democracies is changing along with some of the values that have traditionally dominated educational policies. Voices calling for pluralism and liberalism are more frequently heard, paving the way for new perspectives emphasizing variance rather than uniformity as a prevalent and desirable feature of public educational services. Competition, which traditionally was left out of the educational arena, is suddenly viewed as beneficial for school effectiveness since it allows educational staff to initiate educational programs in line with the needs of schools' clientele and to develop professionally. According to this trend, schools should no longer be domesticated organizations (Carlson, 1964) that have captive clientele who can be taken for granted regardless of the quality of their outcomes. Rather, schools should operate in quasi-market circumstances (Glennerster, 1991; Le Grand, 1991; Le Grand and Bartlett, 1993; Nir, 2003; Whitty, 1997; Woods, Bagley and Glatter, 1996), implying that they need to compete for children and prove their eligibility as educational institutions.

Under such circumstances, the dependency of schools on clients' expectations and needs is likely to increase. Hence, schools need to promote their attractiveness to parents and children of their local community and to present their educational services in a tempting and appealing manner so as to ensure the enrollment of children.

Regardless of the extent to which competition and pluralism dominate a particular educational context, public schools are currently facing four major challenges they must successfully meet in order to maintain their influence and hegemony as dominant social institutions:

*The flexibility challenge*: Flexibility is the mechanism by which schools adjust their services to the particular needs and expectations of their clientele and promote their attractiveness in the eyes of potential students. Flexibility depends on the degrees of freedom that schools have in order to bridge the gap between the novel and the traditional and between central binding regulations and local circumstances, and their ability to adapt themselves to the changing circumstances (Caldwell and Spinks 1988; Cowley and Williamson, 1998). Thus, flexibility is "the desirable organization of learning opportunities to permit wider participation" (Edwards, Nicoll and Tait, 1999, p. 622).

*The authenticity challenge*: If public schools are to gain a head start relative to other private or public institutions that offer educational services, they need to present a unique and authentic educational voice that will be translated into daily school life and will be considered attractive for specific groups of parents and children. In order to maintain their authenticity, schools need to promote the participation of community members, parents and teachers (Anderson, 1998), and to incorporate their inputs into their educational agenda. In this sense, various public schools should not be more of the same, but rather different and preferably unique educational entities.

*The economic challenge*: Although they are sponsored and administered by the state, the continuity of public schools under competitive circumstances heavily relies on their outcomes and their ability to increase their efficiency. Hence, schools operate under a constant need to prove that their outcomes in terms of the proportion of inputs to outputs are better relative to the performance and outcomes of alternative competing institutions (Bradley, Johnes and Millington, 2001). Moreover, at times of governmental cuts in public funding for education, schools must engage in fundraising, marketing their services and knowledge to compensate for the decreased educational funds provided by the state. These funds may also be used to facilitate new experiences and changes in instructional practices and new curriculum initiatives (Lubienski, 2005) assumed to enable schools to improve their outcomes.

*The relevancy challenge*: Finally, and perhaps most importantly, the major challenge for public schools may be viewed in the need to provide educational services that will be perceived by potential clientele as relevant. Relevancy is crucial to justify the paternalistic coercion which forces individuals to enroll in the educational system. This means that each particular school should offer a significant and unique contribution for individuals that may not be obtainable at the same scope and level through other schools or education-providing institutions (Nir and Eyal, 2008).

Although these four challenges are connected with various aspects of schooling, they share one common denominator: they all point at the school as the main actor in providing meaningful education and testify to the importance of sufficient degrees of freedom likely to enable schools to meet their challenges while operating under competitive and ever-changing circumstances.

## MAKING IT HAPPEN: EMPOWERING SCHOOLS

Empowerment is about the delegation of power and authority to the locally operating unit intended to create a liberating rather than constraining environment. In public education, school empowerment refers to the increase of authority at the school site (Clune and White,

1988), and emphasizes maximum delegation of decision-making power to local-level educators within a centrally coordinated framework (Boyd, 1990, p. 90). School empowerment is not merely the passing of central authority to the principal. Rather, it is an attempt to make it possible for the school head to work out the school policies and programs in collaboration with his professional staff and the community. Hence, the school head is expected to serve more as a leader than an agent of the Ministry of Education and to develop collaboratively with the different stakeholders a vision, a mission statement and a set of programs and policies for the school.

Although the transfer of central authority to the school level through school empowerment is controversial, its advantages seem to overcome its assumed shortcomings. The main assertion inherent to school empowerment is that increasing schools' authority and flexibility will increase sensitivity to local needs and, therefore, will better and more effectively enable the conduct of educational processes. Moreover, allowing schools to plan and initiate programs and processes is likely to promote participation of school staff and increase the chances of plans being implemented. Empowerment, furthermore, allows schools to operate more efficiently and rapidly in comparison with the commonly described slow and cumbersome centralized structures. And, finally, empowerment is assumed to professionalize teaching, to enhance teachers' commitment toward school goals and to increase their accountability for their performance and for students' outcomes.

For these reasons, school empowerment may be viewed as a vehicle likely to enable schools to render a general, centrally-determined policy in accordance with local needs. It is believed that delegating authority to schools is likely to improve their relevancy and to promote the productivity and effectiveness of the educational processes they conduct (Caldwell 1990, p. 17; 2003).

Although "to empower implies the granting of power and delegation of authority" (Burke, 1986, p. 50), one cannot overlook the fact that it is rather a *relational* construct (Conger and Kanungo, 1988) in the sense that it heavily relies on organizational members' perceptions regarding their ability to achieve their desired outcomes. What follows is that while empowerment is frequently mentioned and employed in various educational contexts, the features and implications evolving from various school empowerment initiatives may significantly differ.

Empowerment is mainly a top-down process which involves the transfer of central authority to the locally operating unit. Therefore, analytically, it is possible to differentiate among three types of school empowerment initiatives that vary in magnitude and scope:

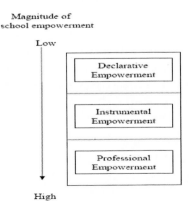

*Declarative empowerment:* This type of empowerment reflects mainly an attempt by policy-makers to appear responsive to voices calling for pluralism and for the need to expand school-level authority and autonomy. The main and at times the only expressions of school empowerment according to this form may be evident in declarations made by high-ranking officials and in written regulations which express a tendency to alter existing circumstances and promote school autonomy. Nevertheless, since this strategy is mostly declarative, it does not impose actions likely to change the circumstances in which schools operate or have the constraints imposed on schools reduced. Obedience is likely to characterize the accountability of school personnel under declarative empowerment since individuals are likely to play by the book rather than to actively search for ways to improve educational processes.

*Instrumental empowerment:* This type of empowerment moves one step further in comparison to the previous one in the sense that it argues for the need to expand the degrees of freedom granted to schools and, at the same time, to change some of the guiding assumptions and patterns of performance that so far have dominated the educational system. Instrumental empowerment is more about granting schools greater autonomy to design and perform various activities based on considerations of school-level educators. Increased financial autonomy is one typical characteristic to this type of empowerment as it delegates to the school principal the authority to decide how to divide and spend some portion of the school budget. Yet, although some changes may be noticed in schools that undergo instrumental empowerment, it is important to note that these changes are likely to be limited in scope since this mode of operation does not significantly alter the way control and supervision of schools are exercised, nor does it grant schools the freedom to fully rely on the professional considerations of their personnel. In central systems, instrumental empowerment is likely to leave most decisions regarding significant school issues in the hands of the state, providing teachers and school principals limited opportunities to design educational processes in accordance with their professional judgement and local circumstances. Instrumental empowerment is not likely to significantly alter the accountability of the school staff since under these circumstances individuals are most of the time required to respond to external impositions.

*Professional empowerment:* This type of empowerment intends to increase authority at the school site and to maximize delegation of decision-making authority to schools within a coordinated framework determined by the Ministry of Education. Although a framework is set by the state, schools are empowered to an extent that allows them to design their curriculum, teaching methods and evaluation procedures in accordance with local needs and the professional judgement of teachers and school leaders. Under professional empowerment schools are encouraged to define and adopt a unique organizational vision in accordance with the circumstances in which each particular school operates. Professional empowerment encourages school educators to initiate new ideas providing sufficient professional freedom to enable them to practice and implement these ideas. Moreover, it shifts the center of gravity for professional considerations from the state to the school personnel and, therefore, motivates the restructuring of school through bottom-up initiatives. One outgrowth of this type of empowerment is likely to be evident in the increased variance among schools comprising a given educational system.

Since professional empowerment allows and encourages individuals actively to search for and implement new ideas, their professional considerations are most likely to shape their commitment and accountability to the school and to children. Hence, teachers' and principals' accountability is assumed to increase since it is in their professional interest to prove their professional eligibility.

## SCHOOL EMPOWERMENT IN CONTEXT

For several decades now scholars and practitioners have expressed their support in policies emphasizing decentralization and school empowerment as means likely better to enable schools to cope with the growing diversity of needs and expectations that the public educational system is supposed to meet and, at the same time, promote the professionalism of school-level educators (Caldwell, 2003).

Increasing local level autonomy is considered better to enable the professional self-actualization of educational staff and students and thus make the teaching and learning processes more relevant and efficient. Moreover, it is assumed to enable the transformation of a national educational policy into something more relevant to local needs and, therefore, to make public schooling relevant and more beneficial for its consumers.

These assumed advantages and the growing disappointment from the performance and outcomes of public schools are among the main driving forces that paved the way for school empowerment policies not only in decentralized states in which decentralization is a dominant feature of public administration, but also in centralized states. However, for states that have traditionally featured a highly centralized structure like those located around the Mediterranean Basin, this proposed change implies a major shift and, as one would expect, the greater the proposed change, the lesser are its chances of being fully implemented.

In spite of the differences in size, culture, history, economy, religion and many other aspects characterizing the nine states described in earlier chapters, when it comes to school empowerment, the similarity among these states is striking. The resemblance may be viewed in particular in three major aspects:

As a starting point, public education in these states has featured a highly centralized structure for many years. Secondly, evidence may be found indicating the growing tendency towards school empowerment in all the countries described. Nevertheless, this tendency is declarative and may be evident mostly in laws, regulations, statements and articulated policies and, to some extent, in the limited restructuring initiatives that have been initiated over the years. In Italy, new laws were articulated granting more freedom to schools regarding the allocation of time, resources, the introduction of new technologies and the enrichment of teaching methods. Schools were allowed to modify 20% of the curriculum. In Greece, various interest groups have led to the legislation of new laws and to the establishment of the Pedagogical Institute as a self-administered organization responsible for the development of school curriculum, and the planning of teachers' training (although it reports directly to the Minister of Education) and to the establishment of Regional Education Directorates. In Spain, a large-scale reform was articulated in 1990 favoring some degree of administrative decentralization with particular emphasis on the local community as stakeholder. In Turkey, based on a new constitution and on the tendency to become part of the Western community and to join the European Market, the Turkish government has attempted to introduce several reforms that will promote the participation of citizens in the educational process and will increase power at the local level. In Malta, the Education Division within the Ministry of

Education issued, in 1995, directives allowing heads of schools a measure of autonomy in deciding purely localized issues without the need to refer to the head office in Valletta. In Portugal, a new regulation was issued in 1996 attempting to promote school autonomy. This reform was eventually denounced and new legislation was issued in 2008 attempting to promote the autonomy of the school principal. In Cyprus, a policy document published in 2007 supports educational autonomy and the need to promote the flexibility granted to schools. Laws and governmental regulations attempting to promote power at the local level to some degree are also the main strategy evident in the French and in the Israeli educational system, where a version of school-based management was implemented in 1998.

In spite of the contextual differences characterizing each of the countries described, these various school empowerment declarations share one major common denominator: They all started as *top-down* initiatives based on legislation or regulations initiated by the government indicating what appears to be the governments' tendency to delegate authority and to transfer power from the Ministry of Education to the schools.

A third feature characterizing these decentralization initiatives and reforms may be viewed in their limited outcomes and lasting effects: In none of the countries described have decentralization efforts reached the professional empowerment stage which may potentially alter the daily conduct of school-level educators. Rather, centralization prevailed and the number of constraints and bureaucratic obligations that school-level educators experienced have increased. Again, some differences may be evident among countries: In Italy, a discrepancy exists between rhetoric and practice, and, although the status of school principals slightly changed following these initiatives, decentralization is mostly administrative. In Greece, the newly-established bodies that were founded did not eventually change the central control of the Ministry of Education on schools. In Spain, in spite of the new legislation and regulations, the authorities being transferred to schools are in fact limited and so is the degree to which local communities influence educational processes. In Malta, school principals do have greater freedom of action. However, this freedom is mostly connected with administrative rather than professional issues. In Portugal, although the issue of educational decentralization has remained on the political agenda since 1990, central control remains the prominent feature of the educational system in spite of the increased opportunity for interest groups to influence. In Cyprus, the many attempts made towards school empowerment have led to some changes in school control over budgets and to an increase of the power granted to educational districts. Still, with these changes, control was retained by the Ministry of Education and the power granted to schools remained practically unchanged. In France, some limited actions toward school empowerment may be identified. Some changes may be evident in the transfer of central budgets to local communities and in the tendency to abandon zoning. Nevertheless, these initiatives did not lead to dramatic changes in school empowerment and schools' freedom to act in correspondence with local needs and expectations. One possible outgrowth of the limited decentralization characterizing French public education may be evident in the strengthening of private education. In Turkey, although school-based management is a declared educational policy, the state remains a dominant actor in the organization, planning and evaluation of the public schooling system. Here, as in other centralized states, it appears that there exists a gap between governmental declarations regarding the need to increase local-level power and the inclination of high-ranking officials to surrender authority to the school level. The same applies for the Israeli educational system where the debate has continued and various efforts towards school empowerment have been carried out since the 1970s, although in fact control in the educational system remains within the Ministry of Education.

To summarize, a rather comparable picture is obtained in spite of the different national and educational settings. In essence, it portrays a rather wide gap existing between official governmental declarations and rhetoric associated with school empowerment and what actually is taking place. Moreover, it is evident that centralized states move in two opposite directions when it comes to school empowerment: The stronger the declarations concerning the power and autonomy granted to schools, the larger the number of centralized measures initiated to ensure sufficient central control over the schooling system. Hence, a paradox emerges.

## Moving beyond Rhetoric: Can the Gap be Bridged?

The similarities among these different centralized states in the extent to which schools are actually being empowered are striking and at the same time puzzling: How can it be that different national settings produce so similar and yet limited outcomes it terms of school empowerment?

The descriptions coming from these nine states testify to the wide range of obstacles that may account for the difficulties in expanding schools' autonomy when operating in centralized systems. Analytically, these obstacles may be divided into two main categories: *Rigid* and *soft*. Rigid obstacles refer to various limitations that are mostly structural, are built-in within the national/educational system and policy-makers' power is not sufficient to alter them. Soft obstacles, on the contrary, are mostly circumstantial and, therefore, may be more easily changed or abolished through new decisions or policies created by high-ranking officials.

Obviously, not all obstacles may be found in all countries: Obstacles vary in quantity and nature. Hence, the greater the number and scope of obstacles which exist in a particular centralized educational system, the less likely are the chances that school empowerment initiatives will progress from the declarative to the professional type.

The descriptions of school empowerment initiatives carried out in the nine states explored provide several examples for what may be viewed as rigid obstacles. One example is the *country's size*. It appears that small centralized states as in the case of Malta and Israel create a unique difficulty. As Farrugia puts it, "Small countries are not down-sized versions of big countries: they have ecology of their own." When describing the Israeli educational system, Inbar explains that small size may be considered a limitation for school empowerment since it "strengthens the perception of the school-level staff of the centralized power of the Ministry of Education, often far beyond its real power."

Lack of *political stability* may be considered another rigid obstacle for school empowerment introduced in a centralized educational system. Moving towards school empowerment in centralized structures requires persistence and long-term planning and implementation. Policy-makers and politicians need to support these initiatives if a new order is to be established and power is to be shifted from the Ministry of Education to schools. However, when centralized countries face political instability, the chances that far-reaching change initiatives will be fully implemented are low. The descriptions coming from Italy and

Greece testify to this difficulty to advance radical and long-term change initiatives and to foster school empowerment initiatives which in many cases contradict the agenda of high-ranking officials who, as civil servants, comprise the educational bureaucracy.

A third rigid obstacle for school empowerment in centralized states is related to the fact that public schools are part of the public administration and, as such, almost all *educational personnel are civil servants employed by the state*. This means that the state is the employer and, therefore, that school principals have practically no power over their teachers. In other words, the state, through its employees (teachers, school principals), may encourage or prevent any local initiatives.

These obstacles may be considered rigid since they set significant limitations for school empowerment and local control; educators or policy-makers who need to cope with these obstacles actually have no power to overcome them.

Soft obstacles on the other hand are more manageable since it is within the power of the educational system to take actions that would create different circumstances and, therefore, alter existing conditions that prevent school empowerment.

One example may be evident in the tendency to maintain *an obligatory national curriculum*. In most cases, the inclination to maintain a national curriculum reflects the tendency of the Ministry of Education to ensure the socialization of the younger generation in accordance to contents and values that the state wishes to emphasize and promote. Nevertheless, it is important to note that when the central office enforces an obligatory curriculum, it actually constrains the ability of schools to design the curriculum in accordance with the particular needs of the children and the community they serve.

Another example may be evident in *external evaluation processes* conducted by the state. Centralized states do not easily surrender their power and authority to lower levels of the educational hierarchy. Yet, when pressures to empower schools increase, centralized systems tend to maintain control by monitoring school outcomes. This may be achieved by employing centralized indicators and testing systems that would indicate the performance level of each particular school. However, a unified testing system implies that all schools have to conduct learning and teaching processes that meet the testing criteria rather than develop unique pedagogical initiatives that do not correspond with the criteria being centrally measured.

A third soft obstacle may be related to the *allocation of budgets from the central office to schools*. It appears that in centralized states, declared policies that emphasize school empowerment do not necessarily lead to increased school financial autonomy. Inevitably, when resources are centrally monitored and allocated, schools are limited in their capacity to spend these funds in accordance with local needs. Here again, schools may find it hard to advance local initiatives when they are allowed to spend only a small portion of their resources without consulting the central office.

A fourth obstacle to school empowerment may be evident in the *lack of sufficient preparation of school principals*. Since school empowerment policies turn school principals into the main actors, it is only reasonable that a preliminary stage to the implementation of school autonomy policy would be the preparation of school principals to operate under these newly created circumstances. This may be true in particular for school principals who operated for many years under centralization. Yet, as the various descriptions suggest, in many national educational systems earlier preparation of school principals hardly ever takes place.

A fifth obstacle may be related to the fact that school empowerment policies in centralized systems are always launched as *top-down initiatives*. Individuals whose authority and autonomy is assumed to increase – school-level educators - are not participating in the process for which a policy plan is set. Paradoxically, central systems enforce school empowerment policies on schools. Such a strategy, clearly, is most likely to promote resentment rather than willingness on behalf of school-level educators to take new initiatives that correspond with local circumstances.

Lastly, but most importantly, the chances of a school empowerment policy to mature and to significantly alter the degrees of freedom granted to schools operating in a centralized educational system is determined to a great extent by the *willingness of high-ranking officials to relinquish their power*. Although this demand seems to derive from the logic that fosters school empowerment, in reality this is not an easy task to accomplish. From the various descriptions it appears that high-ranking officials are reluctant to give away their power and to have their influence over the educational system restricted. As a result, a discrepancy is likely to be found between the declared school empowerment policy and what actually is being implemented. Moreover, school empowerment policies are almost always accompanied by a set of procedures or regulations intended to ensure that high-ranking officials maintain their power over the schooling system.

Although these constraints create significant limitations for school empowerment initiatives, they may be viewed as soft constraints since they may be changed or abolished through new decisions or policies adopted by high-ranking officials.

## The Centralization Trap

The nine descriptions testify to the resemblance among countries both in the process of school empowerment policy setting and in the limited effects that these various policies have for schools. It appears that centralization is a dominant factor in determining the extent to which school empowerment initiatives are likely to materialize and reshape the educational system.

Why are centralized arrangements so difficult to overcome when attempting to empower schools? What are the sources from which centralization gains its support and power? Several sources of support can be mentioned:

Initially, there is the power of habit. Individuals who are used to operating in a centralized system consider this pattern beneficial, although they lack other substantial experiences related to different modes of operation and control.

Centralization also gains power from often heard arguments stating that school empowerment and autonomy will eventually lead to chaos. Increasing school autonomy and legitimacy to operate in accordance with local considerations is thought to undermine the establishment of a shared ethos among the society's future citizens and, therefore, centralization is to be favored.

Disappointment in school outcomes and expectations that schools will become effective organizations may serve as another source of support for centralization. This argument may be explained in considering that centralized educational systems tend to enforce a unified core curriculum, thereby establishing the basis for comparisons among schools.

Centralization is also viewed as beneficial in promoting equity and narrowing gaps among various social groups coming from different socio-economic backgrounds through the enforcement of uniformity.

And, finally, in considering the inherent difference existing between political and pedagogical time frames, centralization is supported by politicians who consider it useful in advancing their agendas. Since pedagogical processes are in essence oriented for the long term and political time frames are rather short, centralization may assist in artificially decreasing the discrepancies between these two time frames by enforcing through various central regulations a political time frame on pedagogical processes.

These various arguments support the notion that centralization offers some common good and, therefore, should be embraced and protected. However, this notion also encourages the establishment of what I shall term "the centralization trap" which may be evident in particular when attempting to reconcile the immanent contradiction existing between the call for pluralism, school autonomy and empowerment and the desire to maintain sufficient central control over schools.

The cobwebs of the centralization trap are grounded in a wide range of contingencies intended to ensure the continuity of centralization. Paradoxically, this trap encourages the tendency to articulate various policy plans that emphasize the importance of correspondence between educational services and the unique circumstances in which a particular school operates and, at the same time, to maintain sufficient central control over the schooling system. This paradox becomes very evident when school empowerment change initiatives are proposed. And, indeed, as the descriptions coming from the nine centralized states located around the Mediterranean Basin indicate, this paradox becomes a central feature of school empowerment policy plans and is evident particularly when rhetoric is compared to practice.

## MOVING FROM A SINGLE TO DUAL MODE POLICY

Based on the descriptions coming from nine states, it may be concluded that centralized states and educational contexts present a different type of challenge for school empowerment initiatives. In national contexts that have traditionally featured a decentralized structure of public administration, it is reasonable to assume that school empowerment initiatives are more likely to be assimilated and to lead to substantial changes in the empowerment of school-level educators. Therefore, a *single-mode* type of policy, which mainly implies changes at the school level, may be sufficient in creating a significant change in the professional conduct of local level educators in considering that the spirit of pluralism and local control already exists in decentralized political and educational settings. Hence, a school empowerment policy which primarily fosters changes at the school level is likely to gain the support of politicians and high-ranking officials as it corresponds to the typical mode of operation characterizing public administration in decentralized states. Moreover, such restructuring initiatives do not suggest substantial changes for the professional conduct of policy-makers who continue to define the general framework for the schooling system and to monitor school performance according to patterns that typically characterize decentralized systems.

When it comes to centralized countries, however, the starting point for school empowerment initiatives is much lower. This last statement may be better understood in considering that the mode of operation that typically characterizes centralized educational systems leaves most control in the hands of high-ranking officials. Under such circumstances, school-level educators are mostly professionals who are required to follow orders and act in accordance with regulations articulated by policy-makers. Hence, centralized countries attempting substantially to promote school autonomy and enable the professional empowerment of school-level educators may articulate a *dual-mode* type of policy. This may be better understood in considering that centralized educational systems face two tightly coupled fronts when attempting to implement school empowerment initiatives.

Initially, such initiatives imply major changes in the conduct of local-level educators and schools. As the various descriptions suggest, moving from central to local control and increasing the degrees of freedom granted to local-level professionals is not an easy and natural shift for individuals who traditionally are used to operating under a tight external control. They need some training and preparation that would better enable them to make use of the increased professional freedom that such initiatives offer and to change their school's organizational norms and educational processes as well as their own professional conduct. In spite of the benefits embedded in professional empowerment, changing past habits is not an easy task, and it therefore requires sufficient support, time and resources to enable proper preparation and adjustment of school-level educators to these newly-created circumstances.

A second front that professional empowerment initiatives need to confront when implemented in centralized educational contexts is at the higher levels of the educational hierarchy. In many centralized states, the calls for local control presented by various pressure groups, the difficulty to centrally monitor schools' conduct and the demand for accountability and achievements push high-ranking officials towards articulating school empowerment policies. However, it should be acknowledged that in many cases they do it reluctantly, since such changes lessen their influence over the educational system and constrain their control. In other words, the greater the professional autonomy granted to school-level educators, the less the policy-makers' strength and capability to shape and influence school-level processes. This may be viewed as the major obstacle for school empowerment initiatives in centralized states. It may also explain why these policies tend to take on a rather paradoxical nature evident mostly in the contradictory policy messages and in the discrepancy often found between the declared policy and the various actions that are carried out as means for its implementation.

A dual-mode type of policy is imperative if a declared school empowerment policy is to lead to actual changes in the professional conduct of school-level educators. Policy declarations supporting school autonomy that are not followed by a redefinition and substantial changes in high-ranking officials' responsibilities and power are likely to end up as fruitless policies and to promote the notion of mistrust between lower and higher echelons comprising the educational hierarchy. It is, consequently, imperative that a policy oriented towards professional empowerment should substantially foster changes both at higher and lower levels of the educational hierarchy.

# MAKING SCHOOL EMPOWERMENT HAPPEN

What follows previously presented arguments is that the tendency to promote school empowerment in centralized settings proposes a different restructuring challenge: It is not a "Model I" kind of change (Watzlawick, Weakland and Fisch, 1974), offering to introduce some minor changes *within* the educational system as in the case of school empowerment policies introduced in decentralized systems. Rather, it suggests a "Model II" type of change (ibid.) implying the restructuring *of* the system and the introduction of some new patterns of operation quite different from previous ones.

Since the introduction of major changes is somewhat more complicated relative to minor ones, it is imperative that school empowerment policies in centralized systems establish a comprehensive set of new arrangements that promote the chances for successful implementation.

A number of practical implications may be portrayed based on the descriptions coming from states around the Mediterranean Basin:

*The perspective of school empowerment policy*: Complicated restructuring initiatives require sufficient financial support and a strategic rather than tactical time perspective for their implementation. While these qualities are essential for the establishment of new modes of operation, these prerequisites do not always meet the perspectives typical to political terms which tend to be much shorter. Since educational agendas are dramatically influenced by political ones, they tend to be fragile and absorb modifications every time a government is replaced and the Ministry of Education is governed by a new minister and director general. This mode of operation undermines continuity. Hence, the perspectives of school empowerment policies should be oriented to the long term, especially when implemented in centralized contexts, and sufficient budgets need to be secured in advance to ensure continuity.

*Coordination of expectations*: The theoretical as well as empirical literature plays a major role in building high expectations regarding the positive effects of school empowerment for the professional conduct of individuals and schools. In general, it may be concluded that granting school-level professionals increased autonomy is likely to promote schools' and children's outcomes. However, it is important to acknowledge that the starting point in terms of degrees of freedom granted to schools operating in a centralized educational system is rather low and, therefore, that the effects of school empowerment are likely to be milder and evident only after a relatively longer period of time. Hence, it is important that such acknowledgement will be part of the articulated policy.

*School principals' preparation*: While the significance of the principal's role in explicating school conduct is well documented, its influence and significance are likely to increase under school empowerment circumstances. Therefore, principals who were operating for many years in a centralized system of education need to adjust to these newly created circumstances and adapt different modes of operation. They need to expand their proficiencies in various areas such as budget allocation and administration, human resource management and the definition and implementation of authentic school vision. The articulation of a school empowerment policy, accordingly, implies the need to prepare school principals in advance and equip them with the needed proficiencies required under school empowerment circumstances.

*Educational staff preparation*: Similar to school principals, teachers are also not accustomed to operating in contexts that allow large degrees of freedom. Rather, teachers spend their daily routine in the implementation of decisions, programs and plans articulated and at times enforced by others. Professional empowerment implies that teachers would be entitled to initiate pedagogical endeavors and to actually make decisions regarding educational processes within their classrooms and their schools. Under these newly created circumstances, proficiencies such as collaborative work, planning, decision making and evaluation are likely to play a major role as means for promoting teachers' professional self actualization. Therefore, initial training that promotes teachers' proficiencies as well as establishes their professional orientation in accordance with school empowerment circumstances is of importance.

*The supervision of schools*: Under centralization, public educational systems typically employ a superintendency system intended to ensure that centrally defined policies are implemented by schools. The superintendents are actually the eyes and ears of the central office at schools. Yet school empowerment implies expanding the degrees of freedom granted to schools, therefore enabling the variance among schools to increase. While the general framework for the operation of schools is still being set by the state's Ministry of Education, the increased variance which follows school empowerment limits the establishment of a common denominator among schools, thus requiring major changes in the role and responsibilities of the school superintendent. Such changes are important not only for the translation of schools' increased freedom to activities likely to meet local needs and expectations of staff parents and children, but also for the superintendents themselves who are likely to experience professional conflict if their role expectations under centralized structure remain unchanged after a school empowerment policy is introduced (Nir and Eyal, 2003).

*Evaluation of school processes and outcomes*: One typical feature of centralized educational systems may be evident in the tendency to conduct external evaluation processes administered in most cases by the state. There are two typical reasons for this tendency: Firstly, school-level educators do not always have the methodological proficiencies required when attempting to create valid and reliable measurements. Secondly, external measurements enable the state to maintain its control over schools and their pedagogical processes through the measurement of school outcomes. This may also be the reason why in many of the descriptions coming from centralized states the establishment of an external measurement authority and/or procedures tends to follow the articulation and implementation of a school empowerment policy. Obviously, unified external evaluations cannot be conducted if schools perform processes lacking a common denominator. School empowerment policies, for this reason, should foster school-level evaluations through building the capacity of teachers and principals to conduct valid educational measurements rather than establish external mechanism that eventually undermine genuine school initiatives.

*The cancellation of zoning*: While school empowerment is assumed to promote the accountability of school-level educators, zoning which guarantees a steady flow of children to a school regardless of the school's outcomes fosters an opposite tendency. School empowerment, among other things, may be viewed as a mechanism that promotes schools' need to develop in some unique venue and, therefore, as a platform encouraging competition among schools. The cancellation of zoning may encourage school staff to create a unique vision for their school and, in this manner, construct too an attractive educational alternative for parents and children who will now have the option to choose among different pedagogical agendas.

*Parental participation*: School empowerment fosters the collaboration between parents and other members of the community and the school. But expanding school control and authority by granting them greater degrees of freedom may also be viewed by parents as an opportunity to enforce their wills and expectations on schools. Evidence suggests that, at times, such circumstances may also encourage parents to act militantly against schools when schools that have greater decision-making power fail to act in accordance with parents' expectations (Nir and Ben-Ami, 2005). It is therefore suggested that the articulation of a national school empowerment policy should also take into account the need to prepare parents to serve as school board members and as facilitators in ways that will enable avoidance of potential conflicts and help establish a school agenda that will best correspond with local needs.

## LOOKING AHEAD

There is much promise in school empowerment as an educational restructuring initiative intended to promote the quality of school processes, the professionalism of educational staff, the relevancy of the public school for its customers and public satisfaction with the schooling system as a whole. These notions are supported by empirical evidence gathered mostly in national contexts that have a decentralized structure of public administration. However, the insights gathered in this book from different centralized educational contexts reveal that much depends on the circumstances where such policies are being introduced. Centralization suggests a set of contingencies that constrain school empowerment, and in this manner increase the chances that such restructuring initiatives will end up as declarations rather than leading to actual changes in schools' autonomy and conduct. It is argued that the larger the gap existing between rhetoric and practice, the greater the mistrust between school-level educators and policy-makers. And, as a result, a school empowerment policy may fail to fulfill its mission and may therefore be mistakenly conceived as misleading.

Can the paradox often found in centralized educational contexts attempting to promote school empowerment be avoided? The answer to this question may be positive provided policy-makers acknowledge this inherent difficulty and articulate school empowerment policies that correspond with the unique circumstances created by centralization. Using a dual-mode type of policy may assist in avoiding the centralization trap and in diminishing the influence of some of the centralized arrangements that constrain schools' degrees of freedom. Moving in this direction should be considered imperative when attempting to develop professional empowerment in centralized educational contexts.

## REFERENCES

Anderson, G. L. (1998). Toward authentic participation: Deconstructing the discourses of participatory reforms in education. *American Educational Research Journal*, 35(4), 571-603.

Boyd, W.L. (1990). Balancing control and autonomy in school reform: The politics of Perestroika. In: J. Murphy (Ed.), *The educational reform movement of the1980's,* Berkeley, Cal.: McCutchan Pub. Co.

Bradley, S., Johnes, G., and Millington, J. (2001). The effect of competition on the efficiency of secondary schools in England. *European Journal of Operational Research,* 135 (3), 545-568.

Burke, W. (1986). Leadership as empowering others. In: S. Srivastra (Ed.), *Executive power* (pp. 51-77). San Francisco: Jossey-Bass.

Caldwell, B. (1990) SBM and management: International developments. In J. D. Chapman (ed.), *School based decision making and management* (pp. 3-38). London: The Falmer Press.

Caldwell, B. J. (2003). A theory of learning in self managing school. In: A. Volansky and I. Friedman (Eds.), *School-based management: An international perspective* (pp. 93-116). Jerusalem: State of Israel, Ministry of Education.

Caldwell, B., and Spinks, J. (1988) *The self managing school.* Washington, D.C.: The John Falmer Press.

Carlson, R. O. (1964). Environmental constraints and organizational consequences: The public school and its clients. In: D.E. Griffiths (Ed.), *Behavioral sciences and educational administration: The sixty-third yearbook of the National Society for the Study of Education.* Chicago, Illinois: University of Chicago Press.

Clune, W.H., and White, P.A. (1988*). School-based management: Institutional variation, implementation and issues for further research.* Center for Policy Research in Education, New Brunswick, N.J.: Rutgers University.

Conger, J. A., and Kanungo, R. N. (1988). The empowerment process: Integrating theory and practice. *The Academy of Management Review,* 13 (3), 471 – 482.

Cowley, T., and Williamson, J. (1998). A recipe for success? Localized implementation of a (flexible) national curriculum. *The Curriculum Journal,* 9 (1), 79-94.

Edwards, R., Nicoll, K., and Tait, A. (1999). Migrating metaphors: The globalization of flexibility in policy. *Journal of Education Policy,* 14 (6), 619-630.

Glennerster, H. (1991). Quasi-markets and education. *Economic Journal,* 101: 1268-1271.

Le Grand, J. (1991). Quasi-markets and social policy. *Economic Journal,* 101: 1256-1267.

Le Grand, J., and Bartlett, W. (1993). *Quasi-markets and social policy.* London: Macmillan.

Lubienski, C. (2005). Public schools in marketized environments: Shifting incentives and unintended consequences of competition-based educational reforms. *American Journal of Education,* 111, 464–486.

Nir, A. E. (2003). Quasi-Market: The changing context of schooling. *The International Journal of Educational Reform,* 12, (1), 26 –39.

Nir, A. E., and Ben-Ami, T. (2005). School-parents relationship in the era of school-based management: Harmony or conflict? *Leadership and Policy in Schools,* 4, (1), 55-72.

Nir, A. E., and Eyal, O. (2003). School-based management and the role conflict of the school superintendent. *Journal of Educational Administration,* 41 (5), 547 – 564.

Nir, A. E., and Eyal, O. (2008). Setting a national curriculum: Bridging the gap between professionalism and politics. In: Casey, J. N., and Upton, R. E. (Eds.), *Educational Curricula: Development and Evaluation* (chapter 9, pp. 235-251).Hauppauge, N.Y.: Nova Science Publishers.

Watzlawick, P., Weakland, J. H., and Fisch, R. (1974). *Change: Principles of problem formation and problem resolution.* New York: Norton.

Whitty, G. (1997). Creating quasi-markets in education: A review of recent research on parental choice and school autonomy in three countries. In: M. W. Apple (Ed.), *Review of research in education 22*, Washington, D.C.: American Educational Research Association.

Woods. P. A., Bagley, C., and Glatter, R. (1996). Dynamics of competition – the effects of local competitive arena on schools. In: J.C. Pole and R. Chawla-Duggan (Eds.), *Shaping education in the 1990s: Perspectives on secondary education.* London: Falmer Press.

In: Centralization and School Empowerment...          ISBN 978-1-60692-730-4
Editor: Adam Nir                                      © 2009 Nova Science Publishers, Inc.

# ABOUT THE CONTRIBUTORS

## Natércio Afonso

Natércio Afonso is an associate professor at the Faculty of Psychology and Education, the University of Lisbon, Portugal. He is a former secondary school teacher, teacher trainer and school inspector, and worked in the Portuguese Ministry of Education as the Head of the Education Inspectorate. He teaches undergraduate and graduate courses in Educational Policy and Administration and in Educational Research Methodology. He coordinates master and doctoral programs in these fields. His major research interests focus on organizational analysis, school management, school evaluation and school inspection. He has a License degree in History from the University of Lisbon (1974), a Master of Education (Ed.M.) in Social Education (1985) and is Doctor of Education (Ed.D.) in Educational Leadership and Administration from the Boston University School of Education – USA (1993). His research focuses on the study of changes in modes of regulation of educational systems, with specific focuses on school evaluation and school autonomy policies. The most recent research focuses on the analysis of the relationship between knowledge and policy, namely the use of scientific knowledge in educational policy-making and political legitimacy strategies, as well as the use of knowledge as a policy tool or in the fabrication of regulation instruments.

His recent publications related to this book include: Afonso, N. (2007). A avaliação das escolas no quadro de uma política de mudança da administração da educação. In Conselho Nacional da Educação, *Avaliação das escolas, modelos e processos.* (pp.223-228); Afonso, N. (2006). A Direcção Regional de Educação: um espaço de regulação intermédia. In J. Barroso (org.) *A regulação das políticas públicas em educação; espaços, dinâmicas e actores.* Lisboa, Educa (pp. 71-98); Afonso, N. (2004). A globalização, o Estado e a escola pública. *In Administração Educacional* , 4, pp. 33-42; Afonso, N. (2004a). L'émergence des espaces intermédiaires de régulation dans l'administration de l'éducation au Portugal : le cas des directions régionales de l'éducation. In *Recherches Sociologiques*, Vol. XXXV, n° 2, pp.121-140; Afonso, N. (2004b). *Approaches to the evaluation of schools which provide compulsory education - Portugal.* Bruxelas, Eurydice (http://www.eurydice.org); Afonso, N. (2003) A Regulação da Educação na Europa: do Estado Educador ao Controlo Social da Escola Pública, In J. Barroso (org), *A Escola Pública, Regulação, Desregulação, Privatização* . Porto, Asa. (pp.49-48); Afonso, N. (2003a). The situation in Portugal. In L. Watson (ed.) *Selecting and developing heads of schools; twenty-three European perspectives.* Sheffield (England): School of Education of Sheffield Hallam University for the European Forum on Educational Administration (pp. 195-214); Barroso, J, Afonso, N. e Dinis, L.

(2006). *Improving school leadership; national report, Portugal.* Lisboa, Ministério da Educação e OCDE.

## Brian J. Caldwell

Professor Brian J. Caldwell is Managing Director of Educational Transformations Pty Ltd in Melbourne and Associate Director of iNet (Global) (International Networking for Educational Transformation) of the Specialist Schools and Academies Trust in England. From 1998 to 2004 he served as Dean of Education at the University of Melbourne where he is currently Professorial Fellow. His previous appointments include Head of Education Policy and Management (1995-1998) at the University of Melbourne where he took up an appointment in 1990; and Head of Teacher Education (1988-1999) and Dean of Education (1989-1990) at the University of Tasmania. International work over the last 25 years includes more than 450 presentations, projects and other professional assignments in or for 38 countries or jurisdictions on six continents. In addition to more than 100 published papers, chapters and monographs, Brian Caldwell is author or co-author of books that helped guide educational reform in several countries, most notably the trilogy on self-managing schools: *The Self-Managing School* (1988), *Leading the Self-Managing School* (1992) and *Beyond the Self-Managing* School (1998), each with Jim Spinks. *Re-imagining Educational Leadership* was published in 2006. *Raising the Stakes: From Improvement to Transformation in the Reform of Schools* (2008) is his fourth collaboration with Jim Spinks. *Why not the Best Schools?* with Jessica Harris will be published in late 2008.

## Jean-Louis Derouet

Professor Jean-Louis Derouet is the head of the mixed research unit, Education and Policies, where researchers from INRP (National Institute for Pedagogical Research) and from université Lyon 2 work together. He is the chief editor of *Education et Sociétés*, an international journal of the sociology of education, and president of the committee Education, Training, Socialisation of AISLF, the International Association of French-speaking sociologists. He collaborates with NESSE (Network of Experts in the Social Sciences of Education and Training) sponsored by the European Commission.

He worked on the evolution of the conception of justice in education and, especially, on the implementation of comprehensive schools. He now works on the territorialization of education and training in France and, more particularly, on the organization of schools.

Main publications: Derouet, J.-L. (1992). *École et justice. De l'égalité des chances aux compromis locaux* (School and justice. From equal opportunities to local compromises). Paris: A..M. Métailié; Derouet, J.-L. (Ed.) (1999). *L'école dans plusieurs mondes* (Schooling in several worlds). Bruxelles: De Boeck; Derouet, J.-L. (Ed.) (2003). *Le collège unique en questions* (The collège unique in questions). Paris: PUF; Derouet, J.-L., and Normand, R. (2007). *L'Europe de l'éducation: entre management et politique* (The Europe of education: between management and politics). Poitiers-Lyon: ESEN-INRP; Derouet, J.-L., and Derouet-Besson, M-C. (2008). *Repenser la justice dans le domaine de l'éducation et de la formation* (Rethinking justice in the field of education and training). Genève: Peter Lang; Information about the work conducted by the Education and Politiques research unit is available at http://ep.inrp.fr <http://ep.inrp.fr/>

# Charles Farrugia

Professor Charles Farrugia started his teaching career in Malta's State schools in 1959, but moved to teacher education in 1967. He studied Education in Britain and Canada, and again at the University of London's Institute of Education, from where he obtained a PhD. In 1978, Professor Farrugia became the founder Dean of the Faculty of Education at the University of Malta, a position he held for fourteen years. He spent the decade 1996-2006 as Pro-Rector of the University, introducing such administrative procedures as University-wide academic audits and the institution's first five-year strategic plan. Currently, he coordinates and teaches in the Post-Graduate Diploma in Education (Administration and Management) course, which awards the qualification mandatory for anyone seeking a Head of School position in Malta's State and Church school sectors. He worked extensively with the British Commonwealth Secretariat and UNESCO on educational policy-making and development in small states. Since 1996 he has chaired the Maltese National Commission for UNESCO.

# Dan Inbar

Professor Dan Inbar is Professor Emeritus of the Hebrew University of Jerusalem. He has a PhD from the University of California, Berkeley. His main research and teaching interests are educational policy, educational planning, and organizational management and leadership. Prof. Inbar served as Director of the School of Education and Associate Dean of the Faculty of Humanities, and is the Chair of Shifman Cathedra of Secondary Education. He has served on many committees in the Ministry of Education, and as the Chair of the National Committee of Parental Choice, and the Chief Educational Scientist of the Israeli Parliament. Prof. Inbar was a research fellow at Stanford University, California, at OISE, Toronto, at the Institute of Education, London University, and at Melbourne University. He taught for four years at the Harvard University Summer School. During the years 1994-1996 he served as President of the International Society of Educational Planners (ISEP). Professor Inbar is now Chair of Strategic Thinking for Education at the Van Leer Jerusalem Institute, and Editor of the scientific journal, *Dapim*, which focuses on educational research and teacher training. Selected publications: Bilski, R. Galnoor, I., Inbar, D., Manor, Y., and Sheffer, G. (1980). *Can Planning Replace Politics?* The Hague: Martinus Nijhoff, in cooperation with the Van Leer Jerusalem Foundation; Inbar, D. (1984). *Responsibility.* Tel Aviv: Sifriat Hapoalim (in Hebrew); Inbar, D. (1996). *Planning for Educational Innovation.* Fundamentals of Educational Planning Series, Vol. 53, UNESCO International Institute of Educational Planning, Paris; Inbar, D. (2000) *Managing Diversity: The Educational Challenge.*Even Yehuda: Reches Publishing (in Hebrew); Inbar, D. (Ed.) (2006). *Toward Educational Revolution?* Van Leer Educational Conference on Dovrat's Report, Van Leer Jerusalem Institute/Hakibbutz Hameuchad Publishing House.

# Amalia A. Ifanti

Amalia Ifanti is an Associate Professor of Educational Planning and Policy in the Department of Educational Sciences and Early Childhood Education of the University of Patras, in Greece. She graduated from the University of Joannina (Greece) Faculty of Philosophy, and did her postgraduate studies at the University of London Institute of Education. She holds a Diploma in Education, Master of Education and the PhD from the Institute of Education. She is an active member of CIES, BAICE, CESE and of a number of Greek Educational Societies. She has acted as a Reviewer for *Comparative Education Review* and *Compare Journals* as well as for Greek peer review journals. Her research interests are in specific educational policy topics such as politics of the school curriculum and of educational changes, educational control, globalization and school practices, teaching as a profession, and health promotion education. She has published a considerable number of papers in Greek peer review journals. Some of her current publications in international journals are: Karamouzis, M.V., Ifanti, A.A., Iconomou, G.V., Vagenakis, A.G., and Kalofonos, H.P. (2006). Medical students' views of undergraduate Oncology Education: A comparative study. *Education for Health: Change in Learning and Practice,* 19, (1), 61-70; Ifanti, A.A. (2007). Policy and curriculum development in Greece. The case of secondary school curriculum. *Pedagogy, Culture and Society,* 15 (1), 71-81; Ifanti, A.A. (2007). The status of undergraduate educational policy at university departments of education in Greece. *KEDI Journal of Educational Policy,* Vol. 4, No. 1, pp. 99-115; Iconomou, G., Iconomou, A.V., Argyriou, A.A., Nikolopoulos, A., Ifanti, A.A., and Kalofonos, H.P. (2008). Emotional distress in cancer patients and the beginning of chemotherapy and its relation to quality of life. *J. BUON,*. 13, (2), 217-222; Iconomou, G., Koutras, A., Karaivazoglou, K., Kalliolias, G., Assimakopoulos, K., Argyriou, A.A., Ifanti, A.A., and Kalofonos, H.P. (in press). Effect of epoetin alfa therapy on cognitive function in anaemic patients with solid tumors undergoing chemotherapy, *European Journal of Cancer Care*; Assimakopoulos, K., Karaivazoglou, K., Ifanti, A.A., Gerolymos, M.K., Kalofonos, H.P., and Iconomou, G. (in press). Religiosity and its relation to quality of life in Christian Orthodox cancer patients undergoing chemotherapy. *Psycho-Oncology.*

## Carlos Marcelo

Carlos Marcelo holds a doctorate degree in Science of Education. He is a full professor at the Department of Teaching and School Organization at the University of Sevilla, Spain.

He has done research in the field of teaching and teacher education, teacher belief and pedagogy. In addition, he conducted research on the problems typical to beginning teachers, and on beginning teachers' induction programs. He has published several books on teacher education and teaching skills.

Recently he is conducted research on the process of learning via internet, analyzing the process of knowledge construction in the asynchronous learning environment.

Selected publications: Marcelo, Carlos (2008). Desarrollo profesional y personal docente. En A. de la Herranz y J. Paredes (Coords.). Didáctica General. La práctica de la enseñanza en educación infantil, primaria y secundaria, Madrid, McGraw Hill, pp. 291-310; Marcelo, Carlos (2007). Propuesta de Estándares de Calidad para Programas de Formación Docente a través de Estrategias de Aprendizaje Abierto y a Distancia. Santiago de Chile, OREALC-UNESCO; Marcelo, Carlos (2007). La formación docente en la sociedad del coocimiento y la información: avances y temas pendientes. Olhar de Professor. Vo. 10, No. 1, pp. 63-90. ISSN 1518-5648; Marcelo, C. (2007). Empezar con buen pie: inserción a la enseñanza para profesores principiantes. Revista Docencia, N° 33, pp. 27-38; Marcelo, C. y Gago, M.J. (2007). Formación para el empleo a través de e-learning en Andalucía. Una experiencia de evaluación. En A. Landera Etxeberría (Coord.). Buenas prácticas en e-learning, Madrid, ANCED (Asociación Nacional de e-learning y educación a distancia), pp. 179-214; Marcelo, C. (2007). Incorporación de las TICs en la formación inicial docente. EducarChile; Vázquez, M.J., Marcelo, C., Lázaro, C. y Álvarez, F.J. (2007). E-learning para la Formación Profesional Inicial en Andalucía: cuatro años de experiencia. Revista de Educación a Distancia. Número 18; Marcelo, C. (2007). Vinte anos não é nada. Preocupações dos assessores diente da sociedades do conhecimento. En C. Monereo y J.I. Pozo (Eds.). A prática de assessoramento educacional. Porto Alegre Artmed, pp. 144-156; Marcelo, C. y Perera, V.H. (2007). Comunicación y aprendizaje electrónico: la interacción didáctica en los nuevos espacios virtuales de aprendizaje. Revista de Educación, N° 343; Marcelo, C. (2006). "Políticas de inserción a la docencia": De eslabón perdido a puente para el desarrollo profesional docente. Informe elaborado para PREAL (Programa para la Reforma Educativa en América Latina), Grupo de Trabajo sobre Profesionalización Docente, y presentado el 23 de noviembre en el seminario "Políticas para integrar a los nuevos profesores en la profesión docente";

Marcelo, C. and Perera, V. (2006). Sequences of Discourse in e-Learning Environments, Academic Exchange Quarterly, Winter Volume 10, Issue 4, pp. 268-273. ISSN 1096-1453; Marcelo, C. (2006). La formación docente en la sociedad del conocimiento y la información: avances y temas pendientes. Ponencia presentada al IV Encuentro Internacional de KIPUS. Políticas públicas y formación docente (Venezuela, 4-6 de octubre, 2006; Marcelo, C. (2006). Pregunta cuando quieras. La interacción didáctica en los nuevos ambientes virtuales de aprendizaje. Biblioteca electrónica de Elearning Europa, Unión Europea. Disponible en: de en fr; Marcelo, C. (2005). Los "otros" profesores. Revista Tarraconensis. Número especial en memoria de Vicente Ferreres Pavía; Marcelo, C. (Coord.). (2006) Prácticas de e-learning, Barcelona, Editorial Octaedro; Marcelo, C. (2005). Las nuevas competencias en e-learning: ¿qué formación necesitan los profesionales del e-learning? En Marcelo, C. (Coord.). (2005) Prácticas de e-learning, Barcelona, Editorial Octaedro, pp. 22-45;

Marcelo, C. (2005). Utilizando casos para un aprendizaje constructivista en e-learning. En Marcelo, C. (Coord.). (2005) Prácticas de e-learning, Barcelona, Editorial Octaedro, pp. 163-175; Marcelo, C. et al. (2005). Propuesta de instrumentos para evaluar la calidad de la formación a través de Internet. En Marcelo, C. (Coord.). (2005) Prácticas de e-learning, Barcelona, Editorial Octaedro, pp. 228-241; Marcelo, C., (2005). Puentes para la formación de profesores en la utilización de tic en el aula, Comunicación y pedagogía N° 203 pp. 45-49.

## Paulino Murillo

Paulino Murillo holds a doctorate degree in Science of Education. Currently, he is an assistant professor at Department of Teaching and School Organization at the University of Sevilla, Spain.

He has done research on school change and innovation. His academic work focuses mainly on the analysis of school improvement processes, attempting to determine the factors that help the school to develop. He also conducted research on teacher development and learning.

Selected publications: Murillo, P. y Altopiedi, M. (2006). How do schools improve? Analysis of the improvement processes and their incidence in the quality of education. Simposio. Second International Congress of Qualitative Inquiry. Universidad de Illinois at Urbana-Champaign; Murillo Estepa, Paulino and Altopiedi, Mariana (2006, Septiembre). Los procesos institucionales de mejora escolar desde la perspectiva del enfoque narrativo [82 párrafos]. Forum Qualitative Sozialforschung / Forum: Qualitative Social Research [On-line Journal], 7(4), Art. 14. Disponible en: http://www.qualitative-research.net/fqs-texte/4-06/06-4-14-s.htm; Murillo, P. (2005). Enseñar y aprender en Educación Superior. Enfoques de Educación, Montevideo (Uruguay), 139-155; Murillo, P. (2004). Hacia la construcción de un nuevo modelo de asesoramiento/supervisión. Educare, n° 5, año 2, 44-57; López, J.; Sánchez,

M. y Murillo, P. (Eds.) (2004). Cambiar con la sociedad, cambiar la sociedad. Sevilla, Secretariado de Publicaciones de la Universidad de Sevilla; Murillo, P. (Coord.) (2004). La formación de equipos directivos. En J. López; M. Sánchez y P. Murillo (Eds.) Cambiar con la sociedad, cambiar la sociedad. Sevilla, Secretariado de Publicaciones de la Universidad de Sevilla, 99-122; Murillo, P. (2003) Estrategias de asesoramiento. Temáticos Escuela Española, n° 7. Madrid; López, J.; Sánchez, M.; Murillo, P.; Lavié, J.M. y Altopiedi, M. (2003). Dirección de centros educativos. Un enfoque basado en el análisis del sistema organizativo. Madrid, Síntesis; Murillo, P. (2003). Experiencias de aprendizaje entre profesores mediante grupos de apoyo. En J. Gairín y C. Armengol (Eds.). Estrategias de formación para el cambio organizacional. Barcelona, Praxis, 51- 518; Murillo, P. (2002). Educación, sociedad y conocimiento. El peso de la realidad en el futuro de la formación. Perspectivacep. Revista de los Centros de Profesorado de Andalucía, 4, 93-109; Murillo, P. (2002). Formas de entender el aprendizaje de los estudiantes universitarios: Teorías y modelos de aprendizaje adulto. En C. Mayor (Coord.) Enseñanza y aprendizaje en la educación superior. Barcelona, Octaedro-EUB, 49-82; Murillo, P. (2001). La problemática de la participación en los centros educativos: una experiencia de colaboración interprofesional. En M. Lorenzo y otros (Eds.) Las organizaciones educativas en la sociedad neoliberal. Granada, Grupo Editorial Universitario, Vol. 3, 2589-2596.

## Romuald Normand

Romuald Normand is a lecturer in sociology. He is working in the mixed research unit Education and Policies where researchers from INRP (national institute for pedagogical research) and université Lyon 2 work together. He collaborates to NESSE (Network of Experts in the Social Sciences of education and training) sponsored by the European Commission. He has worked on the UK/USA and European policies in the area of accountability and management. Currently, he is preparing a book on the long-term influence of the measurement of effectiveness and its epistemic communities on the educational policies at global level.

Main publications: Normand, R. (2006). L'école efficace ou l'horizon du monde comme laboratoire. In: Derouet J.-L., and Lessard C. (Ed.), La construction des politiques d'éducation: de nouveaux rapports entre science et politique. Revue Française de Pédagogie, n° 154, janv-févr-mars 2006 and Revue des Sciences de l'Education du Québec, vol 32, n° 1; Normand, R., and Derouet, J-L. (Ed.) (2007). L'Europe de l'éducation: entre management et politique, INRP-ESEN; Normand, R. (2008). Mesurer la justice en éducation. Esquisse d'une arithmétique politique des inégalités. In: Derouet J.-L., Derouet-Besson M.-C. (coord.), Repenser la justice dans le domaine de l'éducation et de la formation. Genève/Lyon: Peter Lang/INRP; Normand, R., and Derouet. J-L. (2008). French Universities at a crossroad between crisis and radical reform. Towards a new Academic Regime? European Education, Journal of Issues and Studies, vol. 40, issue 1, The Implication of Competition for the Future of European Higher Education (II); Normand, R. (in press). Expert measurement in the government of lifelong learning. In: Mangenot, E., and Rowell, J., What Europe constructs? New sociological perspectives in European studies. Manchester: Manchester University Press; Normand, R. (in press). School effectiveness of the horizon of the world as a laboratory. British Journal of Sociology of Education.

## Angelo Paletta

Angelo Paletta (born 1967) is Professor of Business and Public Administration, Department of Management Studies, at the University of Bologna, Italy.

He is Director of the Master program in Educational Management and Leadership promoted by the Faculty of Economics of the University of Bologna. .He is also President of the Centre of International Studies in Educational Governance, Accountability and Management (EGAM), established in Bologna by the Foundation Alma Mater and the European Association for Educational Law and Policy, in partnership with the Commonwealth Council for Educational Administration and Management (CCEAM).

His academic activities - researches, volumes and articles, workshops, seminaries and conferences - concern strategic planning and management control systems, new public management, university governance and accountability, school leadership and management of educational institutions. Paletta A., (2004) Il governo dell'università. Tra competizione e accountability, Il Mulino, Bologna; Paletta A., (2005) "Performance measurement for strategic management of educational activities", *International Journal for Educational Law and Policy*, Special Issue, October, pp.77-101; Paletta, A., Vidoni, D., (2006) "Italian School Managers: a complex identity", *International Studies in Educational Administration*, vol. n.34, No.1, pp.46-70; Paletta A. (2006), "Financing and Equity of Education. Some economic and managerial implications", in C. L. Glenn, E. Gori, E. Hanushek, J. De Groof, (eds), *Institutional Models in Education, Legal Framework and Methodological Aspects for a new approach to the problem of School Governance*, Wolf Legal Publishers, Tilburg, pp.185-198; Paletta A., (2006) "The Functions of Performance Measurement in Education", in J. De Groof, G. Lauwers (eds), W*orld Conference on the Right to Education and Rights in Education*, Wolf Legal Publishers, Tilburg, pp.301-321; Paletta, A. Vidoni, D. (eds.), (2006) Scuola e creazione di valore pubblico. Problemi di governance, accountability e management, Roma, Armando; Paletta A., (2007) "Network Management and Educational Leadership: linkages between theory and praxis in Italian context", *International Journal for Educational Law and Policy*, Special Issue, *Public Governance of Education system,* pp.1-16.

## Petros Pashiardis

Dr. Petros Pashiardis is Professor of Educational Leadership and the Academic Head of the Studies in Education Program with the Open University of Cyprus. He has also worked at the University of Cyprus from 1992-2006 as Associate Professor of Educational Administration. Professor Petros studied Educational Administration at the University of Texas at Austin as a Fulbright Scholar from 1987 to1990. Before joining the University of Cyprus he worked as a school teacher, an Education Consultant with the Texas Association of School Boards and an Assistant Professor with the University of Texas-Permian Basin where he was deeply involved in research and teaching on the School Principalship, on Strategic Planning in Education as well as other Educational Leadership issues. He has also worked or lectured in many countries including Malta, Great Britain, India, New Zealand, Greece, Germany, South Africa, Switzerland, and the United States. During the periods of January-August 1999, summer 2000, summer 2001, and summer 2002, he was invited as Visiting Associate Research Scientist with the Texas A and M University. On his own or with others, he has authored over 80 articles in scholarly and professional journals many of them on aspects of leaders and leadership. Within Cyprus, this has included research into the role of the principal. He has published a book in Greek on teacher evaluation and papers on the role of the principal in Cyprus. He has also published a book in Greek on the Effective Schools Movement together with his wife. His interests in this area have become increasingly international, stretching to the USA where it all began, the UK, New Zealand, Malta, India and Greece. In his role as vice president for publications for the Commonwealth Council for Educational Administration and Management, he edited a book entitled *International Perspectives in Educational Leadership,* published by the University of Hong Kong-Institute for Education in 2001. Most recently, he co-edited the *International Handbook on the Preparation and Development of School Leaders*, together with Jacky Lumby and Gary Crow. As of October 2004 and until the end of 2008, Professor Pashiardis was elected as President of the Commonwealth Council for Educational Administration and Management.

## Cesare Scurati

Cesare Scurati (born 1937) is Professor of General and Social Pedagogy at the Faculty of Psychology of the Catholic University of Milano, Italy. He has been a teacher and a school principal in elementary schools. He has also been Head of the Department of Pedagogy and Director of the Center for Longlife and Distance Education of the Catholic University. He edits some professional journals for teachers and school leaders and has served in some national commissions charged of preparing national guidelines for the introduction of new curricula at preschool and elementary level. He was President of the Italian Pedagogical Society and of the Regional Institute of Lombardy for In Service and Educational Research and a member of the Administrative Council of the Association for Teacher Education in Europe - ATEE.

His main academic interests concern theories of education, curriculum planning, school management and professional development of school personnel.

Recent publications: C.Scurati (ed.),(2004),*E-learning/Università*,Vita e Pensiero,Milano; C.Scurati (ed.), (2005), *Educazione,società, scuola*, La Scuola,Brescia; C. Scurati (ed.), (2006),*A scuola per l'infanzia*, La Scuola,Brescia; C.Scurati, (2007), *Esperienza educativa e riflessione pedagogica*, La Scuola; Brescia; C.Scurati, (2008), *Il momento pedagogico:bilancio critico*, in C.Sirna (ed.),*Tempo formativo e creatività*, Pensa, Lecce, vol.I, pp.213-230; C.Scurati, (2008),"Professionalità docente e curricolo", *Notiziario UNESU*, Roma, 1, pp.32-42.

## Selahattin Turan

Selahattin Turan received his BA from Ankara University in 1990 and PhD from Ohio University in 1998. He joined Eskisehir Osmangazi University in 1998, where he is a professor, departmental chair of Computer and Instructional Technology in education, and associate dean of College of Education for research and international relations. His primary professional interests are theory in leadership, the organizational psychology of organizations, sociology, sociology of technology and alternative perspectives in applied behavioral sciences and educational administration. He is former president of the International Society for Educational Planning (ISEP) and former chair of the Division A (Administration, Organization and Leadership) Ad Hoc International Committee of the American Educational Research Association (AERA). He has authored and co-authored many books in the field of educational administration and published in a variety of scholarly journals. Moreover, he presented papers at the annual meetings of AERA, ISEP, NCPEA and UCEA. Professor Turan serves as the co-editor of *The Turkish Journal of Educational Administration in Theory and Practice* and on the editorial boards of many Turkish and international journals, including the *International Journal of Leadership in Education* and *Eskisehir Osmangazi, Fırat University Journal of Social Sciences.*

In: Centralization and School Empowerment...
Editor: Adam Nir

ISBN 978-1-60692-730-4
© 2009 Nova Science Publishers, Inc.

# ABOUT THE EDITOR

## Adam E. Nir

Dr. Adam Nir is a researcher at the School of Education, the Hebrew University of Jerusalem and Head of the Educational Policy, Administration and Leadership program. He is also a research fellow at the Van Leer Jerusalem Institute where he is involved in the Educational Policy Research Forum.

He has a BA in Behavioral Sciences (1986) and an MA in Educational Policy and Administration (1989) from Ben-Gurion University of the Negev. He completed his PhD degree in Educational Planning and Policy at the Hebrew University (1996) and his post-doctoral studies at the University of New Mexico (1997).

His academic work focuses on issues of planning and policy making, addressing the connections among organizational structures, contextual features and professional conduct in educational systems. Most of his recent studies have focused on issues of decentralization, empowerment and school autonomy, with particular emphasis on the implications of the School-Based Management policy on the professional behavior of teachers and school principals and on the reciprocal relations between schools and their social environment in centralized settings.

Among his recent publications on decentralization and school empowerment: Nir, A. E., and Ben-Ami, T. (2005). School-parents relationship in the era of School-Based management: Harmony or conflict? *Leadership and Policy in Schools*, 4, (1), 55-72; Nir, A. E. (2006). Maintaining or delegating authority? Contradictory policy messages and the prospects of school-based management to promote school autonomy. *Educational Planning*, 15 (1), 27 – 38; Nir, A. E., and Miran, M. (2006). The equity consequences of School-Based Management, *The International Journal of Educational Management,* 20 (2), 116-126; Nir, A. E. (2006). School empowerment and the centralization trap. In: Dan Inbar (Ed.), *Towards educational revolution?* (pp. 296-309). Tel Aviv: The Van Leer Jerusalem Institute and Hakibbutz Hameuchad Publishing House (Hebrew); Nir, A. E. (2007). The effect of school based management on schools' culture of consumption, *International Journal of Leadership in Education*, 10 (4), 421-436; Nir, A. E. (2007). The antecedents of teachers' perceived effectiveness of School-Based managing schools. *International Journal of Educational Reform,* 16, (4), 436 – 450; Nir, A. E., and Piro, P. (2007). *School based management: From theory to practice.* Jerusalem: The Szold Institute (Hebrew).

# INDEX

## F

**G**

**H**

## S

# T

## W

## Y

## Z